GLENN GOULD

SELECTED LETTERS

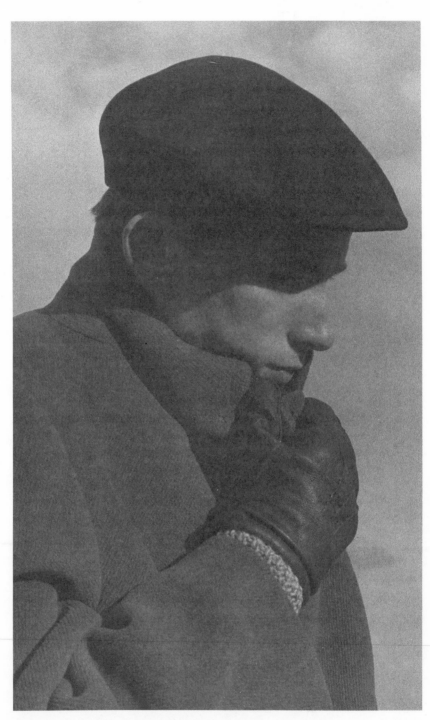

Glenn Gould 1956. Photo by Jock Carroll – copyright.

GLENN GOULD

SELECTED LETTERS

EDITED AND COMPILED BY

JOHN P. L. ROBERTS AND GHYSLAINE GUERTIN

Toronto
OXFORD UNIVERSITY PRESS
1992

Oxford University Press, 70 Wynford Drive, Don Mills, Ontario M3C 1J9

Toronto   Oxford   New York
Delhi   Bombay   Calcutta   Madras   Karachi   Kuala Lumpur
Singapore   Hong Kong   Tokyo   Nairobi   Dar es Salaam
Cape Town   Melbourne   Auckland   Madrid

and associated companies in
Berlin   Ibadan

Canadian Cataloguing in Publication Data

Gould, Glenn, 1932-1982
  Glenn Gould : selected letters

Includes bibliographical references and index.
ISBN 0-19-540799-7

1. Gould, Glenn, 1932-1982 – Correspondence.
2. Pianists – Canada – Correspondence.
I. Roberts, John P.L. (John Peter Lee).
II. Guertin, Ghyslaine.   III. Title.

ML417.G69G54   1992   786.2'092   C92-094539-2

Design: Marie Bartholomew

Typesetting and Assembly: Colborne, Cox & Burns Inc.

OXFORD is a trademark of Oxford University Press

  2   3   4   —   95   94   93   92
Printed in Canada by John Deyell Co.

CONTENTS

PREFACE I   by John P.L. Roberts

Since Glenn Gould's death in 1982, a number of books about him have appeared in English, and several of them have been translated into other languages. Countless articles have appeared in a variety of publications in different parts of the world, as well as television and radio programs and documentaries. Gould has appeared as a character in a novel, *The Loser*, by the Austrian writer Thomas Bernhard, and was the subject of a popular exhibition, "Retrospective Glenn Gould," seen in Paris and other European cities. The Glenn Gould Foundation has established a prestigious international award, the Glenn Gould Prize, in the area of music and communications, and has been associated with a variety of Gould projects, including an "Exhibition Glenn Gould" organized by the National Library of Canada, which has toured Canada and also been seen in Tokyo. This has all been part of what I call the Glenn Gould Phenomenon, because of the ever-increasing interest in Glenn's life and work shown not only by established music lovers but by an emerging generation as well.

Pilgrims come from halfway around the world to visit his grave in Toronto's Mount Pleasant Cemetery, and a steady stream of letters arrive at the Glenn Gould Foundation, saying how much Gould's recordings (which are kept very much alive by Sony Classical) mean to the senders. In addition, the Glenn Gould Society in the Netherlands, with a branch in Japan, plays an important role through the publication of a journal, *Bulletin of the Glenn Gould Society*, containing information on Gould's life and work, as well as scholarly articles.

The closest person to all Gould projects has been Stephen Posen, Executor of the Gould Estate, and when he asked me to take responsibility for a book of Glenn's letters I agreed, because I was convinced it was a project begging to be undertaken. Shortly thereafter I invited Ghyslaine Guertin, who was known to me as the organizer of an excellent international conference in Montreal called "Glenn Gould Pluriel," to become co-editor.

During the days I spent with the gravely ill and unconscious Gould in the Intensive Care Unit of the Toronto General Hospital, I little thought that one day I would co-edit a book of his letters. I was of course hoping for a miracle, one that would restore him to health and to conducting as a new phase in his career. However, this was not to be.

I first met Glenn in 1955, when I was a young CBC music producer in Winnipeg, and our friendship developed in 1957 after I moved to Toronto to become one of two program organizers in the newly-formed national Music Department. In the mid nineteen-sixties, when I became national Supervisor of Music for the CBC, I did something that was not quite legal: I gave Glenn a small office in the Music Department, a move that enabled him to interact with CBC producers and technicians and deepen his technical knowledge of radio recording and broadcasting. It also brought him in close proximity to television colleagues and other creative people in the media.

I think it should be noted that Glenn was fortunate to have been living at the right time and in the right place. Canada was quick to recognize his genius. In fact, by 1955, the year of his legendary debut recitals in New York and Washington D.C., he was already a renowned performing and broadcasting artist on home ground. In Toronto, the CBC gave Glenn the scope to broadcast any repertoire that interested him, and to voice his views on musical and non-musical subjects in various on-going series. As well, it provided him with the opportunity of pushing back the frontiers of documentary making for radio and the possibility of undertaking innovative television projects. Similarly, Columbia Records, which became CBS Records (now Sony Classical), offered him almost unlimited possibilities to make commercial recordings of whatever repertoire he wished, and to do so in Toronto when travel to New York became burdensome. The sad part of this aspect of his career was that exciting recording projects remained unfinished at his death.

During my early years in Toronto I was a frequent visitor to Glenn's parents' house at 32 Southwood Drive, where through late-night sessions in the music room I experienced Glenn's renderings – from memory – of entire Wagner operas, Beethoven's *Fidelio*, and orchestral works by Schoenberg and Webern. Unlike later in his life, when he rarely performed for friends, he eagerly played and talked about countless works, from the *Art of the Fugue* by Bach to a range of other repertoire that extended from William Byrd to contemporary music. Later I helped him in what became a long house-hunting saga. Not wishing to be recognized, he told different people showing him apartments that *he* was "John Roberts" and with a mischievous smile referred to me as "Mr. Gould." When I couldn't be present, whoever else accompanied Glenn on these visits became "Mr. Roberts." At one point – as one of Glenn's letters reminds us – he had his heart set on an absurdly large mansion on which he took out a short-term lease, and at another he had two suites in the now-closed Windsor Arms Hotel and two other apartments, neither of which he kept. Finally, he found a penthouse on St. Clair Avenue West in Toronto which contained an immense living room where he kept the Steinway given to him by his parents, as well as an old Chickering piano. It was here that we held many meetings of a small group of people called the Lower Rosedale Shakespeare Reading Society. Apart from reading plays by Shakespeare and other playwrights, we moved into the area of dramatic improvisations, in the course of which Glenn invented various characters that he used throughout the rest of his life. If he had something sensitive to say about himself or other people, he would sometimes use one of his characters to articulate what was on his mind.

Following my marriage to Christina van Oordt, Glenn frequently visited our home and became godfather to our son Noël. Eventually my wife and I helped refurbish another room in Glenn's penthouse as a second living room. This was necessary because his main living room had become so full of scores, recordings, drafts of projects (both completed and in progress), as well as general clutter, that even moving a short distance across it meant a major exercise. Quite frankly, Glenn lived like Beethoven. His own comment on the state of his penthouse was "at the best of times it looks as though a tornado has just passed through." The amazing thing was that usually he could find what he was looking for. He had a phenomenal memory. Sometimes, when I was looking for a recording, he would tell me it was in a certain pile and that although the jacket said Scriabin I would find the Bach work I was searching for inside.

Glenn made an enormous use of the telephone. Indeed it was not uncommon for calls (which in reality amounted to electronic visits) to last for two or three hours. They very often came in the middle of the night because, generally speaking, Glenn worked during the night and slept in the day. However, there were periods in which he worked for forty-eight hours or longer, with very little sleep, in order to accommodate the working hours of other people. And, of course, he wrote letters, or, to be precise, dictated them – over the years to various stenographers.

There are 184 letters included in this volume. While parts of some of them have been previously quoted in other publications, it is enlightening to be able to read them, and many others, in unabridged form. Most letters were dictated over the phone and some of them contain typographical errors that will be readily perceived because we have decided not to normalize Glenn's spelling and punctuation, but rather to present the letters as they were sent, with misspelled words, sometimes misspelled proper names, missing commas and apostrophes, and even the occasional typographical error and repetitions of words. We have also decided not to pepper the letters with [sic] after each error, distracting readers from the context. This decision, we hope, will give readers a more direct experience of Glenn's letters, which are an extremely valuable addition to "Gouldiana."

The letters reveal many aspects of Glenn's personality, and at least one of them is a genuine curiosity. People he knew at all well were assigned key signatures as an important part of their identity. In one of the letters he reveals a particular association with F minor. This was no whim of the moment, since he consistently described himself as belonging to this key. Gould's description of it as "rather dour" (Feb. 19, 1967) provides only a faint glimpse of the inner man. Finding the meaning of the F minor Gould will be a voyage of discovery for all readers with a penchant for probing musical analogies.

Gould facetiously states that the motto of his family is "Never accomplish today what can best be put off 'till tomorrow" (May 11, 1966), and readers will certainly notice some examples of Gould's procrastination and absentmindedness. He forgets to reply to letters, send recordings, and communicate with people who are counting on him. In a letter to Yousuf Karsh he says, apropos of his training, that he had been equipped with everything "except the kind of solidarity of the ego which is, in the last analysis, the one important part of an artist's equipment" (July 8, 1958). Most observers would say that as Gould's career developed his ego was not lacking in solidarity. However those closer to him knew that he was at once extremely confident and insecure. His ego can best be described as "brittle." It was for this reason that Gould's personal relations were often difficult. He allowed very few people to get close to him, and those who did knew how vulnerable he was to criticism both professional and private. As Gould was an "original" much of the criticism that came his way proved hard to cope with, so he tried to keep it at arm's length and outside his consciousness. Any dark shades in an apparently sunny personality were well hidden, and eccentricities that he tried initially to suppress on and off-stage, in the early days, were quickly allowed to become trademarks of his career. In endeavouring to shut out people who were too critical, confrontational, or probing, Gould went to endless pains to try to control every situation. His telephone existence allowed him the possibility of keeping in contact only with certain people, while avoiding others. After a particularly distasteful interview by BBC Television he resolved to answer only questions that had been previously submitted. However, he clearly preferred self-interviews, which gave him absolute control of any subject under discussion. Indeed in 1982, a few months before his death, we find him saying "I'm quite determined that, in future, all major journalistic efforts will be executed in this fashion" (June 18, 1982).

In many respects Glenn was in advance of his time. The criticism of his performances of sonatas by Mozart, for example, as distortions of the composer's intentions, may be tempered by those who follow us in twenty-five years. Glenn seems to have sensed this himself when he said in a letter "I have suddenly been made aware . . . just how transitionary are our values of performance and how dependent they are upon the analytical approach of the particular generation." Glenn found this a "disturbing experience" because his comment was made after hearing recordings of such pianists of the past as Grieg, Fauré, and Paderewski, which in spite of "some remarkable qualities" reflected "a desire to sectionalize, to play from the passion of the moment in such a way as to jeopardize the larger structures" (May 27, 1963). In other words, in a manner with which Glenn was not in sympathy. However, it is quite possible that future generations will value recorded performances by Glenn that have been roundly criticized in our time. At the very least his provocative performances will be seen as points of departure in re-examining the repertoire and re-evaluating the ethical responsibilities of the performer.

It needs to be stressed that Glenn's performances were in reality recreations. Indeed, he sometimes went as far as to almost recompose the works of others. About Bach, we find Glenn saying "The music of Bach, in particular, because of its curious combination of structural precision and improvisatory options, encourages one to invest it with one's own personality." He adds that the personality injected by the performer "must be, to some degree at least, harmonious with the basic philosophic and/or religious outlook which permeated much of Bach's music, as well as the specific contrapuntal line with which all of it was invested" (Nov. 12, 1972). However, it is clear that Glenn had little or no interest in traditional approaches to performance and felt the performer of the moment had an inalienable responsibility to remake any music in his or her image for contemporary listeners.

Gould's need to stress linear connectedness and de-emphasize theatricality, and his unorthodox tempi, along with a penchant for making the music under his fingers sound totally spontaneous and improvised, were all part of the mindset of his recreations. These characteristics were very much in evidence in his unorthodox recordings of the three last sonatas by Beethoven: opus 109, opus 110, and opus 111. In commenting on them in a letter to Roy Maley, critic of the *Winnipeg Tribune*, it is clear that Gould was trying to "combat the impossibly teutonic and unrelenting manner which is so often applied to not only the stern granitular side of Beethoven but the contemplative side as well" (Dec. 30, 1961). It is also important to understand that his recreations in general circulation were exclusively conceived in terms of electronic recordings, and we find him saying that he has "a preference for those sessions in which one can bring an almost dangerous degree of improvisatory open-mindedness – that is to say, sessions in relation to which one has no absolute, a priori, interpretive commitment and in which the process of recording will make itself felt in regard to the concept that evolves" (June 17, 1972). Clearly, Gould was the first performing musician to develop an aesthetic totally in terms of the electronic media, and in terms of recordings in particular.

The letters also throw light on Gould's thinking concerning two of his idols, Richard Strauss and Arnold Schoenberg. It must be remembered that, in particular, Gould was an international authority on Schoenberg's music and that throughout his life he never ceased to promote it through public performances (in the early days), recordings, radio documentaries, and television programs. In a letter we find Gould saying Schoenberg deserves a wider audience and that "it is only a question of time" before this will happen (Nov. 14, 1966). Clearly, he left no stone unturned in trying to bring Schoenberg's music to a very wide public. He admired Strauss for not having tried to keep up with contemporary music trends as the twentieth century progressed. Indeed, Gould felt Strauss had remained a great composer, and a modern one too, by avoiding the pathways of the avant-garde and by consistently evolving his own musical language, no matter how passé it appeared to younger generations.

In his own way, too, Glenn liked to buck musical fashion. He comments on this in relation to his String Quartet, which because it "superficially at least, revisited the harmonic world of . . . Strauss and Mahler, was an odd sort of creation to turn up in the mid-1950s." Gould adds, "It was nonetheless, and in spite of all the rationalization to the contrary, an unusual work for its time and place, and it would be no exaggeration, I think, to stress that aspect of it through which, in effect, I sought to challenge the zeitgeist." In the same letter he reminds us that "The tyranny of stylistic collectivity in the arts, and, more generally, in life styles, per se, has been, I think, the primary theme in most of the works attempted and, indeed, in a good many of the articles which I have written from time to time about the musical situation." He then makes it clear that in his mind the Quartet is connected to other creative endeavors. "I think that, however far-fetched the connection may appear at first glance, there is a true fraternal link, both in subject matter and technique, between the vocal polyphony of 'The Idea of North' and 'The Latecomers,' and the chromatically concentrated counterpoint of the quartet" (May 23, 1972).

Obviously the links between the creative works lie in their structures. Gould was consumed with a sense of structure and the process that puts it in place. His letters reveal that structural concerns were central to all considerations of the performance of any music and to his creative process. Glenn always had an X-ray view of the music he performed. This is particularly true of his performances of works by Bach, which with their finely chiselled realizations of counterpoint, articulation of overall structure, and rhythmic tension, place them at a high plateau of achievement rarely equalled by others. Although Gould speaks of the glories of Schoenberg's music, again it can be said that he was unendingly fascinated by its structures and by a certain asceticism which comes from working within the discipline of serialism and its creative limitations as exemplified not only by Schoenberg, but also by the other members of the Second Viennese School. Toward the end of his life we find Gould waxing enthusiastic about the Norwegian composer Fartein Valen. He commented that his music "provides the most 'refined' . . . utilization of conventional 12-tone technique this side of Alban Berg" (Oct. 23, 1971). Once again, it was a matter of being attracted to a certain composer because of structural concerns in his music.

The question of organic unity was something that preoccupied Gould's mind and work. To take one example, it was this concern for organic unity that was the reason given for his extremely unconventional and controversial approach to performing the Piano Concerto No. 1 in D minor by Brahms, with the New York Philharmonic Orchestra and Leonard Bernstein. Certainly in Gould's time it was the longest performance on record because of the inordinately slow tempi of the first and last movements. Speaking of his television program "The Well-Tempered Listener," Glenn makes a point of emphasizing "we did indeed attempt to compose the program in such a way as to make it, in and of itself, an organic structure, to avoid telegraphing (i.e. telescoping) the various . . . illus-trative episodes . . . and to treat them as though they were in fact a spontaneous complement to the basso continuo provided by our conversation" (March 5, 1970). In certain documentaries he placed a particular emphasis on contrapun-tal radio – various counterpoints of voices speaking simultaneously – as part of his quest for organic unity. As well, other forms borrowed from music were employed. His concern for structure superseded all other considerations in the documentaries. Gould called them "mood pieces" because they do not preach. In fact, he was loath to emphasize one point of view over another. He said, "I would do less than justice to my role as producer if I were to deliberately sacrifice the 'contrapuntal' integrity of one value-system in order to enhance another" (Aug. 3, 1971). Some might argue that achieving organic unity at the expense of presenting some striking revelation or new point of view can be construed as a weakness in his approach to documentary making. Nevertheless, it must be understood that Gould thought of his documentaries as a form of music, and any evaluation of them needs to take Gould's aesthetic into consideration.

Gould also commented on the tyranny of public taste in relation to composers who fall in and out of favour with audiences. We find him saying "I have always felt that among the earlier generation of romantic composers – Chopin, Schu-mann, Schubert, et al – the most sadly underestimated is Felix Mendelssohn. As you know, Mendelssohn's music has gone in and out of vogue with some regularity (very much 'in' for the English Victorians, for instance; very much 'out' for many people today who find it rather 'square' and perhaps a bit cautious) but, in my opinion, the precision of craft which Mendelssohn exhibits – especially in his orchestral music – is equalled by few composers in the 19th century and that craft, moreover, is put at the service of an extraordinarily touching, neo-devotional attitude which I find particularly alluring" (April 5, 1971). Since Gould felt so strongly about the neglect of Mendelssohn's music we may wonder why he did not make an effort to record a sampling of it. Certainly at one moment he was considering recording some examples of the piano music. However, it has to be understood that in analyzing and assessing compositions Gould believed totally that "every facet of a work has to prove itself of structural necessity," which explains why the music of Wagner meant so much to him.

While Gould knew it was perhaps not viable to apply this "Schoenbergian type of molecular analysis" to late-nineteenth-century music with its "more open structures" (May 27, 1963), he nevertheless kept a safe distance from much of the rich piano repertoire of the nineteenth century. In short, he was not very attracted to it and in any case he regarded the piano as primarily a polyphonic instrument most suited to revealing tight linear structures, and that is why the "jewels" in Mendelssohn's piano music eluded him.

Gould, like Marshall McLuhan, developed visionary ideas based not on empirical research but on intuition and perception. He was convinced of the therapeutic value of music and was impressed by a "pressured Madison Avenue-type executive" (March 5, 1970) whom he found coping with tension by listening to the recording by Albert Schweitzer of the G minor fugue by Bach as background while he worked. In March 1980 he observes, "I most certainly agree with you about the therapeutic effects of music and musical performance; I have always believed that if this relationship does not exist, it *should* exist" (March 30, 1980). Glenn certainly liked to think that his recordings were of therapeutic value, and he took it as the greatest compliment when told so by others. However, he knew very little about the developing area of music therapy per se.

Gould's "the concert hall is dead" views were based not on research but on the conviction that the best music-making can be done in a studio and not in a concert hall. "I have always preferred working in a studio, making records or doing radio or television, and for me, the microphone is a friend, not an enemy and the lack of audience – the total anonymity of the studio – provides the greatest incentive to satisfy my own demands upon myself without consideration for, or qualification by, the intellectual appetite, or lack of it, on the part of the audience. My own view is, paradoxically, that by pursuing the most narcissistic relation to artistic satisfaction one can best fulfil the fundamental obligation of the artist of giving pleasure to others" (Feb. 15, 1961). In another letter we find him saying "the real virtue of the recording process is not in its inherent perfectionism but in the after-thought control by which one can operate upon the raw material of performance. For me, the best of all possible worlds would be one in which the art of performance supplied raw material only and the process of assembling or reconstructing the work occupied the major portion of the performer's activity" (April 24, 1967). While we must be grateful that after 1964 Gould put so much emphasis on working within the electronic media – without it his legacy would not have been nearly as rich – in the larger view it is clear that he had given little thought to the economic underpinnings of the music profession. After all, orchestras and opera companies are only able to record because they are primarily concerned with public music-making in traditional venues, and most performing ensembles and artists derive a great part of their income from public performances.

However, Gould's perception may prove to be more correct in the future than many people can now comprehend. Already there is indisputable evidence to suggest the audiences for certain live music events are declining, and there can be no doubt that the greatest use of music continues to be through the electronic media. As we move into the twenty-first century it is extremely difficult to forecast what sort of equilibrium (if any) will exist between live music and music in the electronic media as a result of sociological, economic and other forces.

There are letters that deal with Gould's now much discussed shoulder injury inflicted by a piano technician in 1959, his illnesses, travels, pianos, mannerisms, pre-concert rituals, lack of interest in food, the process of selecting music for concerts, radio, television and recording projects, as well as his beliefs and convictions as they related to a variety of subjects, mostly concerned with music. The contradictions in Glenn are revealed to some measure in the letters. To take one example, he said of major romantic works of the nineteenth century, "if one is to do them, one should surely do them straight" (Sept. 14, 1966). However, his realization of Chopin's Sonata in B minor was decidedly unorthodox and anything but straight. And it is fascinating to discover that after spending several hundred hours on his radio documentary on Leopold Stokowski, who had been a greatly admired colleague for many years, we find Gould cautioning against allowing Stokowski to actually hear the completed project for fear that he would insist on a re-mix (a remaking of the documentary), something that Gould was "not able or willing" to do. The Maestro had withheld permission to turn the documentary into a recording on the grounds that he did not approve of "montage as a documentary technique." Finding himself thwarted this way, Gould admits to being "ever so slightly infuriated" in view of "the Maestro's fondness for concocting symphonic syntheses" in the past. However, Gould consoles himself by saying that because Stokowski is "a nonagenarian . . . one must make allowances" (June 28, 1974).

There are also letters concerned with plans and proposals that did not see the light of day. Among them is a television program with Herbert von Karajan and another television project that would have dealt with the "birth, development, decline and death" (Sept. 3, 1971) of the piano concerto. A radio documentary on China was briefly considered and the idea of making one or more recordings with Yehudi Menuhin was a cherished thought which kept recurring. The most curious proposal of all was one that finally came to fruition. Glenn wanted to make a special recording as a parody of the public recital. His plan was to "fake" a concert so that it sounded as though the venue was situated in the far north of Canada, and Glenn's own playing was to be interspersed, and even interrupted, with a tubercular-sounding audience and howling wolves. Initially his recording company received the idea with polite silence. However, after persisting over a period of years, he was finally allowed to undertake the project, *A Glenn Gould Fantasy*, as part of a project to celebrate his Silver Jubilee as a recording artist. In satisfying his obsession, Glenn produced a parody that was far more extreme than the original proposal. It was inspired by Vladimir Horowitz's return to the concert stage. (Gould's public concert is set on an oil rig in the Beaufort Sea in the Canadian Arctic.) Not surprisingly, CBS Records made sure that there was not even one veiled reference to Horowitz.

Those readers looking for personal letters will find there are very few indeed. Except for a few letters to his parents, and an on-going correspondence with Kitty Gvozdeva, a language coach for singing students he met during his Russian tour in 1957, most of the letters in this collection deal with making music in various facets – which, after all, is what Glenn chose as the center of his life. However, one of these letters will certainly arouse interest. There is an unfinished draft of a letter to Dell – a woman with whom he is in love. It appears to be intended for someone else – a person who would bring Glenn and Dell together. Dell seems to be someone he knew as a young man. But she remains a mystery. All attempts to uncover her identity have failed. If there were other letters concerning Dell, no trace of them has so far been found.

Glenn once said of Marshall McLuhan, "he remains, I think, an intriguing and important figure" (May 14, 1966). Surely as we approach the next century, nothing less can be said of Glenn. Throughout his letters, with the strengths and weaknesses they reveal, a multifaceted image of Gould appears which will intrigue all those trying to develop an understanding of this extraordinary musician, media artist, thinker, visionary, and complex human being.

No book of letters can be assembled and researched without the help of many people. First, I would like to thank Stephen Posen and Lucinda Vardey for their assistance and encouragement with the project. In terms of researching the footnotes, I consulted people too numerous to list here. Nevertheless, I would like to express my gratitude to them. Particular thanks must go to the following individuals: Russell H. (Bert) Gould, C. Winston Fitzgerald, Christian Geelhaar, Walter Homburger, Otto Joachim, Deborah MacCallum, Paul Myers, Howard Scott, and Henry Z. Steinway. In addition, I must thank my co-editor Dr. Ghyslaine Guertin for her meticulous work and for her devotion to the book, and our research assistant Valerie Verity for her investigative thoroughness, invaluable hard work and endless patience. Dr. Guertin and I feel very privileged to have worked with Dr. Richard Teleky and I would like to seize this occasion to express our gratitude to him. We must also give special thanks to Dr. Timothy Maloney and Dr. Stephen Willis of the National Library of Canada in Ottawa for their assistance over a period of two years, and also to Ruth Pincoe, who organized and catalogued all the letters in the first place. As well, I would like to express my thanks to Barbara Clarke of the CBC Archives in Toronto, and to the University of Calgary for the support and encouragement I received from colleagues during the gestation period of this work. Finally, I would like to thank my wife Christina Roberts van-Oordt for her assistance with the manuscript and my secretary Barbara Chibambo for her patience and typing skills.

PREFACE II

by Ghyslaine Guertin

The letter and the recording studio represent two places where communication can occur in the absence of others. For Glenn Gould they were essential to the realization of his desire to make sense – to be better understood, better heard. If the recording studio served as his workshop for the production of musical meaning, the letter was his tool for defining it, for clarifying and justifying it, and for explaining the conditions – physical, sociocultural, psychological, and esthetic – that made it possible. The letters permit us to understand the why and how of his creative behavior as musician, theoretician, and communicator.

The correspondence of Glenn Gould is not a contribution to *belles lettres*. Nor does it offer the kind of secrets or confessions likely to satisfy the voyeur that lurks in most readers. However it is astonishing simply in quantitative terms. Shortly after Gould's death the letters in his personal archives – in seemingly hopeless disorder – were classified and then deposited in the National Library of Canada. The collection includes 2,030 letters written by Gould, and 2,798 written to him.[1] Gould kept copies of all of the letters he sent, which were typed with carbon paper by various secretaries from dictation based on notes. Gould would then correct and, in theory, mail them, though often not until after a considerable lapse of time. He had ample justification for his ironic claim that his family motto – "Never accomplish today what can best be put off 'till tomorrow" (May 11, 1966)[2] – was perfectly appropriate to his habits: "I am a very sluggish correspondent" (May 31, 1960). In some cases a telephone call preceded the letter: "Although I expect to be on the phone with you before this arrives in New York or even, given the not infrequent breakdown in my dictation-thru-mailing production line, before it gets sent off" (Jan. 26, 1969). In fact, Gould's letter-writing had its counterpart in the many exchanges he carried out by phone.

The one-hundred and eighty-four letters chosen for this edition of Gould's correspondence are taken (with few exceptions) from the letters in the Glenn

Gould Collection of the National Library of Canada. The research that accompanied this selection required several steps. First, each of the outgoing letters had to be analyzed in relation to the incoming ones in order to clarify questions of context, date, and meaning. Efforts to trace certain missing letters – outgoing as well as incoming – led us to examine other archival documents from the Gould Collection, notably his personal journal and "keepers."[3] The discovery of rough drafts of unfinished letters, undated and sometimes illegible or written in the form of abbreviations (like the letters to Susan Koscis and Dell) confirmed the necessity of such research. In addition, one would have to determine whether other unknown Gould letters exist as the jewels of some correspondents' personal collections.

The selection of letters for this book was determined by our desire to provide a general overview of Gould as correspondent rather than to highlight any specific theme, let alone his correspondence with any particular individual. In other respects our choice was guided by the evolution of Gould's thought in conjunction with the diversity of his creative activities; the unity of its formal preoccupations; and the originality of its connections with technology and the media. If we have focused on the friendly, prosaic, administrative, pedagogical, technical letters with some esthetic and musicological content, that is because they also allow us a glimpse into the life, the character and personality, of the writer/ musician who was inseparable from his work.

Another step consisted in classifying the letters according to the chronological order assigned to them by the archives. This chronology clarifies the meaning of each letter while at the same time situating it in a historical context. The first letter and the last are like two pillars framing this unfolding of meaning through time. Although forty years separate the Valentine to his mother and the 1982 letter to Theresa Ximenes, they are linked by an identical passion for the animal world.

The yearly quantities of Gould's letters, from 1956 until his death, are illustrated in Figure 1.[4] Although this distribution is based only on the data recorded in the archives, it does allow us to trace a preliminary trail by suggesting a relation between Gould's letter-writing and his other creative activities. If the letters contribute to our understanding of the work, the work in turn helps to explain the letters. Examination of this graph identifies three periods to which the letters correspond: (1) 1956-1964, from the beginning to the end of his concert career; (2) 1964-1976, covering his developing recording career, productions for radio, television, and film, and theoretical writing; and (3) 1976-1982, from a year after the death of his mother to his own death, his last productive years. The letters selected for this volume cover all of these periods.

(1) The letters from the first period describe the public man, the virtuoso with his many national and international commitments. They convey the distress and discomfort that, bound up in a way of life that was contrary to his thinking,

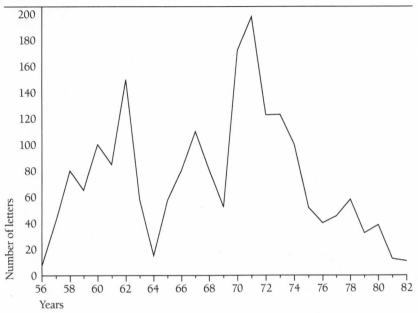

would accompany Gould until his final decision, announced in the letter of April 17, 1962, to abandon the concert stage.

The symptoms of this discomfort are already evident in the letters of June 3, 1957, Oct. 18, 1958, Nov. 4, 1958, and June 20, 1961: sinus trouble, colds, hay fever, chronic bronchitis, weight loss, nephritis, rheumatism. Nor is this list complete: an injury to the left shoulder, sustained at Steinway & Sons in 1959, caused him much anxiety and real suffering (Jan. 27, 1960, Feb. 17, 1960, March 10, 1960, May 31, 1960). In other respects, however, this experience was providential, for it helped Gould to recognize his attraction to television and the recording studio, as well as his future direction (April 17, 1962, Feb. 15, 1965), and to question the incompatibility of his life as a concert pianist with his insatiable perfectionism (Feb. 15, 1961) and the meaning that he attributes to music. Certain letters suggest the formal, structural demands that music imposes. His ideas on interpretation and fidelity to the composer (Dec. 16, 1959), the primacy he attributes to the analytical approach, the qualities he looks for in his instrument (Dec. 27, 1956), his concept of tempo (April 17, 1962), his choice of repertoire (June 14, 1961), his favorite composers, Bach and Schoenberg, on whom he was preparing a radio documentary – all point to the romantically-tinged formalism of the man himself: "You know what an uncurable romantic I am anyway" (Jan. 25, 1961).

These early letters from the period of the public man bear witness to the musician's literary inclinations and the pleasure he took in writing. The letter to Edith Boecker (Jan. 27, 1960) becomes a veritable short story; the letter to Yousuf Karsh (July 8, 1958), an autobiography; the letter to John Roberts (April 6, 1961) shows the imagination and humour that could come to life in the presence of friends. Moreover, the correspondence reveals how Gould connected with other people: in particular, his letters to Kitty Gvozdeva (Dec. 30, 1961), and Silvia Kind (Jan. 10, 1965) suggest the affection, warmth, and thoughtfulness he was capable of.

As the chart shows, this period ended in 1964. But Gould's letter-writing had already begun to slow down, starting in 1962. He wrote to Kitty Gvozdeva on Feb. 15, 1965: "The last year has been quite eventful for me. I've written a great deal for one thing – many lectures and magazine articles of one kind or another, and my first book – a small one on Schoenberg, so you won't approve!"

(2) The shift from public to private, from the stage to the studio, constituted a new departure in which the artist's creative potential found complete freedom of expression. This was the period, between 1964 and 1976, of the great achievements and the fulfillment of an esthetic ideal in which the relation between the listener and the music itself is inseparable from use of the media (radio, television, film, recording) and technology. The symptoms described in the letters of the earlier period seem to have disappeared entirely. Anxiety gives way to pleasure and a passion for creative work for which the only condition is solitude. The letters are no longer bulletins on his health. On the other hand, the journal fills that function: statistics on hours of sleep achieved under various conditions, systematic summaries of his high blood pressure, observation and description of new symptoms, and analysis of medical reports appear alongside scattered notes and sketches for various projects. Throughout this second period the main theme is the work under way, the work to come. The letters become less literary and more technical, with esthetic and musicological connotations. Often they reflect the passion that animates their writer. The sentences that go on forever – for example, the last sentence in the second paragraph of his letter to Lee Brown (April 5, 1971), with its parentheses – borrow their rhythm from Gould's telephone conversation, as Geoffrey Payzant describes it: "Once when he was telling me about his music for the film Slaughterhouse Five he plunged, in a single sentence, into fourteen levels of parentheses, subordinate clauses, qualifiers, asides, asides within other asides."[5]

The graph for this period, 1964 to 1976, shows two peaks indicating a rise in letter-writing, each followed by a decline that in the second case, following 1972, would continue through 1982. From 1964 to 1969, the resumption of letter-writing coincides with an enthusiasm for creative activity that was distinguished by the use of television, radio, and recording. The letters reflect this enthusiasm, expressing on one hand Gould's desire to see the use of television in terms of strictly musical ends and, on the other, the conviction that recording would revolutionize the concept of interpretation. This period of high activity corresponds to the creation of his first radio documentary, centering on the theme of solitude and based on observation of people who had lived in the Arctic or subarctic (Sept. 1, 1967). This documentary on the Canadian North is the pretext for experimentation with "the most promising" new radio techniques. Gould's aim is to analyze the effects of solitude and to demonstrate its role in all creative activity. Hardly is this documentary finished than he moves on to another radio project around the same theme, this time focusing on the people of Newfoundland (June 22, 1968). This is to be the second part of the "Solitude Trilogy."

In addition to describing these activities, the letters define Gould's concept of interpretation through recording (April 24, 1967). He justifies the use of the piano for the works of Bach (Sept. 25, 1968), a composer he has always venerated (his letter of May 22, 1967 is a perfect example). As for interpreters, he admires Leon Fleisher for his originality (Nov. 14, 1966), while in a whimsical letter to Diana Menuhin he expresses his affection for her husband (April 25, 1966). The time devoted to these projects would appear to explain the reduction in letters in 1968 and 1969. On July 6, 1969, he writes: "I'm presently locked into a C.B.C. schedule which involves a weekly radio show plus one hundred and sixty-eight (repeat, 168) hours of editing on a documentary-drama about Newfoundland between now and the first week of August."

In contrast, the period from 1969 to 1971 shows a spectacular increase in correspondence, as illustrated in the sharp grade of the graph. Revolving around an avalanche of work completed or under way, these letters not only describe these projects but explain Gould's approach to them. They also represent an opportunity to express his conception of art and the esthetic principles underlying it. On the subject of a television program that he has just completed, "The Well-Tempered Listener," he declares that he put it together with an eye to "organic structure" (March 5, 1970). The radio documentary on Leopold Stokowski is intended to pay him homage; Gould hopes "that something of his remarkable kindness and generosity of spirit as well as his relentless dedication to art comes through in this program" (Jan. 5, 1971). The same letter describes the methods used in this stereophonic effort. Then he is mapping out a new radio project on the Mennonites, which he sees as the logical follow-up to the earlier dramatic documentaries "The Idea of North" and "The Latecomers" (April 5, 1971). Gould's enthusiasm for television resurfaces with the wish that such productions might be broadcast several times and, above all, reproduced on video cassette. At the same time, production of the sound track for the film version of Kurt Vonnegut's *Slaughterhouse Five* is under way (Dec. 21, 1971). Gould's interest in Schoenberg shows up again in a project to celebrate the centenary of his death (Dec. 10, 1972).

Another radio production in 1972, entitled "The Scene," provides Gould with the opportunity both to elaborate his ideas on competition and to analyze the role of the media and "celebrate the praise of the objectivity" that should be their defining characteristic. By June 14, 1973, the radio documentary on Pablo Casals is almost finished, and Gould is working on the series of broadcasts with Bruno Monsaingeon. In the same period, "The Age of Ecstasy," a television program on music in the first decade of the twentieth century, is also completed. Featuring works of Scriabin, Debussy, Schoenberg, and Berg, it is the most harmonious marriage ever of music and the camera (March 11, 1974). In the same series, 1975 would see the completion of "The Flight from Order," which included Gould's own transcription of Ravel's *La Valse* (Dec. 6, 1974).

Recording was equally central to his creative activities. The works of the Elizabethan composers Byrd and Gibbons occupied a special place in his repertory, particularly in view of their pedagogical value as the ideal initiation to the contrapuntal music of Bach (May 13, 1971). Another project emerges with a passion for the complete sonatas of Haydn (Dec. 21, 1971). In addition, the recording of Bach's French Suites is almost finished, while that of the English Suites is still to come. As for twentieth-century repertory, a technical experiment with multi-track recording is in progress. The music of Fartein Valen, "a kind of Norwegian hermit," is Gould's latest discovery, confirming the principle that should lie at the root of all creative activity: "I do feel quite convinced that one's creativity is enhanced primarily by the more-or-less single-minded pursuit and development of one's own resources without reference to the trends, tastes, fashions, etc. of the world outside" (Feb. 14, 1973). In the same year, Gould completes his transcriptions of Wagner; he says that the tempi are "alarmingly conventional" (Oct. 27, 1973).

The letters describing the repertory also permit a better grasp of Gould's concept of recording, which should serve the perfection that is the goal of all artistic activity. His beliefs regarding this mode of interpretation remain firm. Recording is not the documentary reflection of a public concert: the first take is not necessarily the best, nor is it dishonest to insert material from different performances (June 17, 1972). The recording studio remains at the service of creative interpretation (Sept. 12, 1972). In addition, the letters show the coherence of Gould's choices and, in particular, the fascination he has always felt for counterpoint, as illustrated in the letter to Kimiko Nakayama (Nov. 12, 1972). If his correspondence in this period is of a more technical nature, his letters to Stephen Posen (Nov. 30, 1972) and to John Roberts (Jan. 28, 1973) make it clear that his imagination and sense of humor have not disappeared.

This fertile period ends in 1975 with Gould's reserved announcement, to the composer Ernst Krenek, of the sudden death of his mother. This painful event contributed to a reduction in all his activities, including correspondence. Nevertheless, he says he has been monopolized by another, more theoretical form of writing: "I have several pieces due within the next 6 months notably an article about Ernst Krenek's 75th birthday celebrations and another about the theologian Jean Lemoyne" (June 26, 1975). His telephone bills[6] suggest another pertinent explanation for the direction of the graph at the end of this period.

(3) From 1976 to 1982 Gould's correspondence generally continues the decline that began in 1971. In the last years of his life Gould became sedentary (July 4, 1978). The telephone took the place of travel and made it possible for him to conduct the interviews required for his last radio documentary: "The Bourgeois Hero," on Richard Strauss. In various letters he defines and clarifies his objectives (April 14, 1976) and explains the method, structure (Jan. 30, 1979), and content (May 25, 1976). Musicology is at the very center of his argument in this documentary. But his interest in making radio documentaries seems to have diminished in favor of film production. A new project is proposed, this time on China – he could have helped to make the "Solitude Trilogy" a quartet (July 4, 1978) – but it does not materialize. In this last period Gould takes the opportunity to reaffirm his convictions, among them the importance of the link between music and the media (May 29, 1976) and the immorality of the competition process (c. 1977). Another letter allows him to correct certain biographical details (Sept. 9, 1981). The letters written in the last months of his life show the same capacity as ever for expressing affection, friendship, and gratitude to colleagues and friends.

Gould's correspondence is an invaluable aid to explaining the whole of his work – as is the work itself for the letters. In effect, the outline of his work that I have traced shows the creative imagination of the musician and the wealth of his multidisciplinary activities, as well as his ability to pursue several projects at the same time. It also reveals the esthetic thinking underlying the latter, and suggests clues to Gould's character.

Our notes to Gould's letters are intended to guide the process of signification set in motion in each reader, who in turn will add the personal notes on Gould gleaned from his or her other personal reading and listening to the whole of Gould's work. We have chosen not to offer long notes about Gould's many eminent colleagues, from Leonard Bernstein to Marshall McLuhan to Elisabeth Schwarzkopf, who will be familiar to readers; instead, our notes focus on the less familiar figures, who were equally important to Gould. The principal source of these notes is the analytical catalogue produced by the archivists Ruth Pincoe and Dr. Stephen Willis and published by the National Library of Canada. We are very grateful for their cooperation. It should also be noted that the only references to discography are the dates of recording and original release, given the first time a record is mentioned.

I would like to acknowledge my co-editor John P.L. Roberts, whose intimate acquaintance with Gould was a rich source of information. In addition, the contribution of research assistant Valerie Verity, who for three years followed the twists and turns of the Gould manuscripts, was invaluable. She helped in the selection of letters and undertook the thankless task of technical research for the footnotes. The archivist Gilles St-Laurent helped with the audio-visual documents of the Gould collection and, with Cheryl Gillard, assisted with the checking of archival data; the archivist Raymonde Litalien helped us to understand the nature and function of the correspondence as an archival document. Phyllis Wilson did the word-processing of the letters and Ming Bao did the word-processing for the footnotes. Mathieu-Emmanuel Bélanger provided pertinent information regarding the quantitative distribution of the letters. Sally Livingston translated my introduction into English. I am especially grateful to Richard Teleky for his assistance in preparing this edition, and Jean-Jacques Nattiez, who arranged publication of the French version in the collection of which he is co-editor (with Pierre Boulez) for the publisher Christian Bourgois in Paris. I hope that all of those cited above will accept our warmest thanks.

Research on the correspondence of Glenn Gould was made possible by the cooperation of Stephen Posen and the financial support of Glenn Gould Ltd.; the Québec organization F.C.A.R. (Fonds pour la formation des chercheurs et l'avancement de la recherche – programme Aide aux chercheurs des collèges), which for five years subsidized my work on Glenn Gould; the Collège Edouard-Montpetit; and the faculty of music at the Université de Montréal.

[1] These figures refer to the entire Gould correspondence, including greeting cards, undated letters, and dated letters starting in the 1940s. The correspondence is divided into two groups in the Gould collection of the music division at the National Library of Canada, Ottawa, according to the following codes: outgoing letters (two boxes) 1979 – 20, 31, 32; incoming letters (four boxes) 1979 – 20, 33, 34, 36, 37.
[2] Dates in parentheses refer to the letters in this edition.
[3] A variety of documents, so named by Gould himself.
[4] The chart shows *dated* letters starting from 1956, and does not include correspondence before that year.
[5] Payzant, "Interview: 'Yes, But What's He Really Like?'", in *Glenn Gould Variations* (Toronto: Doubleday Canada, 1983), p. 80.
[6] For example, his telephone bill for Jan. 4, 1975, totalled $1,404.78; for March 4, 1975, $1,185.93. The bills for 1973 and 1974 came to similar amounts. On the other hand, the years 1980-81-82 generally show much lower figures, between $100 and $800 a month.

TO FLORENCE GREIG GOULD[1]   [c. 1940]

1. Dear Mistress[2]
   Sometimes I'm as bad can be,
   I run away quite often;
   But when I give you my sad look
   I know your heart will soften.
2. and when I'm home I try to show
   I'm really not so dumb,
   and when I get a pat from you
   I know you love me, Mum.
3. E'en when I'm given a gentle shove,
   and Master Glenn says 'bother,
   Get out of here you big old hound',
   I know I've got you, Mother.
4. 'Cause every day throughout the year
   your good to me dear Mummy
   You fix my ears, and let me out
   and make my dinners yummy.
5. I really do appreciate,
   and here have tried to say,
   How much I really love you
   For your care from day to day.

Your setter,
Nicky

[1]Glenn Gould's mother.
[2]Doggerel valentine written by Gould to his mother, at about seven years of age, on behalf of his dog, Nick.

1

TO OTTO JOACHIM[1]

32 Southwood Dr –
Toronto –
[c.1955]

Dear Otto,

Reach for your most reliable sedative. You are about to receive a blast! As you will no doubt recollect – the quartet[2] has been in your possession for nigh on 2 months. As yet I have had no word that work has begun. You will remember that I wanted to come to a rehearsal while it was still in the formative stages of preparation – It is not, as you will admit, I'm sure, an altogether uncomplicated work and I feel it is sufficiently important for us to go over the score that I am willing to come to Mtl. preferably the last week of Feb

I have waited with exemplary patience, not usually identified with my temperament. And, in the past couple of months, I have given you guys a helluva lot of free publicity. Your performance? of it has been mentioned in numerous interviews on my trips – Naturally, all this stems from motives of the greatest altruism. But even the benign charitability of my nature has plumed its abyssmal recess. And now the Gould ire so long sublimated with friendly forebearance gives sign, and symptoms of severe inflamation. (A condition against which terramycin is woefully ineffectual)

I know that you will be in Toronto on Feb 9 however my recording session begins the preceeding day and I shall be away for several weeks. The quartet by the way, is to be done (at least, I should say, it is 96% certain) in a concert of contemporary music at Town Hall in N.Y. next season. Feel free to laugh about the adjective 'contemporary'!!

Seriously, I am sure you will see the problem. A – that this year is rather a full one for me and if I am to come to Mtl – I should like to arrange it to our own mutual convenience. B – That I am anxious (I think understandably) about the quartet since it is important to me to have some foreknowledge of its first performance.

It only remains to appeal to you to reply at the earliest possible occasion.

Yours, for high fevers, and more intoxicated climaxes.
Richard Strauss[3]

---

[1]Born in Germany in 1910, and naturalized a Canadian in 1957, Otto Joachim is a composer, teacher, and violist/violinist, and founder/member of the Montreal String Quartet, in which he played the viola.

[2]The Montreal String Quartet made a transcription recording of the String Quartet, Op. 1, by Gould, in 1956. In 1960, the quartet was recorded for commercial release by the Symphonia Quartet of Cleveland at Severance Hall.

[3]A Gould pseudonym, used here because the quartet was influenced by Richard Strauss.

2

TO WALTER KAUFMANN[1]

November 7, 1956

Mr. Walter Kaufman
Winnipeg Symphony Orchestra
Winnipeg, Manitoba

Dear Walter:

May I offer my very sincere compliments on the opening broadcast of the Winnipeg Symphony. I don't know whether I have always listened to the wrong performances and recordings, but, believe it or not, I had never before heard the overture to Meistersinger at a tempo in which every contrapuntal excursion was transparently manifest.[2] For the first time I realize that it is quite possible, while maintaining one tempo, to provide the full impact of contrast between such rhythmecally similar motives. The whole effect, particularly with the superb triple counterpoint, was griping in the very best sense of the word.

I was not able to hear all of the Fifth, but admired the same lucidity here also. Looking forward to next month.

Sincerely yours,
Glenn Gould

[1]Conductor, ethnomusicologist, composer, and teacher, Kaufmann (1907-84) emigrated to Canada in 1947. He was the conductor of the Winnipeg Symphony Orchestra when Gould wrote to him.
[2]Gould transcribed and recorded Wagner's *Die Meistersinger* Prelude in 1973 (Columbia).

TO C.W. FITZGERALD[1]

December 27, 1956

Mr. C.W. Fitzgerald
Steinway and Sons
New York, New York

Dear Winston:

This is a delayed precis which was requested by your office after our conversation held some weeks ago in regard to C.D. 90.[2]

An explicit summary of my complaint can scarcely fail to do justice to the incredible negligence on the part of your firm, of which I have been victim since our first dealings 18 months ago.

Surely no artist of the undersigned stature has ever received such lack of consideration, and so conspicuously failed to reap those advantages of personal consideration which, through popular legend, have become a trademark of Steinway and Sons.

3

In brief however, my dispute with C.D. 90 centres on the following promise; – the piano is, without doubt, too loose in action. With my own flair for mechanical adjustment, I have made innumerable alterations which have been, of course, to the incalculable advantage of C.D. 90. These alterations have taken the form of deepening the key draft somewhat, in the hope of producing a reaction tentamount to a heavier touch. However, it does not seem that, in this case at least, my theories of keyboard alignment have been altogether successful. Indeed, I am now totally unable and unwilling to play for even the briefest period on this instrument. I need only mention parenthetically that my admiration, indeed my enraptured awe, at the interpretative versatility, the corrective faculty, the sheer exuberance of tonal palate offered by my subsidiary instrument, the worth Chickering remained undaunted.

There remains only two concerts this season for which I should use CD 90. They are both during the latter half of February. Consequently, if there is any possibility of having your expert technicians do a leading job or some such similar offence, it would have to be accompleted during the coming month.

I noticed when playing the new Steinway in Vancouver (which, but the way, I liked very much indeed) that that instrument had leads inserted in the fore-part of the key just beneath the beginning of the black key. They, I imagine, were a compensating weight for a heavier set of leads in the rear and so this defies the protestations of the uniformity so often declaimed by the distinguished representative of your firm.

In faith and in conclusion, this operation suggests to me the only possible solution of my present predicament, if it should fail to be successful or if you should fail to acquiesce to these most reasonable suggestions, I shall be left no alternative but to avail myself of your oft-repeated offer to assist me in selling this nine foot delight and to return once more to my old standing as a Heintzman artist.[3]

Cordially yours,
Glenn Gould

[1]Winston Fitzgerald was Artist Liaison in the Concert and Artist Department of Steinway & Sons New York.
[2]CD90 refers to a Steinway piano.
[3]Gould was extremely even tempered, and this letter is one of the few examples of him in a rage. He had a profound knowledge of the mechanical aspects of pianos and their actions, and before performances often spent an inordinate amount of time with a piano tuner, making certain that the action of the piano he was about to play was totally to his liking. After having tried various Steinway pianos, Gould settled on one that he greatly cherished for most of his professional life. It was CD 318, now in the National Library in Ottawa. He briefly owned a German Steinway and also kept the Steinway given to him by his parents (which was not a full concert grand) in his Toronto penthouse for practice purposes. Miraculously, it rarely needed tuning. It is now in Rideau Hall, the residence of the Governor General of Canada. Gould also used an old American Chickering

(the instrument referred to in this letter) as a practice instrument, but over the years he let it fall into lamentable condition. Towards the end of his life he purchased a Yamaha in New York and used it for his second recording of Bach's *Goldberg Variations*. (He used a Steinway for his first recording of this work.)

TO THOMAS McINTOSH[1]

GOULD'S CLINIC FOR
PSYCHO-PSEUMATIC THERAPY

32 Southwood Drive
Toronto, Ontario
January 21, 1957

Mr. Thomas McIntosh
Washington, D.C.

Dear Thomas:

I am delighted to hear that Dr. Gould's perscriptions as usual proved efficacious. Due to my long experience with internal medicine practice I am unusually alert to the problems of neurotic artists. Whenever you are planning a trip up to Canada my nurse will be glad to arrange an appointment.[2]

The yellow sleeping pills are called Nebutol. The white sedatives are called Luminal. I believe that both will have to be obtained through your doctor. Luminal is perfectly harmless and can be taken generally three times a day: – one after the noon meal and two at bed time. I strongly advise however that you do not make a habit of Nebutol. It should definitely be reserved for the nights before special occasions and to break chronic sleeplessness.

I spoke with Winston[3] on the phone this morning and he tells me that you received very favourable notices, so many congratulations. I am sorry that I couldn't be there.

The person of whom I spoke in connection with the Marlboro School is Prof. Harvy Olnick, c/o Royal Conservatory, 135 College Street, Toronto, Ontario. All good wishes.

Sincerely
Glenn Gould

[1]A pianist friend.
[2]Gould had difficulty sleeping and took sedatives before going to bed. Eventually he could not sleep without taking Nembutol, but finally he gave up the habit by changing his work pattern. In the latter part of his life he worked throughout the night and slept as best he could during the day.
[3]Winston Fitzgerald.

TO JOHN ROBERTS[1]

32 Southwood Drive
Toronto, Ontario
February 15, 1957

Mr. John Roberts
Canadian Broadcasting Corporation
Winnipeg, Manitoba

Dear John:

Many thanks for the recording. I haven't heard it as yet because the 78 arm on my record player is out of order but I'm looking forward to hearing it very much indeed.

I do wish that you had enclosed the bill which is certainly my responsibility. Nevertheless I am extremely grateful.

I am delighted to hear that you are doing the two programs of my recordings. In regard to the Beethoven Sonatas:[2] they have, as you know, received both extravagant praise and devastating condemnation. I can only say that those alterations of dynamic or tempo indication with which I took licence were the result, not of whims, but of rather careful scrutiny of the scores and bear, up to the moment at any rate, an optimistic conviction.

Since so many listeners and critics (trustworthy ones too) have taken exception to my conception of late Beethoven I cannot claim that it is the most convincing recording that I have made. However, I do feel that, if only as a personal manifesto, it is the most convinced.

Kindest regards.

Sincerely yours,
Glenn Gould

[1]From 1955 to 1957 John Roberts was a music producer for CBC Radio and assistant music director for CBC Television in Winnipeg.
[2]Recorded in 1956: Beethoven Sonata No. 30 in E major, Op. 109; Sonata No. 31 in A♭ major, Op. 110; Sonata No. 32 in C minor, Op. 111 (Columbia, issued in 1956). Gould described music as "a malleable art" but his unorthodox performances of the three last sonatas, with changes of tempi and dynamics, upset critics and colleagues.

TO MOUSE POSSUM BANK[1]

Wien June 3/57

Dear Mouse-Possum-Bank –

As you will see I did manage to get to Wien. I thought in case you worried about my being sick in Frankfurt I should let you know everything was okay now. (I am assuming you have seen the letter sent to Mrs. Wadge.[2])

Actually I spent a pretty miserable day with sinus pain – much like the time I came home from Texas and was deaf, remember (last November). Aeroplanes can wreak havoc with a cold. Anyhow, I stayed in Frankfurt (which is a very beautiful city from what little I saw of it) for the week-end – then took the train last nite to Wien.

But it seems that this just wasn't my weekend because this morning at 6.30 the porter came around to give me back my passport when we had crossed into Austria and as I was opening the door of my compartment he suddenly pushed it shut again on my left thumb and said thumbnail is now turning slightly blue and making it a bit difficult to write – Hope it will be allright by Friday.

Otherwise I was glad I look the train because if provided an opportunity to see something of the countryside. Our route was through Wurzurg, Nurnberg, Passan and Linz. The countryside of Upper Bavaria which I saw for about two hours until dark is just indescribably lovely. Endlessly rolling hills, rivers, beautiful forests and any number of quaint little towns dominated by baroque churches. The most wonderful pastorale imaginable. I stayed up till 11.30 specially to sing *Die Meistersinger* as we went through Nurnberg.

But the countryside of Northern Austria this morning was less eventful. (I was up at 5 AM window gazing.) Not nearly so prosperous, dried up streams, rather shabby villages, every square foot of usable land planted – it was a little reminiscent of parts of French Canada.

You remember Walter[3] running into Steinberg[4] in Switzerland last summer. Well last night I went one better – I was getting on the train at Frankfurt when I noticed a distinguished looking white-haired man on the platform taking the air (the train was the Amsterdam-Wien-Express) I looked twice to make sure, then said – "Excuse me, but isn't it Mr. Stokowski."[5] He winced as though he thought I were a reporter or an autograph-hunter and without turning to look at me mumbled "It is." I ploughed ahead and said "Permit me to introduce myself, sir. I am GG." Suddenly he smiled "Are you Glenn Gould!" Whereupon like a benevolent long-lost grandfather he came into my compartment and chatted for half an hour.

A real character but very charming. He wanted to know all about Russia – Had I seen Ulanova?[6] Did I hear Richter?[7] Had I met him? Do they still serve wonderful tea and terrible coffee? The answer to all these being "Yes" he then told me about his tour of Russia 30-odd years ago.

Anyway we had a great time. Saw him again this morning. He is conducting at the Festival.[8]

Walter and I wish you had sent the Records-reviews from Holland. Were they all that bad? We did want to have an idea how the reaction was there.

Don't know what will become of me after Wien. If I can get an international driving permit (which I have just found out you can *not* get in Wien) I shall possibly rent a car and pursue *either* of 2 routes which appeal to me at the moment of writing.

(1) Salzburg – Munich – Stuttgart.
Frankfurt – Colonne – then fly to London.
(2) Trieste or Venice (or both) – Milan
Geneva – then London –

If I do get the car please rest assured I shall not speed and shall generally exercise utmost caution. If I don't get it – you will likely see me home a lot sooner than expected. I am not a good tourist – I'm afraid – I never have had the energy to traipse about from village to village. When I am settled in one place I am happy but I still hate moving about [Attention H. Wadge][9] This does not minimize the fact that I have had a wonderful time in Europe. In fact I am seriously thinking of taking up residence here for 6 months of 58-59.

Now, may I close with a suggestion for you two – Why not plan and save now for a trip in Europe. Forget about going west – this is much more exciting. You (I address this to Daddy) are always talking about being a good traveller and not being tired by long trips, so you could certainly enjoy driving around as I hope to do. Besides, if my plans of the moment go through I shall be establishing my European residence (sounds imposing what?) probably in Germany in the early fall of '58 (concerts permitting) and you could come over and visit me.

Leon Fleischer[10] and his wife are living in Italy this summer where they have 2 servants pulling down high wages – the equivalent of $1.00 per day each. To give another example – last nite I had dinner in my room as usual in Frankfurt where the food was 1st class. Steak, vegetables, fruit juice, ice cream with all kinds of trimmings, coffee – the sort of dinner that would cost $7.00-8.00 in N.Y. hotels – for 10 marks – i.e. $2.40. And in Germany things are relatively expensive.

So take the advice of a world traveller – Rent the cottage, if need be.

Love,
Glenn

PS. (over) Your letters just arrived. Glad to hear that Ann[11] has the Dutch reviews in hand. She should send them on to Walter as soon as possible.

You mention Grandma – I did send her a card from Leningrad – one of several I wrote on my last day there and gave to Henrietta[12] to post. The others were to the music scribes in Toronto. I'll write again because I bet 'Henri'[13] forgot all about it.

I think that bit about Susan[14] running away is awfully funny – though not to her parents, I guess. I hope my exploits don't affect many youngsters that strongly.

You ask about cars in Russia. There are by our standards very few, indeed. Trucks and buses outnumber them, or so it seems. They produce only 4 different types of automobile, ranging from the equivalent of the small Nash, say, to the luxury model operated by govt bureaux and approximately the big Desoto airport limousine type. In body style they are closer to the pre-war La-Salles, which, since you know my affection for LaSalles is not meant to be derogatory. The Ministry of Culture cars were usually of this ilk – curtains on the windows rugs on the floor – tres snazzy. But the average person does not own a car. Hope that answers the Question Department for today.

Hound   Mouse   Possum on a dead tree trunk

P.P.S. Will let you know by wire where I will be going as soon as I know myself. In any case I will be home by the end of June.
P.P.P.S It is absolutely impossible to get much practise in here – So many concerts going in all the halls. I should have stayed in Berlin.
P.P.P.P.S. Thanks for sending the clipping of the Telegram Soviet reviews[15] – They were *all* ones that we had not seen and I was delighted with them – The quotes from the musicians in Leningrad were from people I got to know and talk to while there – Walter sent a letter off to the Star with that delayed 'Busoni' review from Berlin – He thought they wouldn't pay for another telegram. That one was much the best review I have ever had and by a tough critic too!

Appendix and Errata Thurs.
Greetings once again,
    The letter as so often happens with me has sat around all week and not been mailed. Sorry!
    However it may be just as well because now you can relax for it seems that I cannot get a drivers lisence. The only place one can get one is in London.

Frankly, though you will no doubt be relieved I am very disappointed. You cannot see too much of the country without a car. So as of this writing I still don't know for sure what I will do but the chances are, if I can get a reservation I will go either to Switzerland (Geneve or Zurich) or to London or perhaps both but I am afraid my leisurely trip through the Bavarian countryside is out – I can't be bothered fooling with train schedules et al.

In any case I will now definitely be back here because this morning Walter had an excellent offer for some concerts in Germany[16] and besides that Dr von Karajan[17] has offered to introduce me to any city where he happens to be conducting if our schedules fit. So things are in good shape for Germany in the future.

I find Vienna much less attractive than I imagined it. Too much rococo architecture for my rather severe tastes.

My cold is still with me and gives signs of becoming the annual hayfever. You'll hear from me by wire.

Love
Glenn

P.S. I recorded an interview this afternoon with Ted Viets from Detroit whom you met up at Stratford[18] last summer. Ted arrived here yesterday. The CBC told him if he got something interesting to send it back. So we talked a little about Russia. Don't know when it will be on, if at all. They would probably use it for News roundup or something like that.

---

[1]Gould wrote this letter to his mother (Mouse), his father (Possum), and his dog (Bank, after Shakespeare's Banquo from *Macbeth*).
[2]Mrs. H. Wadge, a musical admirer in Uxbridge, Ontario.
[3]Walter Homburger.
[4]William Steinberg (1899-1978), German-born American conductor.
[5]Leopold Stokowski (1882-1977), British-born American conductor.
[6]Galina Ulanova (b.1910), Russian dancer.
[7]Sviatoslav Richter (b.1915), Ukrainian-born Soviet pianist.
[8]The Salzburg Festival.
[9]Mrs. H. Wadge, as above.
[10]American pianist, conductor, and friend, Fleisher (b. 1928) was admired by Gould.
[11]A friend.
[12]Gould's official interpreter during his stay in the U.S.S.R.
[13]Henrietta, as above.
[14]One of the children taught music by Gould's mother.
[15]Gould's schedule in Russia: May 7, 1957, a recital sponsored by the Moscow State Conservatory, Grand Hall, Moscow State Conservatory, Moscow; May 8, a concert, Moscow Philharmonic Orchestra, Tchaikovsky Hall, Moscow; May 11, a recital, Tchaikovsky Hall, Moscow; May 12, a recital and demonstration/lecture, Moscow State Conservatory, Moscow; May 14, a recital, Bolshoi

Hall, Leningrad; May 16, a recital, Glinka Hall, Leningrad; May 18, a concert, Leningrad Philhar-monic Orchestra, Bolshoi Hall, Leningrad; May 19, an informal concert recital, Leningrad State Conservatory, Leningrad.
[16]May 24-26, 1957. Concerts with the Berlin Philharmonic Orchestra, Konzertsaal, Hochschule für Music, West Berlin.
[17]Herbert von Karajan (1908-89).
[18]The Stratford Festival in Stratford, Ontario.

TO C.W. FITZGERALD

September 20, 1957

Mr C.W. Fitzgerald
Steinway and Sons
New York, New York

Dear Professor Fitzgerald:

Further to our conversations of a few moments ago – I have now contacted your ambitious salesman and local representative, Mr. James Graham, who, of course, is firmly convinced that the entire project is the conception of a fevered brain, but who, in the best tradition of Steinway's good relationships with their artists, has agreed to humour the undersigned's present notion.

Mr. Graham requests from you an order for the piano which he can present to customs here in order to expedite its clearance. The piano, as I mentioned, is joshingly referred to as #266,[1] since the poor piano has never been given the honour of bearing the illustrious trademark of Steinway and Sons – a CD insig-nia. Indeed is is regrettable that one of the finest flag ships of your fleet should be so deprived. It would be a gesture entirely worthy of the noble dedication of your company if, during the October visit of your most celebrated artist and your most glorious instrument if a diner were held at which a bronze plaque might be unveiled on the lyre of #266 (which, Mr. Graham tells me, has been lost ever since I had it in Toronto last week) bearing the inscription "this instrument maintained for the exclusive use of our favourite son, Vladimir Gouldowsky).[2] If you will inform me as to the hour and place of this dinner (the Oak Room at the Plaza would be appropriate) I will start to work on my address which I shall endeavour to keep within modest limits – certainly not exceeding $2^1/_2$ hours.

Yours with ever renewed friendship,

[1]#266 was a piano Gould had discovered – and taken a fancy to – at Steinway & Sons New York.
[2]A Glenn Gould pseudonym.

11

TO E.A. WRIGHT

Mr E.A. Wright,
Paris, Ontario.

Dear Mr. Wright:

I wish to acknowledge the receipt of one of your folding chairs (#503) which you sent me for inspection. I have decided to keep this chair and would be grateful if you would forward your bill to me.[1]

For my purposes (as you may recall, I wanted a chair suitable for use at the piano) the only defect is that the back tends to be a bit straight, i.e., there is approximately a 90° angle where the back adjoins the seat. This has the rather uncomfortable tendency of forcing one to sit unusually erect and is augmented by padding at the back of the seat. I was wondering whether you happen to have another model of folding chair similar to this one but on which the back would slant at a somewhat more leisurely angle. In comparison, the #100 chair of the London firm, of which we spoke, is somewhat more comfortable because of an angle greater than 90°. If you could alter one of your present chairs slightly in order to compensate for this angle, I would be very happy if you could let me know, and I could then try out the altered version.

Thank you very much for your cooperation.

Yours truly,
Glenn Gould

[1]Gould liked to sit low at the keyboard. Because piano stools did not allow for this, his father decided to provide him with a portable chair. Bert Gould bought the lightest folding chair he could find and attached brass fittings to the legs, which allowed his son to adjust them as he wished. There was an upholstered seat that gradually disintegrated, and finally had to be discarded. From time to time Gould tried to find other chairs that would prove as successful as his father's, and this letter is concerned with such an attempt.

TO YOUSUF KARSH[1]

July 8, 1958

Mr. Jousuf Karsh,
Ottawa, Ontario.

Dear Mr. Karsh:

Herewith are the answers[2] I promised you, or at least if they do not constitute answers they represent fantasies of my own construction which may be of some use.

1) During the two weeks in Russia,[3] I was originally scheduled to perform on the programs only two contemporary works – sonatas by Hindemith and Berg.[4] Both of these might be considered fairly conservative representations of Western music but both were unfamiliar to the Russian audiences and were received with no noticeable frigidity on their part but they were ignored almost altogether in the review articles.

However, during the course of the visit, I was invited to play for the students and professors of the Conservatories in both Moscow and Leningrad. I accepted with great delight but with the stipulation that I be allowed to play just whatever came into my head at the moment and that there would be no formal program. After some discussions with my manager and the people at the Embassy, I decided to play for them a program composed entirely of contemporary music, most of it belonging to what is loosely referred to as the Viennese school – the Arnold Schoenberg, Anton Weber tradition. I began by re-playing the Alban Berg sonata which I had included on one of the regular programs and which, in some ways, starts at the very threshold of contemporary music or at least at the very threshold of atonal music. It was written in 1908 and provided a wonderful point of departure from which to play for them and talk to them about the more serious facets of twelve tone music. I talked to them, by the way, with the assistance of no less than four different interpreters – one was officially provided, one was from the Embassy and two were students who spoke flawless English. These four supplemented one anothers vocabulary of technical terms and we made out amazing well – at least the audience mostly laughed in the right places and I assumed I was being translated accurately, although one can never tell. When I first announced that I was going to do, i.e., that I was going to play the sort of music that has not been officially recognized in the U.S.S.R. since the artistic crises in the mid thirties, there was a rather alarming and temporarily incontrollable murmuring from the audience. I am quite sure that many of the students were uncertain whether it was better for them to remain or walk out. As it turned out, I managed to keep things under control by frowning ferociously now and then and the only people who did walk out were a couple of elderly professors who probably felt that I was attempting to pervert the taste of the young. However, as I continued playing music of Schoenberg from his earliest years almost until his death and following that, music of Webern and Krenek, there were repeated suggestions from the student body, mostly in the form of discreet whispers from the committee on the stage but occasionally the odd fortissimo suggestion from the audience that they would prefer to spend their time with Bach and Beethoven.[5]

By and large, however, it was an experience which I will remember for the rest of my life as being the most exciting musical occasion in which I have taken part. The students and the professors are as a whole so wonderfully attentive and receptive that you are dealing with the sort of audience that is amenable to any well presented idea. It was a sensation equivalent to that of perhaps being the first musician to land on Mars or Venus and to be in a position of revealing a vast unexplored territory to some greatly puzzled but very willing auditors. It was a great day for me!

2) You ask if I feel that artists have an obligation to present contemporary works. I feel that they do only if they have a genuine enthusiasm for a certain segment of contemporary music which they are presenting. I think that there is no use whatever in presenting it for its own sake without the same kind of conviction that would be present in a performance of Mozart or of Brahms.

3) It is, unfortunately, true that in my own case I have in the past few years been seriously hampered in concentrating very much time on composition, which is the field in which eventually I feel I must devote my energy. Concentrating so much on a touring career has decided limitations which are not all offset by the practical compensations of earning a living. Though I should hate to be held to this prophecy, I hereby go on record as announcing that while I will never stop playing the piano, indeed could never stop playing the piano, within five or ten years I will have made a major shift in the time which I allot to each facet of my career. I must add that I went on record once saying to a reporter from the Toronto Telegram that I would retire at 23. Unfortunately I said it when I was 22 and he reminded me of it when I was 24, so perhaps you should take the above with a grain of salt!

4) Your question about repeated performances is a very penetrating one and one that touches upon the psychology of the concert business. I must say that I am totally incapable of understanding how it is possible for a theatrical per- former to chalk up, say 500, consecutive performances of the same role on Broadway or on tour. They say that such things become completely instinctive, which is probably true, but it does not alter the element of boredom or stagna- tion which, it seems to me, will inevitably take its toll. For my own part, I alternate programs as frequently as is physically possible and within the frame- work of the same repertoire I make frequent rearrangements – anything to preserve some vitality and enthusiasm!

5) My reading has been governed to a certain extent by a sort of informal plan but it is never quite as exclusive to any one period or writer as perhaps the press book which you have suggested. At the present, I am on a history kick!

6) You ask about my being self-taught since the age of 19. I would be very reluctant to say that this is a blueprint which others could follow. In my own case, it was an invaluable experience. I had been for nine years a student of Alberto Guerrero,[6] for whom I have much admiration, but I felt that at a certain

point I was equipped with everything, except the kind of solidarity of the ego which is, in the last analysis, the one important part of an artist's equipment. It seems to me that even if one does the wrong thing at any time there is a kind of absolute right about making ones own wrongs. This is what I experienced with great benefit at that time.

7) I really have no particular preference about sizes of auditoriums except as related to certain portions of the repertoire and, even then, I can think of some extraordinary exceptions to the rule. Generally speaking, one would prefer to play music of earlier times, Bach for instance, which was intended for instruments much less powerful than our own, in a very intimate surrounding or at least a moderate size auditorium. But, as recently as last March, a concert for the University of Kentucky was held to my horror in an arena which seated some 12,000 people. This happened to be one of th biggest subscribed concert series in U.S.A. with an audience of some 7,000 which improved the acoustics to a certain extent. But the main problem was not one of projecting to the man in the back seat but rather not projecting to the man in the back seat. Though I was simply terrified about the whole thing, I resolved to resist the temptation of putting everything in the score up 50% in order to compensate for the hall in which I was playing. Instead I deliberately played for myself trying to conceive the performance as though it presented no more dynamic problems than a broadcasting studio or a living room. The only compensation which I made was the pacing of the performance on a slightly broader scale in order to allow for the echo potentials of the hall. But I must say probably because of the fine instrument on that occasion and the very sympathetic audience, it turned out to be one of the most enjoyable experiences of the entire season.

It was a great pleasure to meet you again last night at the Frontenac[7] and I hope that the above will prove useful. Again may I say how pleased and honoured I feel to be included in your book.[8]

Most sincerely,
Glenn Gould

[1]Yousuf Karsh, the internationally renowned Ottawa-based photographer, had taken a photograph of Gould early in his career. (Later Gould thought of the photograph as being too monumental and official.) Karsh was extremely interested in Gould's trip to the Soviet Union in 1957.
[2]In his letter dated June 26, 1958 Karsh had asked Gould to send him the answers to an enclosed questionnaire.
[3]Gould was one of the first musicians from North America to perform in Russia, in May 1957, and his visit caused a sensation. Because of the difficulty of students obtaining tickets to his concert, Gould gave free concerts for them in both Moscow and Leningrad.
[4]Paul Hindemith's Sonata No.3 B♭ major, and Alban Berg's Sonata, Op. 1.
[5]A live recording was made without Gould's consent on May 18, 1957, in the Bolshoi Hall, with the Leningrad Government Philharmonic Orchestra, Ladislaw Slovak conducting. J.S. Bach Concerto No. 1 in D minor, BWV 1052, and Beethoven Concerto No. 2 in B♭ major, Op. 19 (Melodiia).

⁶Born in Chile in 1886, Guerrero became a leading musical figure there before emigrating, first to New York and then Toronto, in 1919. Three years later he joined the Toronto Conservatory of Music, where he taught until his death in 1959. He said of Gould, "The whole secret of teaching Glenn is to let him discover things for himself."
⁷The Château Frontenac Hotel, in Quebec City, where Karsh stayed while photographing Maurice Duplessis, then Premier of Quebec.
⁸Gould's photograph appears in *Karsh Portfolio* (Toronto: University of Toronto Press, 1967).

TO JOAN BONIME¹   August 5, 1958

Miss Joan Bonime,
New York Philharmonic,
New York, New York.

Dear Miss Bonime:

Yesterday I phoned in the timing of the Mozart C minor, K 491, which, according to my clock, was bout 30 minutes. I am sorry that I was so long in replying to your letter but quite frankly, I had forgotten about it until a few days ago.

I now see that you have requested from Walter² the suggestion for a harpsichord concerto to be included on the program. I assume that you mean the harpsichord concerto be included with the Mozart concerto (would it also be with the Beethoven C minor on the Sunday?) My suggestion would be either the Bach F minor concerto or the G minor concerto, which is a transposition of the A minor violin concerto. The timing of the F minor is approximately 10 to 11 minutes. I am not certain of the G minor but the advantage of the latter would be that in the event of civil strife or acts of God preventing my appearance, any back desk man from the fiddle section could fill in for me. I hope that you pass this information along to Lennie³ and see what he would like to do.

The cadenza to the first movement of the Mozart C minor is by Hummel. There are two brief moments of cadenzas in the slow movement which are improvised by me, to the horror of all musicologists, and which are so slight as to be undeserving of an asterisk.

I shall be in New York at the end of this month, to be specific August 27th, and I shall give you a call and see what has been decided.⁴

Best regards,
Glenn Gould

¹Joan Bonime, of the New York Philharmonic Orchestra, was trying to finalize Gould's contribution to two programs.
²Walter Homburger.
³Leonard Bernstein.
⁴Gould performed Mozart's Concerto No. 24 in C minor, K 491, on April 2, 3, and 4, 1959; on April 5 he played Beethoven's Concerto No. 3 in C minor, Op. 37.

TO LEONARD BERNSTEIN

August 29, 1958

Mr. Leonard Bernstein,
New York City.

Dear Leonardo:

The address of somebody or others Vineyard was given to me in New York where, of course, I left it, so I hope this is duly forwarded to you. I also trust that you have now recuperated from the South American trip and are once again able to function at sea level.

The advance plans for the Philharmonic look marvellous. I feel it is going to be the most exciting one in its history. I had some misleading correspondence from Joan Bonime – something about doing a harpsichord concerto. I assume, of course, that she meant a harpsichord concerto on the piano and suggested Bach F minor or G minor. It now turns out that she meant – rather you meant – Handel and meant it on the harpsichord, which presents a certain problem of muscular co-ordination for me it is within the same 48 hour period and I am attempting a piano concerto. My only possible alternative suggestion would be to do a Handel concerto on the organ, but most certainly not on the Carnegie Hall organ. If we could find a cute little neo-baroque Kisto Whistles it would be fun, but I still would approach it with some temerity.

Somehow I think that Mozart and Beethoven is a big enough assignment but being a hard-working hack, I am always ready to spread my talents with a lavish hand. I think maybe I should just be a pianist this year!

I see by the Musical America[1] that you are conducting in Milan in the middle of November, which is exactly the time that I am playing in Florence, Turin and Rome. If it is at all feasible, I shall descend upon La Scala (or is it Le Scala?) and take a few conducting lessons.[2]

All the best,

[1] *Musical America*, Vol. LXXVII, No. 9, August 1958, p. 131.
[2] Gould did not go to Milan.

TO WALTER HOMBURGER[1]

Hamburg
October 18 [1958]

Dear W.H.

By the time you get this I may have spoken to you by phone again but in any case here is the pertinent information which we can thus save a few long distance dollars by mutually comprehending. – I have a chronic bronchitis in the right lung. This we found out by X-rays yesterday. Since I don't know too much about this I am not sure that the practitioner who is seeing me is the best person for the job. (The X-rays of course were done by a lung specialist) But the daily doctor is very much a Nature-Boy type – milk and honey, cold cloths on the right side – all that sort of thing. I'm sure this kind of doctoring would suit you perfectly but it doesn't seem to be getting me any improvement.

Along with this as I told you on the phone the other night I have a high fever every evening (last night up to 100.8) but it doesn't begin to go up till around dinner time. I think you will admit that an ascent of 2 or more degrees is not quite the usual evening rise. The doctor is not sure that the fever is entirely connected to the bronchitis – though no doubt contributory. And of course since he comes in every morning around 10 and finds me with my fever down or gone altogether he didn't quite believe me, I think, until I showed him a thermometer this morning saved and unshaken from last evening's crest. He was dutifully impressed but still doesn't know to what extent they are related.

Consequently if, on Monday, things are not really looking up, I shall try to find a diagnostician or someone like that. Tomorrow's and Monday's concerts with NDR[2] were, of course cancelled – that is my part in them.

I spoke with Kollitsch[3] twice today – he is solicitus and kind as always but is of course worried as to whether I can do his recital on Friday. I told him that as long as this exotic fever with the accompanying aches, and weakness lasts I can not or will not leave this bed. (Fortunately it's quite a comfortable one)[4]

One last skeletal detail I have since arriving in Stockholm lost 20 pds, and this with the 10-15 I lost after Salzburg puts me back to the poundage of my delicate years – 150. And while I don't mind returning to the figure and spirit of those ingratiating times, I would prefer to do it a bit more gradually.

Now to the central point we've all been waiting for. A few more days of this and if I see no hope of speedy recovery, I am going to cancel the works and head for Die Zamberburg[5] (for goodness sake, don't quote that last or the local yokels will have me with FB[6] in no time. It would not have to include Israel – yet – on whose deaf ears so many wise warnings have already fallen Frau Geotte of the Konzert Dir. here is already aware that her recital stands in jepordy so that would leave only Vienna (I don't really mean that only) and Italy, which pleasant task we would leave to Miss Camus.

I think I can already see you picking up impassioned pen and writing me not to be a fool, or similar sentiments couched in softer, more soothing Homburger-ian tones. But the facts remain that it is far more difficult on the local mgr. to find a replacement two days before the concert, and for that matter it does my reputation much more harm this way also.

And, most important of all, I am afraid of sacrificing this winter's tour and health at the shrine of this month's gallantry.

I believe I have now rendered my views in a manner which does them the justice of poetry, and I shall now apply another wet towel to my right side and put this away.

Please express my customary but infirm, passion to Mlle Sandercrook.[7]

Wishing you, sir, the full retention of your customary vigours and exhuberant step.

I am, with affection,
GLENCHICK

[1]Well-known impresario, and Gould's agent. Homburger became Managing Director of the Toronto Symphony in 1962 and subsequently established a reputation as an arts administrator. When Gould was little more than a child, Homburger had been quick to recognize his outstanding abilities.

[2]Norddeutscher Rundfunk. It has headquarters in Hamburg.

[3]Wolfgang Kollitsch, an impresario who had arranged Gould's engagements in Germany.

[4]Gould had been feeling unwell since late September but continued his concert tour until Hamburg when he was confined to bed. He sought a medical diagnosis and an estimate of the convalescence period required. He had already developed a reputation as an artist prone to cancel concerts.

[5]Der Zauberberg is a sanitorium in Thomas Mann's novel The Magic Mountain.

[6]For "FB," a typographical error in the original, read "TB."

[7]Walter Homburger's secretary, Verna Sandercock.

TO VLADIMIR GOLSCHMANN[1]   November 4, 1958

Dear Vladimir,

I have been exalting for two days now in our Beethoven #1 which was sent to me – I hope you have heard it and are as proud of it as I am.[2] There is a real joie-de vivre about it from beginning to end. Usually I become disenchanted with any new record by the second playing but I have now listened to it about 6 times and like it better each occasion.

Quelle accompaniment!! I ran into my old friends Sir Ernest[3] and Lady Mac-Millan here this morning – played it for them and Sir Ernest, who is always somewhat reserved in his appreciation, was full of admiration for the beautifully articulated playing of the orchestra. If I have anything to say about it this is not the last record we make together.

I trust you are now settled in New York and commuting to Tulsa – I was very sorry that we couldn't work together there this year but hope it will be possible next season.

At present I am in semi-permanent residence here[4] (having been here 3 wks. and 1 more to go) I came from Sweden where I picked up something called nephritis and have been undergoing tests and diets ever since. But in another week I should be able to resume the trip to Italy. (So far 9 concerts cancelled).

I think I shall sign off and go and play the record for the 7th time. My best to Odette and love to you both,

Glenn

PS Since writing, I have played the Beethoven for Dr. Helmut Storjohann, the Oppenheim of Germany (Deutsche Phillips). He was greatly enthusiastic and I think he might issue it over here. Why not make me your manager? You'll never meet a better press agent!!

[1]French-born American conductor (1893-1972).
[2]Gould's recording of the Beethoven Piano Concerto No. 1 in C major, Op. 15, with Golschmann conducting the Columbia Symphony Orchestra, was released in 1958. Some critics were startled that Gould included his own cadenzas because they sounded more like Richard Strauss than Beethoven (Columbia).
[3]Sir Ernest MacMillan (1893-1973) was an important figure in the musical history of Canada. Conductor of the Toronto Symphony Orchestra from 1931 to 1955, he was also a composer, organist, and administrator at the University of Toronto.
[4]This letter was written on stationery from the Hotel vier Jahreszeiten, in Hamburg.

TO GLADYS RISKIND[1]

32 Southwood Drive
Toronto 8, Canada
June 30, 1959.

Dear Old Shenner:

Many, many thanks for your letters. As I warned you, I am a very haphazard correspondent but please don't let that compromise your maidenly pride and write as often as you can.

Your description of your first day on the job was very sad and affecting but I think not really unexpected and I am equally sure that by now you have found a greater security in the work and are getting along famously. I would love to know how your interview with Julie Andrews came out. By the way, your fame as foreign correspondent reached its zenith with a picture on the front page of the Globe & Mail, in which, doggoned, if you didn't look glamourous as hell! I assume that your mother saw it and sent it to you. If not, let me know and I shall try to dig up a back issue of the Globe from you – it was the one at the UNESCO conference or whatever.

When I arrived home at the airport on friday afternoon, I immediately phoned Gordon Spears[2] and told him about the indiscretion about the two hotel suites.[3] He sounded rushed off his feet and we only spoke for a minute but he did say that he was not sure about the fate of the story and did not seem to want to elaborate beyond that. I was rather puzzled by this and didn't notice until the

20

following day that in Friday's paper, they devoted an editorial to me, a very flattering and gracious editorial, but written in the manner of an apology. It took the tone that the London press had overstated my mannerisms and that all good Canadians would rise with irate displeasure at the slighting inference that I was anything other than the archtype of the well scrubbed, gentlemanly boy next door. It seemed odd that it was also the Star that reproduced the Manchester Guardian to the exclusion of all others. I still think that your story struck a sane balance between the two poles and was, moreover, entertaining, and extremely well written and I think it would have done much more to straighten out the misconception of the Neville Cardus reproduction than the editorial, which most people probably missed seeing anyway.

For the past week I have been on top of the world. I have been luxuriating in the glow of the NFB movie spotlight and I believe that I have finally found my true place in this world. I am, forsooth, an actor, something my public has long suspected anyway. We have been doing sequences in New York this past week and tomorrow we begin the scenes at Uptergrove.[4] I will tell you about the thing in detail when I see you in August and I only hope that I am still supported by this lofty cloud of ego on which I ride at present. This movie-making has done more for my morale and indeed enthusiasm for life in general than anything else within memory.

Finally let me say what a great pleasure, a really great pleasure, it was to see you and talk with you so much in London. I hope that you found our talks of some benefit; I know that I certainly did, and I also hope that you are finding the desired balance between your social and business life and that your enthusiasm for London is unwavering.

Affectionately,

[1]A friend of Gould's, Riskind was a journalist.
[2]Borden Spears was Managing Editor of the *Toronto Star*.
[3]During his stay in London, Gould maintained two hotel suites; he slept in one and used the other as a practice studio.
[4]Location of the Gould family cottage on Lake Simcoe, north of Toronto.

TO LUKAS FOSS[1]   June 30, 1959

Mr. Lukas Foss
c/o Berkshire Festival
Lenon, Mass.

Dear Lukas:

I am getting the quartet[2] off to you finally and I apologize for being so late about it. I was in Europe for some weeks and fell behind in my promises. I hope you like the quartet – it is a work that I am proud of but not altogether happy with. It was my first attempt at writing for strings and my old organist's habit of seeing the cello line as a pedal-board induced me to keep it for long stretches on the C string, among many other faults.

Your concerto[3] languished in Canadian Customs for many weeks but it was recently rescued, however, I have not really had time to examine it too carefully. I find that I love the first movement – it is marvellously well constructed – but I am not so certain about the finale. I hope that we can get together for some talks soon.

All the best for a good summer and let me know if there is any chance of running into you in New York soon.

Sincerely,

[1]German-born American composer, conductor, and pianist (b. 1922).
[2]This was the first, and only, string quartet that Gould composed.
[3]Probably Foss's Piano Concerto No. 2, written in 1949 and revised in 1953.

TO LOUIS LANE[1]

June 30, 1959

Mr. Louis Lane
Cleveland Heights, Ohio

Dear Louis:

Thank you very much for your letter of June 4th.

First of all, let me say that I see no problem in coupling the Bach and the Schoenberg on the same half of the program.[2] I did it this way with the New York Philharmonic last year[3] and it worked quite well. I am quite sure that two rehearsals will be sufficient for the Schoenberg and I am looking forward to doing it with you very much.

I have asked my publishers, Barger & Barclay, to send you a score of the quartet[4] as well as a set of parts so that your resident quartet can look at it. I think they should know, however, that it is a rather formidable work – in terms of length and physical demands – and besides that, it is in a good many instances badly written for strings. It was my first attempt at writing for strings and my old organist's habit of seeing the cello line as a pedal-board induced me to keep it for long stretched on the C string. Nonetheless, it is a work that I am quite proud of and I would be delighted if they decided to do it.

Now then, while addressing women's associations are not one of my favourite pastimes, I am more than happy to barter a lecture on Schoenberg for a perform-

22

ance of the quartet. As a matter of fact, I have done three such lectures in Toronto in past years, one of them devoted entirely to an analysis of the concerto. On that famous occasion, I was a guest lecturer on a series at the University here and was asked to prepare a 50-minute talk. Somehow or other, it extended into one hour and 35 minutes and the Assistant Principal of the Royal Conservatory finally strode on stage and informed me that I was infringing on the time of the annual Christmas party and even if I hadn't got around to discussing the inversions in the last movement, would I please shut up and go home! So your poor ladies may be in for more than they bargained for. I would like, however, to have a piano available if we do this and perhaps with the coffee they can hand around serviettes inscribed with the tone-row of the concerto.

All the best for now and let me know how the quartet strikes you.

Sincerely,

[1]American conductor (born 1923). In 1959 he was assistant conductor of the Cleveland Orchestra, under George Szell.
[2]Gould performed in Cleveland on November 26, 1959: Schoenberg's Piano Concerto, Op. 42, and Bach's Brandenberg Concerto No. 5, in D major, BWV 1050.
[3]On March 13, 14, and 16, 1958 Gould performed Bach's Concerto No. 1 in D minor, BWV 1052, along with Schoenberg's Piano Concerto at Carnegie Hall with Dimitri Mitropoulos and the New York Philharmonic Orchestra.
[4]Gould's String Quartet, Op. 1.

TO CHRISTIAN GEELHAAR[1]   December 16, 1959

Mr. Christian Geelhaar,
Berne, Switzerland.

Dear Mr. Geelhaar:

I want to thank you very much for your interesting and very detailed letter of October 11 and I want to apologize very sincerely for having taken so long in replying to you. All of your questions in regard to my performances I found extremely interesting and I only regret that I, frankly, do not have the time in answer them in the detail that they deserve.

You ask about a suitable introduction to the music and world of Arnold Schönberg. I think that perhaps, in a general way, the best volume dealing with Schönberg and with his major pupils is Rene Leibowitz's book "Schönberg and His School. "[2] This was written in french, later translated into English and I would imagine also into German, though your English is really remarkably fine and you have no reason to apologize for it or I should think search for a German translation of a technical work such as this. In the United States it is published by

23

the Philosophical Library. Another work which strikes me as being of some value to you is Dika Newlins' "Bruckner, Mahler and Schönberg"[3] in which she traces with great authority and clarity the emotional ties of Schönberg to the Viennese tradition.

I cannot think of any one particular recording that I would recommend except, in a general way, I suggest that Schönberg is most excessible when approached through his early works and there are several excellent recordings of the two Chamber Symphonies, of the first two String Quartets and so on. If you can still find them, the old and out-of-print recordings of the first String Quartets by the Kollisch Quartet are perhaps the most beautiful and authentic document of Schönberg interpretation up to the present time.

As to the matter of interpretation and the artist's fidelity, or lack of it, my approach has always been a rather relaxed improvisatory one when dealing with those eras out of the repertoire in which the performer's role was, in part at least, that of an elaborator. On the other hand, many of the liberties I have taken with the Mozart K 330 I cannot attempt to defend on any grounds other than those of instinct. However, when I do arbitrarily change a phrase marking or dynamic indication, I do attempt to integrate it into the concept of the work as a whole and not to allow it to be simply and exclusively a notion of the moment without relation to the total conception.

Finally, as you were kind enough to inquire about future recordings, I am able to tell you that this winter recordings of the Third Beethoven Concerto with Leonard Bernstein, the first two Bach Partitas and the Italian Concerto will be released.

Again, I thank you very much for your letter.

Cordially,
Glenn Gould

[1]Geelhaar is a specialist in the relation between the history of art and musicology. He is the author of *Paul Klee and the Bauhaus* (Greenwich: New York Graphic Society, 1973), as well as other works.
[2]New York: Philosophical Library, 1949.
[3]New York: King's Crown Press, 1947.

TO NICHOLAS GOLDSCHMIDT[1] January 13, 1960

Mr. Nicholas Goldschmidt,
Vancouver Festival Society,
Vancouver, B.C.

Dear Nicky:

After our lovely Christmas Day talk, I called the first violin of the Symphonia Quartet in Cleveland and asked him to send you their repertoire. Did you get it?

He explained to me that they are involved with their summer season during all of July and August but since the conductor in charge, Louis Lane, is a good friend he was quite sure that any time that was necessary for the trip could be worked out. I spoke to him on the basis of three programs which I think is also what you had in mind – (1) a chamber music program with me, (2) an evening of quartets by themselves, and (3) participation in the performance of "Ode to Napoleon" on the Schoenberg concert.[2]

I had an immediate reply to my letter to Kirsten Meyer[3] in which she said that she would be most happy to sing a couple of early lieder as well as the Hangen-den Garten. She was going to take a look at some of the titles I suggested to her and choose the ones she found most suitable. This being the case, we could quite easily let her have the whole first half of the program, i.e. three or so early lieder and then the Hangenden Garten. This should comprise about 30 to 32 minutes. The second part of the program could then consist of the Opus 25 Suite for Piano (or perhaps the Opus 19 Miniatures and the Opus 25), and could conclude with the "Ode to Napoleon." This would make the second half about 35 minutes long, which, considering the fact that either before Part I or just after intermission I will be doing considerable talking, is I think plenty long enough.

I have thought a good deal about your excellent suggestion of reviving the Eroica Variations[4] and the more I think about it the better I like the idea, and I agree with you that unless I think of a better conclusion to the program, it should definitely be the Eroica. As you wanted a composer list for the recital program without final selections, you might announce Byrd, Bach and Beethoven, and if you really feel it is the right choice, Morawetz.[5] I do feel, however, that if you decide to program his Symphony on Steinberg's program, it would be less urgent that I play a piano work of his and therefore it might be possible for me to do something late romantic or modestly contemporary, e.g. the Berg Sonata, which I have never played in Vancouver.

Do let me know what you decide in regard to a narrator in the "Ode to Napoleon." If it is at all possible, I should like to get together with whoever it may be (assuming it was a person from Vancouver) when I am out in Victoria the end of March.

All the best for now,

Sincerely,

[1]Conductor, administrator, teacher, and founder of several important music festivals in Canada, Goldschmidt was born in Czechoslovakia, in 1908, and became a naturalized Canadian in 1951. As Artistic Director and Managing Director of the Vancouver International Festival he had engaged Gould to perform in 1960. In spite of his statement to the contrary in this letter, Gould was already afraid that he might be forced to cancel his trip to Vancouver because of his shoulder injury.
[2]On July 27, 1960 Gould performed with the Festival Chamber Orchestra, conducted by Louis Lane: Bach's Concerto in G minor and Beethoven's Concerto No. 4 in G major, Op. 58. On

August 2, 1960 Gould gave a recital with Kerstin Meyer and the Vancouver Quartet of works by Schoenberg: *Das Buch der Hängenden Gärten*, Op. 15 and *Ode to Napoleon Buonaparte*, Op. 41. ³Swedish mezzo-soprano (b. 1928), Meyer was both a colleague and a friend of Gould's. ⁴On July 29, 1960 Gould gave a piano recital of works by Beethoven and Berg: Beethoven's Sonata No. 17 in D minor, Op. 31, No. 2, the *Eroica Variations*, Op. 35; and Berg's Sonata for Piano, Op. 1. ⁵Oscar Morawetz (b. 1917) is a Canadian composer and teacher. Gould admired Morawetz and performed and recorded his Fantasy in D minor, written in 1948 (Columbia).

TO EDITH BOECKER   January 27, 1960

Dear Edith:

Many thanks for your Christmas greetings. I did not send mine earlier because I had no way of knowing whether or not you still resided in Husumer Strasse. I had speculated that you had probably moved and, indeed, when I last heard from you, you were by no means sure that you would remain in Hamburg. Are you, by the way, still affiliated with Philips?[1]

Now then, allow me to ease some incredibly goring pangs of conscience on the subject of whether or not I ever did extend my felicitations to you on the occasion of your marriage. I remember clearly receiving the announcement, complete with Bach chorale, which I came across again in my "Buddenbrook" file the other day, but did I ever write you at the time? If 'yes', chalk this interrogation up to the senile ramblings of my advanced years but, if 'no', your delayed acknowledgement of "The Last Puritan" is completely exonerated.[2]

Now to some bracing news. By now you have probably read that I will not be in Hamburg on February 10, indeed will not be in Europe at all during the winter. A little over a month ago I sustained an injury to my left arm and shoulder in what may gallantly be called an "accident" at Steinway Hall in New York. As the "accident" however was entirely due to the idiocy of one of Chez Steinway's senior employees and as it may yet result in some legal move being taken, I cannot speak of it without wincing. Next time I see you I shall give you all the details (it has its funny side but, for the moment, only the results). The initial injury was to the left shoulder and when x-rayed the shoulder blade was shown to have been pushed down about one-half an inch. That problem has basically been cleared up now but has caused a secondary reaction much more troubling. The nerve which controls the fourth and fifth fingers of my left hand has been compressed and inflamed or whatever with the result that any movement involving a division of the left hand, as a sudden leap to the left side of the keyboard, is, if not actually impossible, accomplished only by a considerable effort of will. Now if this had only happened in Hamburg I could have blamed it all on poor Herr Richter! I am not, however, just sitting by and idly letting this run its course, in fact, I have been having two treatments per day on different aspects of it – one medical and one chiropratic – while no one seems to feel that it is likely to become permanent, I must say I am becoming rather dissatisfied with the relative lack of improvement.

Quite apart from this little excitement, this past season has been one fraught by all kinds of curious adventures. Several months ago I began to develop a longing for grandeur which my establishment at Lake Simcoe was not fully able to satisfy. So, more or less on a whim, I became the tenant of an estate some fifteen miles above Toronto, known as "Donchery." It was love at first sight and it lasted until the day after the lease was signed! The estate, let me tell you, had 26 rooms, if one counts the 7 bathrooms, the breakfast room, the scullery, the dog kennel, and every other partition which could conceivably be construed as a room. It also had on the property, which by the way was beautifully wooded with a river running through it, a swimming pool and tennis court. The swimming pool was surrounded by a four-car garage and boys and girls dressing rooms (no bacchanalian revelries for us!). The house was situated some 60 steps above the river (known as the Don) and the view from down below looking up and especially at night with flood lights was like looking at Salzburg castle from your own strawberry patch. Oh yes, there was one of those too on the other side of the Don.

Anyway, the lease was signed on December 13 and on December 19 I was suddenly struck with the realization of what I had done as well as with the intriguing puzzle of what I would ever do with 26 rooms in the first place. Of course everyone here put their own interpretation on it and the most fascinating stories were circulating about Toronto. Unfortunately someone let the news of this operation get to the newspapers and from that moment on the house began to be enlarged by one wing every day. The last time I was accosted on the street about it someone asked me whether it was really 40 rooms or just 38!! Mr. Homburger, I think, was terrified that I was giving up the piano to devote myself to the role of country squire and his secretary was convinced that I was having an affair with the upstairs maid (who hadn't yet been engaged – to do house-work, that is) and my mother, I'm sure, was convinced I was secretly married.

On the second day of the lease, I sent out on a gigantic buying spree in a vain attempt to furnish 26 rooms in two days and, with all the ferocity of the plague at Oran, I descended with a group of advisors on one of the large department stores. It was my first exposure to household purchasing and I must say that I was rather intimidated by it. It was relatively easy in the kitchenwares where I was able, for the most part, to stand with my head inside an oven ostensibly examining the broiler and even in the towel and bathmat department, I managed to pick out some subdued specimens which I felt would go well in the master bedroom suite. (By the way, the master bedroom suite possessed a fully broad-loomed bathroom!) But it was really in the bedroom furnishings that I began to show signs of weakness and, although mattress testing has always been among my favourite private pastimes, I began to feel rather conspicuous when a group of salesmen began to persuade me of the advantages of "Beautyrest" vs "Posturepedic." This little vignette was made the more dramatic because I was accompanied by a most elegant young lady, who was left over from the kitchenware blitz, and who tested the mattresses with such dignity that all of the salesmen were addressing her as "Madame."

The following day I was back at "Donchery" to welcome the movers as the various purchases began to arrive. I was alone at the time in the 26 rooms and at first, as the larger items such as the refrigerator and the stove arrived, I was grateful for the space which they filled and optimistic about the possibility of polishing off the other 25 rooms. But then suddenly it happened – the brooms and the pyrex dishes arrived and I was filled with all the horror of the domestic idyll I had been courting. Suddenly "Donchery" represented a snare, my lease commitment, the pyrex dishes – permanency – and my only escape seemed to flee with my trusty Buick, into which I sprang, and I streaked for Toronto.

Only last week, at considerable expense to the management, was I able to purchase my release and so now, when not occupying a newly acquired apartment in Toronto, I return with my tail between my legs to Lake Simcoe which somehow seems quite grand enough.

I am not really minding the enforced leisure too much. In the last weeks I have been studying most of the Bruckner symphones with an eye to doing an essay I have had in mind for sometime and besides that, I am preparing to produce "Hamlet" tomorrow evening at the regular meeting of the Lower Rosedale Shakespeare Reading Society.[3] I believe I spoke to you of the splendid work of the Society! Tomorrow evening, as well as officiating as technical director (I am the only one who owns an Ampex), I shall also be a dynamic Laertes and a cockney gravedigger. We must try and spread a little culture in the colonies!

If you are still with Philips, would you please give my best regards to Dr. Storjohann and tell him that I have a new recording of the third Beethoven concerto with Bernstein being released this month.[4]

All the very best,

Affectionately,

---

[1]Boecker had moved to Heidelberg and was no longer affiliated with Phillips.
[2]Gould referred to himself as the "last puritan," after the title of George Santayana's novel *The Last Puritan.*
[3]The Lower Rosedale Shakespeare Reading Society consisted of Gould and a small number of friends. It was organized in 1957 at the apartment of John Roberts on Edgar Avenue in Rosedale, an affluent Toronto neighborhood. Later, meetings took place in Gould's penthouse on St. Clair Avenue West. It was not a formal society but rather friendly gatherings at which the plays of Shakespeare were read and enjoyed. Gould always undertook several roles, and because he had a

sophisticated Ampex tape recorder, assumed the role of technical director. Other plays were eventually read, including those by Oscar Wilde and George Bernard Shaw. The society also branched into character improvisations.
⁴Concerto No. 3, in C minor, Op. 37, recorded with the Columbia Symphony Orchestra, conducted by Leonard Bernstein.

TO WINSTON FITZGERALD   February 17, 1960
Mr. Winston Fitzgerald,
Steinway & Sons,
New York, New York.

Dear Winston:

It was good to hear from you and I admit my guilt in not having written to you before. Frankly, I have been in such a bad humour that I felt that the main topic of conversation would be altogether too painful.[1]

I must say I was a little surprised at the tone of your letter in so far as you seem to express some bafflement about the nature of my malaise (or did I misread between the lines?). I can appreciate the predicament in having to make up suitable alibis for me but, at the same time, I can tell you that the only reason my arm condition was allowed to be construed by the papers as a "fall" was to avoid a fuller explanation which would perhaps cause some embarrassment to Steinway & Sons and which would, in any case, require more character delineation of the employees of said firm that would be practical for the limited spaces of the New York Times.

I can assure you that I, too, have no wish to see this extend itself into a "Horowitzian Legend," but neither have I any wish to represent myself publicly in performances that are necessarily deficient because of this arm injury. I don't know what is going to happen to the balance of the season.[2] At the moment it looks very grim – I am consulting with all kinds of orthopaedic people and others but they are all understandably reluctant to give positive assurances as to when and how. I am toying with the idea of cancelling all recitals for the balance of the season and perhaps doing a few concerto performances which are less strenuous and in which to an extent the inadequacies of the left arm can be disguised (I have never been an inveterate pedaler but I may have to become one!) I have set an arbitrary deadline of this weekend as to the time when I shall make a final decision as to what will happen to the concerts in March. I can't bear the thought of passing up such a lucrative month but, as of this moment, it looks like more cancellations.

If a miracle happens and the arm radically improves I will be in touch with you immediately on the subject of pianos for the various places. You might in any

29

case, as a safety measure, remind Sherman Clay in San Francisco that I reserved No. 122 (?) for the Los Angeles recital on March 23.[3] In all probability I will not cancel all the concerts at once, probably the first two weeks of the month and then see what happens so that Sherman Clay should still continue to hold the reservation for me.

If you have anything to alleviate the gloom, do write.

Best,

[1]This letter refers to what Gould described as a "slap on the back" by an exuberant employee at Steinway & Sons in New York. Although the intent was undoubtedly innocent, the result was an injury that caused Gould physical problems and considerable anguish. Recovery from the injury was so prolonged that many engagements could not be undertaken, and Gould was afraid of not being able to continue his career. (The injury resulted in financial compensation from Steinway & Sons.) The injury was deleterious in another way. A natural performer, Gould really did not know how he played the piano from a physical point of view. Generally, Gould avoided pianists as much as possible and loathed pianistic talk. Thereafter he started considering physical aspects of performance in increasing depth, and this became a negative factor in his life.

[2]Gould retired from the concert stage on April 10, 1964, in Los Angeles, California.

[3]No. 122 refers to a Steinway piano. The Los Angeles recital was cancelled.

TO SCHUYLER CHAPIN[1]   March 10, 1960

Mr. Schuyler Chapin
Columbia Records,[2]
New York, New York.

Dear Schuyler:

I took due note of your letter in which you suggested the D major, E major or the F major concerti of Bach for recording with the CBC Symphony with Bob Craft or Susskind. None of these three are in my active repertoire though the mention of the F major, which I seem to recall being a transcript for piano fo the Fourth Brandenburg Concerto, prompts me to dig it out of the library and have a look at it. I do feel, however, that for facilitating another recording, i.e. April or May, a concerto in my repertoire is essential. I am lukewarm about the idea of the G minor Bach concerto because it doesn't really lie very well on the piano and I feel, all things considered, the best coupling for the Schoenberg would be the Mozart C minor, K 491. Not only is it one of my star pieces but I think it might help the sales potential of the Schoenberg concerto considerably.[3] My own preference would be to do this with Walter Susskind if it were done in Toronto and I would suggest that it could be done with a group of players chosen from the ranks of the CBC Symphony. They possess very capable first desk woodwinds which, of course, are necessary for the slow movement of the Mozart. If you decide on this coupling, it seems to me that we might arrange a session shortly after the Schoenberg session, which I assume will be April 30 (Saturday). My next concert after that is in Detroit on May 6 (Thursday) so that were it convenient for you and for the CBC, it might be possible to do such a recording of the Mozart in the period between May 2 and 4. I am assuming that it is useful to do both recordings at the same time. If this is not of much importance or saving to you, we could always do the Mozart later on.

I had a note from Bob Craft recently in which he asked if I would consider the Berg Triple concerto for the reverse side of the recording.[4] It is a work that I have never played although I have looked the score through several times and it is a work which, frankly, I am not very fond. I am going to communicate this to him. However, if you prefer to maintain the recording as an example of the Viennese Twelve-Tone School, I would have no objections to only being involved on one side of the recording, i.e. having some other pianist do the Berg concerto on the other side. I do feel though that in view of what we have talked about in relation to an exhibit of music in Canada doing a classical concerto, such as the Mozart K 491, with Canadian forces is a good and sound idea. I consign all this, sir, to your characteristically impeccable judgement.

I must tell you that the arm is very, very much better. The cortisone is having a truly miraculous effect, except that it makes me wretchedly nauseous but I have developed a system of taking it one day, being sick the second day, eating the third day, taking the cortisone the fourth, etc. At any rate, the improvement is wondrous and I must say, retrospectively, that I have, because of the enforced abstinance, discovered a whole new enthusiasm for music and music-making. I am dying to make recordings now and the more the better. I do hope we can get together with Eileen Farrell[5] when I am next in New york, and I am definitely planning on two Beethoven albums for recording this summer; the sonata albumn, which we have talked about, and the three sets of Variations, which I mentioned to you last week.[6] At the moment I am writing and re-writing the script for next week's television show on Beethoven and I must say I never realized before quite what a gift it is to possess innately the ability to say things in generalities and not suffer inhibitions in so doing.[7] The more I try to simplify this thing, the more hopeless it gets because, in reducing the verbage, it simply becomes mercilessly compact and pressured and I have now been advised to inject into it a fine old Madison Avenue formula: "Tell them what you are going to say, say it, and tell them what you've said."

All the best,

[1]In 1970, Director of Masterworks.
[2]Later CBS Records, now Sony Classical.
[3]This recording was produced at Toronto's Massey Hall and released in 1962. It consisted of Schoenberg's Piano Concerto Op. 42, with the CBC Symphony Orchestra, conducted by Robert Craft, and Mozart's Piano Concerto No. 24 in C minor, K. 491, with the CBC Symphony Orchestra, conducted by Walter Susskind (Columbia).
[4]American conductor, writer, and music scholar (b. 1923). After 1948 Craft was closely allied with Igor Stravinsky, collaborating in many concerts, recordings, and publications.
[5]Gould did not record with American soprano Eileen Farrell.
[6]Gould's first recording of the Beethoven sonatas was issued April 1965. It included No. 5 in C minor, Op. 10, No. 1; No. 6 in F major, Op. 10, No. 2; No. 7 in D major, Op. 10, No. 3 (Columbia). *Thirty-two Variations in C minor* recorded in 1966; Six Variations in F major, Op. 34, (Columbia, issued in 1970).
[7]February 6, 1961 on "Festival/61 CBC." "The Subject is Beethoven" with American cellist Leonard Rose (1918-84). Together they performed Beethoven's Sonata for Cello and Piano, No. 3 in A major, Op. 69. As well, Gould played Beethoven's *Eroica Variations*, Op. 35.

TO ROBERT CRAFT

March 10, 1960

Mr. Robert Craft
Hollywood, California

Dear Bob:

Thank you very much for your card. I am happy to be able to say that the arm is finally beginning to respond. I have been put on cortisone, which makes me feel rather wretched and nauseous, but it is having an amazing effect on the arm. I am still, quite frankly, uncertain as to whether I will be able to play in Los Angeles on the 23rd or not. If not, I will let them know within the next few days. I resumed my activities last week with a concerto performance in Baltimore but I have otherwise postponed all recitals scheduled for the first half of March.[1]

At the moment, despite the improvement of the arm, the problem is one of fatigue over more extended periods of playing and I still doubt my ability to get through a whole recital evening. I have managed, so far, to postpone most of the scheduled solo recitals into May and if the worst comes I hope that might be possible with the Los Angeles engagement also.[2] Anyway, I will write directly to Miss Huttenback within the next couple of days.

As of this moment and prospecting continued improvement in the arm, the performance of the Schoenberg on April 29[3] and the recording on April 30 is very much on and I am certainly looking forward to working with you. I must tell you, quite frankly, that the Berg Triple Concerto is not by any means a favourite of mine. I wish it were because it would be an advantageous coupling but, as it is not, I really must decline to play it and I am leaving the ultimate decision of what to put with the Schoenberg to Schuyler Chapin.[4]

I would be delighted to take a look at Mr. Stravinsky's new work[5] so if you can spare a copy, please bring it with you to Toronto – or send it earlier if you prefer. Please give him my greetings and best wishes.

And, also all the best to you,

Sincerely,

[1]On March 2, 1960 Gould performed the Beethoven Concerto No. 4 in G major, Op. 58, with Peter Herman Adler conducting the Baltimore Symphony Orchestra.
[2]This performance was cancelled.
[3]The Schoenberg was paired with Mozart's Concerto No. 24 in C minor, KV 491, with Walter Susskind conducting the CBC Symphony Orchestra.
[4]Schuyler Chapin was Executive Co-ordinator of the Masterworks Division of Columbia Records, New York.
[5]Gould is referring to Stravinsky's *Movements* for piano and orchestra, composed in 1958-59. However, Gould was not interested in this work and, generally speaking, he was not interested in Stravinsky's music. At one point there was some talk of Gould recording the *Capriccio* for piano and orchestra by Stravinsky. However, Gould was cool to the idea. An unstated problem with recording anything by Stravinsky was that with the composer alive and too close for comfort, Gould would not have been able to make the music his own.

TO WILLIAM B. GLENESK

May 31, 1960

The Rev. William B. Glenesk,
Spencer Memorial Presbyterian Church,
Brooklyn, New York.

Dear Bill:

It was awfully good to hear from you again.[1] Your letter did not indeed find me preparing for Stratford or at the moment anything else. I have been somewhat out of condition with a shoulder injury for the last six months and, for the last month and a half, I have been in Philadelphia taking treatments with a famous orthopaedic surgeon. I have not cancelled all concerts this winter but a very large percentage of them and all solo recitals because the fatigue from playing a whole evening of music was simply too much. The shoulder was injured in a rather fantastic circumstance which took place in Steinway & Sons last December and sometime when I see you I shall tell you all about it because it really needs some fanciful narration to get all the crazy aspects of the story across. However, I am hoping to begin full activities with the Stratford and Vancouver Festivals this summer.[2]

I was very interested to read about the series of lectures you are arranging and very impressed with the list of lecturers. I must say, however, that in order to say something individual on the subject of ecclesiastical influence on Bach, or on the Baroque music generally, I feel that a more specialized study is necessary than that which I have devoted to Bach. As you know, when I do get around to writing something or lecturing, I really take the project seriously, perhaps too seriously, but I feel that on the subject that you suggest, a great deal could be said afresh, as it were, but I also feel that it would require someone to do a considerable amount of research into the Bach bibliography dealing with the subject and more especially into the cantata literature.

I have been involved the last couple of years in a study of Bach from one particular angle, that of disposition of modulation in Bach's music. On two of the concerto recordings which I made, I devoted a good deal of space on the record jackets to feeling around the edge of this problem and it is something which I hope within the next year to two to develop into a lecture and subsequently into an extended essay.[3] I might possibly give this lecture at Stratford this summer in conjunction with an evening of Bach concertos which we are planning to do but this is by no means certain.[4] I mention all this simply to say that that particular aspect of Bach (an aspect which has remained surprisingly unexplored and the ignorance of which, I think, is the largely lamentable tradition of playing the more extended Bach movements as though they were simply moving in endless circles of modulation rather than following a course carefully charted and marked by specific points of harmonic emphasis clearly governing the total shape of the work though not given a special formal shape, such as the later Sonata-Allegro, for example) has already taken a great deal of thought and study and preparation in order to permit me to feel that I am saying something which has not quite been said before and, as this subject is one which is more readily available to me as a practising musician than the quasi-philosophical one which you propose, I really feel that for your purposes you need someone much more experienced and knowledgeable in the command of the 17th century church-state-social concepts.

But I really do wish you the best of luck with this series and I sincerely hope that you will find someone who will fit the bill a little better than I. Please keep me informed of your activities. I am a very sluggish correspondent but it is very good to know what you are doing.

All the very best,

[1]In a letter dated May 25, 1960, Glenesk invited Gould to lecture on Bach and the factor of religion in his works. Gould declined, but he did write on this subject in a letter to Harriet Ingham (April 19, 1962).
[2]Gould was co-director of musical activities at Stratford from 1960 to 1963, during which time he

gave eleven performances, the last on July 28, 1963. During July and August 1960, he gave three performances at the Vancouver International Festival.
³Gould's record-jacket notes appear on the following records: J.S. Bach's Piano Concerto No. 1 in D minor, BWV 1052, with Leonard Bernstein and the Columbia Symphony Orchestra (Columbia) and J.S. Bach's Piano Concerto No. 5 in F minor, BWV 1056, with Vladimir Golschmann conducting the Columbia Symphony Orchestra (Columbia).
⁴The lecture was not given.

TO NICHOLAS GOLDSCHMIDT

May 31, 1960

Mr. Nicholas Goldschmidt,
Vancouver Festival,
Vancouver, B.C.

Dear Nicky:

Thank you very much for your letter of May 20. I have just returned from Philadelphia and regret to say that although I am, in your terms, an "outcast," the treatment there was by no means wholly successful.¹ I am not telling you this incidentally to indicate that there is the slightest chance of my not playing this summer, so please do not be alarmed, but purely for your own information the case was by no means a total success. There has been, however, some improvement in the arm, I believe, and I am beginning to wear a metal cervical collar which is intended to hold my neck in place while playing the piano. Needless to say, I am not intended to wear this during any concerts.

As I just returned to Toronto yesterday, I have not yet had time to comply to your request for a 200 word introduction on Schoenberg but I shall be more than happy to do so and shall get it done this week, and hope to have it off to you no later than next week, if that is convenient.

I could give you right now the opus numbers, movements, etc. of the program which we projected earlier in which I intend to include, as you recall, a Byrd group, Bach Partita, Beethoven Eroica Variations, Berg Sonata, etc.² However, if you will bear with me for just a few more days, I would like to try doing a little playing in my cervical collar, which I have not yet done, to find out just how well it would work. The reason for this delay is that certain works were easier for me to play in view of my shoulder condition than others and the most difficult to play under these particular circumstances was music such as Bach with an evenly distributed contrapuntal line texture between the hands, and the easiest was Beethoven with a homophonic distribution. Consequently, if you don't mind waiting a few days, I would like to try a few things and make sure that the mixed program that we spoke of would not pose any undue strain.

I have not yet heard from Kirsten Meyer as to her decision regarding doing the early lieder at the opening of the program before the Hangenden Garten.[3] I assume that you have not had a reply either as you would probably have let me know. So, in this case, I am going to be very blunt about it and simply request that she program the following songs: Waldsonne, Opus 2; Traumlieben, Opus 6; Verlassen, Opus 6. All of these songs should lie perfectly for her voice since I have done them all before with singers of approximately the same range of voice and none of them are certainly very difficult and should present no unusual preparatory problems. Do try to get her to confirm this and let us, one and for all, settle the order of the program. I feel that it should be as follows:

  I. Three early songs (as above)
  II. Talk by G. Gould
  III. Hangenden Garten Lieder, Opus 15 Intermission
  IV. Talk by G. Gould
  V. Suite for Piano, Opus 26
  VI. Ode to Napoleon

I hope this meets with your approval. Last week I dispatched the recording of "Ode to Napoleon" which I hope you have by now.[4] Do give my regards to Donald Brown and the quartet, and I hope the recording is of real use to them. But do let me know about Meyer. I feel it is terribly important to do something of the earlier years and, unfortunately, apart from "Verklarte Nacht," there is nothing except the lieder.

Love to you and Sheila,

[1] Gould had been in Philadelphia to see the distinguished orthopedist, Dr. Irvin Stein.
[2] He performed the Beethoven Sonata Op. 31, No. 2, the Berg Sonata, Op. 1, and music of Byrd and Bach on July 29. (On July 27 he played Beethoven's Piano Concerto No. 4 in G major and Mozart's Piano Concerto in C minor, K 491, in an orchestral concert.)
[3] The all-Schoenberg concert took place on August 2, 1960 and included *The Book of the Hanging Gardens*, Op. 15; *Suite for Piano*, Op. 26; and *Ode to Napoleon Buonaparte*, Op. 41.
[4] Released in 1967, with the Juilliard String Quartet and John Horton, speaker (Columbia).

TO ABE COHEN

June 7, 1960

Mr. Abe Cohen,
Israel Philharmonic,
Tel Aviv, Israel.

Dear Abe:

Thank you very much for your letter. I only wish that I could write and tell you that all was now well with my left arm and that I was expected to experience no further difficulties and problems with it. I have just returned from spending six weeks in Philadelphia under the care of a very highly regarded orthopaedic surgeon. Four of those weeks were spent with the arm immobilized by a full body cast, the remaining two weeks were devoted to physiotherapy, etc. When the arm was completely at rest in the cast, there was indeed a great deal of relief but, unfortunately, when it was taken out and once again required full support from the shoulder, the problem returned. The doctor naturally was very disappointed and has since made a cervical collar which I am to wear while practising. Although it may be too soon to tell, this has had little or no effect.

As I indicated to you last winter, this does not mean that I am completely out of action. For four of the five months since it happened, I cancelled all concerts; for one month, March, I played a limited schedule of orchestral engagements only and all of these were quite successful. The problem is essentially one of endurance. Due to the stretching of the muscle complex of the shoulder, the arm fatigues terribly quickly and I am not able to play, for example, a full recital program and all rehearsals have to be kept to a bare minimum.

As for next season on this continent, it is perhaps too soon to make predictions. I hope that it will somehow have responded to the various treatments I am taking now and permit me to play, as scheduled, a full series of concerts – both with orchestras and solo recitals. If not, I will try to play some orchestral engagements in any case, since it is about time that I started earning some money again. It may well be that by the time that we originally spoke of for my visit to Israel, i.e. next May, all this will long since be water under the bridge. I sincerely hope so. But I can only say once again that the requirements of your schedule are rather special and that both from your point of view and from mine it would be very hazardous to make any promises, any commitments or sign any contracts right now.

As you quite rightly point out, I could play as frequently or infrequently as I wished, depending how long I planned to stay in Israel so that the problem of fatigue due to constant playing would not be insurmountable. But you must also remember, as it has happened several times in North America, I have been forced to cancel several months of concerts after having played just the week before. In other words, what I am trying to say is that I feel it is vastly unfair to you to journey to Israel with any condition which given the laws of averages would necessitate cancelling a sizeable percentage of the tour there. I feel that I should definitely wait until this condition is one hundred percent cured or until I have made up my mind to take it as it is and live with it. But I am not ready to surrender yet.

I only want to say again that there is no place to which I would rather return than Israel and you have, as you know, my good wishes always.[1]

Sincerely,

[1]Gould did not, however, return to Israel.

TO WINSTON FITZGERALD

June 22, 1960

Mr. Winston Fitzgerald,
Steinway & Sons,
New York, New York.

Dear Professor Fitzgerald:

This is just a note to remind you that before you leave on Part I of your vacation, before in other words the efficienty of Freros Steinway plummets noticeably, I would be grateful if you would make sure that all is in readiness for the arrival of CD 318.[1] I don't have to ennumerate for you the many admirable qualities of this klavier, suffice it to say it was the piano which assisted in many of the memorable moments in my career as child prodigy. For this reason alone I expect it to be given a place of honour in the basement and that Morris Schnapper[2] will be required to bow twice each time he passes it. For the exhibit in your showroom, I could if you wish send a picture of myself in the Lord Fauntleroy suit – the sort of garb with which I was usually decked out by my doting parents for performances on 318.

When I am down in two weeks, I also would like to take a look at the tack-hammer piano with a view perhaps to taking it with me to Stratford for our Bach concerto evening. It is a crazy idea probably but just crazy enough to be a great one. In any case, I will not decide that until I get there. Failing that, however, I will have to have CD 318 in Stratford for the concert on the 24th and preferably for rehearsals on the 21st and 22nd. This I realize will be something of a feat and will indeed test the metal of the shipping department especially since I will be using it in New York until the 14th. However, I am sure you will agree that association with me has frequently drawn from the rank and file of your employees deeds of which one would hardly have thought them capable, and with a little urging I am sure it can be done. You might also remind Steve that I am looking forward to his help with the Berlin Steinway – in any event on Saturday the 9th and perhaps on Friday the 8th if he can manage it and if the studio is free.[3]

I must say, sir, that my mind has never been far from the sad plight of our dear mutual friend, Miss L. Do you feel as I do that you and I working together should attempt to save her from herself? After all, we are both men of the world and vastly experienced in handling difficult cases of this kind and I do feel that we can yet bring a ray of hope into the wretched existence of this poor unfortunate girl.

Yours for lechery,
G. Herbert Gould[4]

[1] After 1960 Gould played this piano exclusively. He had it reconditioned, and bought it in 1973. After his death in 1982, the piano was acquired by the National Library of Canada (1983).

²Morris Schnapper was the concert tuner at Steinway & Sons.
³Steve Borrell was Steinway's chief concert technician.
⁴Gould's middle name was Herbert, a name he never used except in letter writing of a bantering nature.

TO WALTER HOMBURGER   July 15, 1960

Dear Gomburger:¹

I have just returned from what was supposed to have been four days' recording in New York. When I went there last week my arm, I think, was in the best shape it has been since last winter. I have been wearing the collar at all times when practising and having a great deal of physiotherapy, and I was quite sure that I could get through the recording with no difficulty. First of all, we made a film clip with Lieberson for Debbie² and I think that went very well and on a Monday I began recording. The Monday session went very well indeed. I did Opus 31, No. 2 on my German piano and I think it will be a superb recording³ but by Tuesday with the exposure to air conditioning (possibly), without the help of the collar (which I found somewhat inhibiting for the recording) and without as much physiotherapy as I had been used to, the arm had tightened up again in exactly the same way and finally on Wednesday we abandoned the recording of the Eroica Variations, cancelled Thursday's session and will take up again the end of August.

This is, needless to say, very disappointed because I had certainly expected better results by this time. The symptoms are exactly the same as before – same knot, same aches, same fatigue. Next week Stratford begins and I am determined to try to get through it, as well as Vancouver too, but at this point I frankly don't see how.

When you get back to New York you will have several other little amusements to deal with beside WNTA. Dave Oppenheim⁴ wants me to do a half-hour Omnibus. We are going to get together again in August and draw up some idea of what it will be but among the suggestions which I offered, the one that they like best and the one which I feel is most suitable for them is one which I have thought of doing for some time – "A Piano Lesson from Glenn Gould."⁵ This, needless to say, would not involve a technical discussion of piano playing but would cover quite a different and, I think, rather amusing area. I would write my own script, of course, and they want to see an outline of it in August. Dave will be on vacation when you get back but don't worry about the matter of fee negotiation. I didn't say a word (nor did he) and it will be entirely left to you.

The other amusement for your concern is the fact that RCA and Columbia have both been bidding for Mr. Richter's service to make an American recording. As usual, RCA outbid Columbia and Hurok apparently assigned them the rights. Schuyler was very annoyed about this because he was not given a second chance to raise his bid and contact a couple of guys who are opening next fall a distributing agency for Soviet recordings in New York. (According to Schuyler, they are planning to put out Soviet pressings in packages that will make Angel look like pikers.) These two guys apparently live in the Park Avenue penthouse belonging to the mistress of one of them (i.e. in the most bourgeois setting imaginable) but commute back and forth between the US and the USSR and are in direct relation with the Ministry of Culture, though they are not apparently Russian citizens. In any event, Schuyler approached them and was told that Mr. Hurok had no business to assign the rights for Richter's service as recording artist to anyone since he had not been granted them in the first place and they further said that, as far as they were concerned, the deal was far from closed and that Columbia in fact could still negotiate. "However," they said, "there is a price tag to this." When Schuyler asked what it was, they replied, "That Mr. Gould and Mr. Stern must both make a recording strictly for use of the Soviet people."

This would apparently be done in New York, probably with Columbia's facilities, but the cost and I assume the payment to me would be borne by the Soviets. In one way, it is of course very complimentary; on the other hand, there is the same irritating two for one bargain that the Russians always manage to drive. Nonetheless, Schuyler and Lieberson both would like me to do it if I can see my way clear and I know that having Richter record means a great deal to them. Debbie sees a wonderful publicity angle in the exchange recording hookup and I think she is right. How do you feel about it? Incidentally, it would apparently have to be repertoire which I would not otherwise release in North America in the next few years.[6]

I think that this is about all the news. Keep your fingers crossed that my arm holds out for the Festivals and I hope to hear from you when you arrive.

All the best,

[1] Walter Homburger.
[2] Goddard Lieberson, CBS President, and Deborah Ishlon, CBS employee in the Department of Creative Services.
[3] Beethoven's Sonata No. 17 in D minor, Op. 31, No. 2 (Columbia, released in 1973).
[4] Music executive at Columbia Records. He asked Gould to sign a contract with Columbia Records for the first recording of Bach's *Goldberg Variations*, and in this way was instrumental in establishing Gould's international recording career.
[5] Nothing came of this project.
[6] No such recording was made.

TO ROBERT WOLVERTON[1]   September 14, 1960

Mr. Robert Wolverton,
Los Angeles, California.

Dear Mr. Wolverton:
Thank you very much for your letter and for your kind comments. In reply to your question concerning my pre-concert rituals, I do indeed find that hot water is a most efficient muscle relaxant and it is true that I do wear gloves of special design twelve months of the year. The purpose of these gloves is, however, not intended for public amusement but simply as a very practical measure to insure a constant temperature of my hands when in chill auditoriums.
May I wish you all the very best for your career,

Sincerely,
Glenn Gould

[1] A fan.

TO SILVIA KIND[1]   January 25, 1961

Dear Sylvia:
Thank you so much for your letter and especially for the tape. It is really a delight. The performance is so wonderfully animated. I played it the other night for Greta Kraus,[2] a very gifted harpsichordist in Toronto, and she was thrilled with the performance and with the instrument and wanted me to be sure to ask you what instrument it was. By the way, Greta goes to Switzerland every summer and would love to meet you since I told her that you also were usually there.
I am happy to say that my arm is much better, much better – I travel now mostly with my own physio-therapist in attendance – and I have once again been able to resume all my activities although occasionally I still have to cancel a concert when there is some difficulty with the shoulder. As a matter of fact, since writing to you I have received the test pressing of my latest recording – the first one made since the shoulder trouble – and I really think it is perhaps the best piano playing I have done. It is a whole album of Brahms Intermezzi[3] and I think that you will be quite surprised not only with the repertoire but also with the style of playing which is, if I might say so, rather aristocratic. Come to think of it, I don't think you really will be surprised either. You know what an uncurable romantic I am anyway. I am sending you the recording of my String Quartet which was released a couple of months ago and, which, despite its atmosphere of faded elegance and rather bittersweet fin-de-siecle idiom, has received on the whole marvellous critical notices. There have been a few 'fashionable' reviews

which have pointed out that it is rather inappropriate to revive the spirit of Richard Strauss in the age of Karlheinz Stockhausen (or is it really his age), but the 'progressive' voices have, fortunately, been in the minority and have helped to stir up a reasonably healthy controversy.

I had a note from Dick[4] at Christmas and he seems to have settled comfortably into life in Canada once again. If he comes to Toronto, I will be sure to play him your tape and that should bring back lots of pleasant memories for him, as it did for me.

Love,

[1]Internationally renowned harpsichordist from Berlin and Switzerland, Kind (b. 1907) maintained an on-going correspondence with Gould.
[2]Eminent harpsichordist, born in Vienna in 1907, Kraus became a naturalized Canadian in 1944. Also a pianist and teacher, she performed at the Stratford Festival while Gould was Musical Co-Director.
[3]Ten Intermezzi for Piano by Brahms (Columbia, issued in 1960).
[4]Richard O'Hagan was a member of the Canadian Diplomatic Corps.

TO RUDOLF SERKIN[1]

January 25, 1961

Mr. Rudolf Serkin,
Curtis Institute of Music,
Philadelphia, Pa.

Dear Rudolf Serkin:
Many, many thanks for your very kind and thoughtful and warm (no pun intended) gift from Japan.[2] It has made a handsome addition to my winter wardrobe which now consists of a seal hat and a coon coat. The latter is of the classic vintage 1925 which has been handed down in our family until all, except me, were ashamed to be seen in it.

I do hope we can get together sometime this year. I would love to hear about your trip to Japan.

All the very best,

[1]Austrian-born American pianist (1903-91).
[2]Gould's clothes were often commented on by the press – especially his penchant for wearing winter coats and gloves in summer. Here Gould refers to a raccoon coat he seldom wore in Toronto. This coat had belonged to his grandfather and was worn more to amuse friends than to ward off the cold, although he liked to wear it in the country.

TO MRS. H.L. AUSTIN[1]

February 15, 1961

Mrs. H.L. Austin
Ile D'Orleans, P.Q.

Dear Mrs. Austin:

Thank you very much for your letter and for your enthusiastic comments about the Beethoven programme.[2] I am very happy to hear that you enjoyed it.

I hope sometime we can get together and have a real knockdown-dragout discussion with the matter of communication to and from an audience.[3] I, also, have been witness to a sort of misalliance between an artist and audience that you describe but it seems to me that these artists who are affected by such currents are probably too dependent on extramusical stimulation in the first place. Strangely, I have always preferred working in a studio, making records or doing radio or television, and for me, the microphone is a friend, not an enemy and the lack of an audience – the total anonymity of the studio – provides the greatest incentive to satisfy my own demands upon myself without consideration for, or qualification by, the intellectual appetite, or lack of it, on the part of the audience. My own view is, paradoxically, that by pursuing the most narcisstic relation to artistic satisfaction one can best fulfil the fundamental obligation of the artist of giving pleasure to others. Maybe when you get to Ireland and find the time and the repose for it, you can fire off another salvo of dissent.

It is always nice to hear from you.

All the best,

[1] A fan.
[2] CBC-TV program entitled "The Subject is Beethoven."
[3] Mrs. Austin had written, "I must also step lightly on your toes and disagree with something you said in an interview. That is, your statement that you considered an audience negligible – more precisely, that an audience had no effect on you."

TO JOHN P.L. ROBERTS

April 6, 1961

Mr. John P.L. Roberts,
Music Department,
CBC,
Toronto, Ontario.

Dear Mr. Roberts:

I have long heard it said that it is the policy of the CBC Music Department to rescue starving musicians by graciously offering them work when their financial needs are critical. Therefore, I am most happy to receive your letter of March 16 in which you request that I write a commentary to accompany my String Quartet performance on CBC Wednesday Night, June 21.

I cannot tell you, sir, how much this assignment and its colossal attendant fee means to myself, my good wife, my ill-clad children and my dog. This will be our first cheque in five months and it will be such a relief to provide for them for the month of June, or possibly July should the cheque be delayed, the bare necessities of life. I am sure you, as a family man yourself, will appreciate the emotion now surging in my breast and I beg you to express my humblest thanks and most sincere appreciation to the CBC for their generosity.[1]

Yours sincerely,
G. Herbert Gould,
Freelance Writer & Composer

[1]Gould's humor, though not always sophisticated, was infectious. He had been asked by Roberts to record a commentary for the broadcast of his String Quartet. Gould, who received high fees as a concert pianist, was prepared to work for a modest honorarium if he knew the budget of a particular CBC program was small, and if the project meant a great deal to him. In this case, the payment was so small Gould regarded it as hilarious.

TO KITTY GVOZDEVA[1]   April 27, 1961

Mme. Kitty Gvozdeva,
Leningrad, Centre, U.S.S.R.

Dear Kitty:

As you see, I am very much alive and I am very sorry to hear that you have been worried about me, but flattered to know that you do worry. I must apologize for not having replied to your kind New Years message. Frankly, I have been very busy this winter (though that is no excuse I know) doing my concerts which were scheduled for this year and trying also to make up, in addition, some of those which I had to cancel last year. And that brings me to the story of what happened to me this last year and what possibly was behind the rumour that you heard.

More than a year ago now my left shoulder was seriously injured in an accident in New York and during most of last season I had to give up my concerts and, in fact, was only able to play the piano for very short periods of time. I was treated for this injury by a famous doctor in Philadelphia and spent a month with my arm in a cast (though it was not broken). Finally, this past fall I was able to begin playing though it still forced me to cancel quite a number of concerts and, even now, I am required to take treatment for it and massage practically every day. I am, however, very optimistic about a complete recovery and so, I should add, is my doctor.

I must tell you that now that I am able to play the piano again I have much more excitement and enthusiasm in doing so than before this happened. Not being able to play for a while made me more appreciative of the piano. As I think you know, there are many aspects of the concert world which do not appeal to me very much – travelling, for instance, which I hate – and it is sometimes easy to assume that these disenchantments represent a certain ennui for music itself. So perhaps taking the philosophical view, this injury may have proved to be an almost valuable experience.

It has not, however, been an idle year for me. In addition to the many concerts which I am doing now, I have done quite a number of television programmes which I find very exciting. Some of them are performances and discussions of music, the script of which I write myself. Another rather nice thing which happened this year has been the recording of my String Quartet, Opus 1,[2] which I am sending to you under separate cover. I hope this arrives safely and that you enjoy it.

Do let me hear from you again and bring me up-to-date on all the news from Leningrad.

Mr. Homburger joins me in sending our warmest wishes.

Love,

[1]Ekaterina Gvozdeva Cergueieuna was one of Gould's translators during his Leningrad recitals in May 1957. An octogenarian of great culture, she was a private tutor with the Rimsky-Korsakov Conservatory for more than thirty years.
[2]Recorded by the Montreal String Quartet (Radio-Canada Transcription Program 142), in 1956; and in 1960 by the Cleveland Symphonia Quartet (Columbia).

TO ROBERT CRAFT   May 9, 1961

Mr. Robert Craft,
Hollywood, California.

Dear Bob:

First of all, thank you for your card and particularly the lines from Mr. Stravinsky[1] which I very much appreciate. I am dropping him a line in your care.

My shoulder was in wretched shape that week, in fact, I cancelled the San Francisco Symphony a few days before and only did Los Angeles[2] because

I couldn't bear the thought of disappointing Mrs. Huttenback once again. It was one of the more disturbing setbacks but it seems to be coming around nicely again, nonetheless, it was about the least happy performance I have played all year.

Last month Joe, Howard[3] and I listened to the Schoenberg[4] and I must say I was extremely pleased with it. I think you did a wonderful job in putting it together. One thing that surprises me a little, at least listening to it as I did in a small cubicle upstairs, was that the sound of Massey Hall, normally so resonant, was extraordinarily immediate, even a bit dry. Joe says that he miked the brass very closely and this may have a lot to do with it. We listened to it twice and, after the shock wore off, it really had a wonderfully analytical clarity – almost a textbook diagram of Schoenberg. Anyway, I am very proud of it and my congratulations to you.

All the best,

[1] Gould mentioned this letter to friends because Stravinsky had been extremely complimentary about his performance of Beethoven's Sonata No. 31, Op. 110. The few lines from Stravinsky meant a great deal to Gould because so many critics had disapproved of his approach to the late Beethoven sonatas. A year or two later, when asked if he still had the letter, Gould said it was "mislaid." His apartment was always in total disarray and the letter was never found.
[2] On April 25, 1961 Gould performed in Los Angeles: J.S. Bach's *Goldberg Variations* BWV 988; Anton Webern's *Variations for Piano*, Op. 27; Beethoven's Piano Sonata No. 31 in A♭ major, Op. 110; and Alban Berg's Sonata, Op. 1.
[3] Joseph (Joe) Scianni and Howard Scott were producers at Columbia Records in New York.
[4] Released July, 1962: Schoenberg's Piano Concerto, Op. 42, with Robert Craft conducting the CBC Symphony Orchestra (Columbia).

TO NATHAN TWINING[1]   June 14, 1961

Mr. Nathan Twining,
Oberlin, Ohio.

Dear Nathan Twining:
Thank you very much for your letter. It was good to hear from you. I have always enjoyed our backstage chats very much indeed.

I don't really know what to suggest in regard to your repertoire problem since not having heard you play it is hard to tell exactly where your primary sympathies lie. In general terms though, it is most certainly possible to avoid the Tchaikowksy, Greig, etc. repertoire and I only wish that more people would take the trouble to think up presentable alternatives to the late 19th century warhorses.

Since you are starting out on a concert career, I would think that a particularly welcome repertoire suggestion from you would include an imaginative contemporary concerto. By this I do not mean necessarily something of the order of the Bartok or Prokofieff concerti since everyone plays them anyway, but what I had in mind was something more or less off the beaten track, yet from an established master like Krenek,[2] for instance. There are not, in my view, any very important contemporary concerti; most of those of today's older and middle generation have been at a loss to write intelligibly for the piano with full orchestra, in fact, I am quite sure that the piano concerto as such is a dead form. Nevertheless, you might try looking into the Krenek concerti. The Fourth Piano Concerto of Krenek, which is the only one I can find at the moment and which is not one of his best, is published by Bärenreiter-Verlag, Kassel, Germany. I do not know whether the other concerti are published by the same people but they could probably tell you. These utilize the piano more or less as an obligato and hence are not works which will display any virtuoso precocities. Has Humphrey Searle written a piano concerto?[3] I seems to me he has but I am not sure. Wolfgang Fortner has, though it's not called a concerto (I forget what it is called) and is not terribly interesting either.[4] I did not hear the new concerto by Ben Weber which Masselos played this winter but that might be worth looking into.[5]

In any event, what I began to suggest was that you might consider coupling such a work with a classic work such as Mozart or an early Beethoven concerto. I think that it always helps at the beginning of ones career to have rather special and imaginative repertoire suggestions (not that I am in favour of getting stoggy later on) and it might well be that some conductors would have special interest in programming a pair of such works.

I do hope that everything goes well for you and when you feel like it, please feel free to drop me a line.

All the best,
Glenn Gould

[1] Young American pianist.
[2] Ernst Krenek (b. 1900), Austrian-born American composer, whose music Gould promoted. He interviewed Krenek for his series of ten programs on Schoenberg, and also recorded his Sonata No. 3, Op. 92, No. 4 (Columbia). While in Moscow Gould played the Sonata No. 3, which was recorded without his permission.
[3] English composer and writer on music, Searle (1915-82) wrote a Concerto for Piano in D minor, 1944.
[4] German composer and teacher, Fortner (b. 1907) wrote a Concerto for Two Pianos in 1933 and a Piano Concerto in C major in 1943.
[5] American composer, Weber (1916-79) wrote a Concerto for Piano, Wind Instruments, and Cello in 1950.

TO WALTER HOMBURGER

June 20, 1961

Dear Gomburger:

As seems to be the rule on your European sojourns, I have not heard a peep from you so I shall take the initiative in sending the news from this end. There isn't much really except that I cancelled Chicago for the third time not, as you suggested in your letter to Verna[1] (which I peeked at) because I felt like it but because I had and have a sort of rheumatic thing in my left arm (not wholly related to the other business perhaps) but something which is beginning to give me considerable worry since it has now been going on for two and one-half weeks. If it's not improved in a few days I am going to call Stein.[2] Harry Zelzer[3] was much upset, I suspect, but I think he was reconciled to the idea when I offered to reduce my fee for him next year to one-half – whether this will mean $1,000 or $1,250 we will have to figure out when the time comes. Needless to say, he accepted it gratefully. Frager[4] substituted by the way. I think it is fine that I can spread a little employment in the world.

The reviews of the Brahms,[5] which are now beginning to arrive in force, are almost unanimously glorious – so glorious indeed that Verna chokes on most of them when reading them. The only exception is the unpredictable Mr. Kolodin[6] who is violently opposed and says that my view of Brahms' last year is clearly of a stodgy mooning old codger – or words to that effect. I will now give you a run down of a few reviews:

Musical American called it "The Record of the Month," and said "Only Gould and Richter. . . ."[7]

The Chicago Sun, which arrived this morning said, "Gould has the kind of exceptional musicianship that can make him a specialist in any type of music he wishes to cultive."

And one of the Cleveland papers said "one of the most felicitous piano recordings in a long time."

Schuyler is very pleased and it seems to be selling well but it is really too early to tell.

I have been inordinately creative the last couple of weeks – knocking off two essays (good ones too), planned a third and drafted much of the first scene of my opera.[8] I just hope the mood holds.

Got a letter this morning from your Mr. Leavy[9] in New York and I am annoyed, I must say. A cheque was enclosed for $280 (I have already received $800) with the following comment:

"Enclosed herewith is cheque representing your proportionate share of an additional investment return on the touring companies of "The Andersonville Trial" and "The Pleasure of His Company." If any further monies are received together with a final statement I shall advise you accordingly." What in earth does he mean by 'if.' Either he knows that there are further monies to come or that there are not. And does, as it would seem from his letter, the arrival of a final statement also merit an 'if.' Frankly, I think this is a disgraceful way to conduct business and I can assure you that unless a final statement is forthcoming from him immediately, I am going to (a) raise a row and (b) think twice about any investment of that kind in the future. I am sure your other contributors likely feel the same way.

All the best for now,

[1] Verna Sandercock, secretary.
[2] Dr. Irvin Stein, the Philadelphia physician who treated Gould's shoulder injury in 1959.
[3] Harry Zelzer, concert manager in Chicago, who presented Gould in his "Allied Arts Series."
[4] Malcolm Frager, American pianist.
[5] Intermezzi Op. 76, Nos. 6 and 7; Op. 116, No. 4; Op. 117, Nos. 1-3; Op. 118, Nos. 1, 2, and 6; Op. 119, No. 1 (Columbia, released in 1961).
[6] Irving Kolodin, Editor of *Saturday Review*.
[7] June 1961, p. 15.
[8] From time to time Gould started compositions that were never completed. This opera was one of them.
[9] A New York lawyer, Leavy raised money for the Broadway production of *The Pleasure of His Company*. Both Gould and Homburger invested in this financially unsuccessful production.

TO HUMPHREY BURTON[1]   December 5, 1961

Mr. Humphrey Burton,
B.B.C.,
TV Studios,
London, England.

Dear Humphrey:

I thought I would bring you up-to-date on what has happened re TV here and the plans for the next few months. I have already taped the first of my series which has the title "Music in the U.S.S.R."[2] It went, I think, extremely well, gorgeous sets – Mme. von Meck's palace, icons, samovar, et al. – and the works were Prokofieff's Third Sonata and three movements of the Shostakovitch Quintet, plus twenty minutes of talk. Next month we tape the second of the series which is Bach with the Fifth Brandenburg and Cantata No. 54.[3] I will conduct from the "harpsipiano"[4] which I think I told you about with Russell Oberlin[5] as soloist in the Cantata. I would dearly love to have your thoughts on these two and I hope that you can get the CBC to send them over in due course.

I have not at all forgotten your invitation to come and do something for you and perhaps if these first shows of the series do not meet your requirements, we can talk about my coming over some more, but I would like you to take a look at them if you can.

Do let me hear from you. All the best,

[1] Television producer with the BBC.
[2] Aired on the national television network of the CBC on January 14, 1962, "Music in the USSR" consisted of performances of most of the Piano Quintet, Op. 57 by Shostakovich, with the Symphonia Quartet, and Prokofiev's Sonata No. 7 in B♭ major, Op. 83, and not Sonata No. 3, as indicated in Gould's letter. Gould's commentary was interspersed with excerpts from music by Balakirev, Glinka, and Tchaikovsky. Gould liked to tell friends that the set was so sumptuous looking that questions as to its cost were raised in the Canadian Parliament.
[3] "Glenn Gould on Bach," broadcast on April 8, 1962, on CBC-TV's "Sunday Music."
[4] A piano altered to sound like a harpsichord.
[5] American counter-tenor and teacher (b. 1928).

TO KITTY GVOZDEVA

December 30th, 1961

Madame Kitty Gvozdeva,
c/o Leningrad Conservatory of Music,
Leningrad, U.S.S.R.

Dear Kitty:

Thank you very much for your New Year's greetings and in return my best for 1962 to you. I was terribly sorry and very worried to read about your heart attack. Are you back at work full time now? I hope you are doing everything possible to take the best care of yourself and that you are not working as hard as I know you usually do. I hope to hear soon that you are much, much better.

I was both amused and delighted with your comments on my String Quartet and quite frankly I was pleased by the comparison with Taneyev.[1] He is a composer who is very little known in the West though such of his music as I have heard has impressed me very much. He certainly was one of the most important academic figures in the Russia of his time, wasn't he? In any event, even though and quite rightly, many of your colleagues were surprised by the conservatism of the style of the work I still count among the strongest influences of my musical development the work of Schonberg. I think that although one likes his music or detests it the fact remains that for most of us his influence has been enormous. Actually there is much of his music which I, myself, find rather cold and relentless, but even in those instances the technical command which he possessed, for all the austerity of the style, was still impressive.

The other great influence on me,and I fear an influence which it is no longer fashionable to admit, was the music of Richard Strauss. As a matter of fact, I don't know the current state of his reputation in the U.S.S.R., but in North America, especially among people of my own generation, it is presently quite fashionable to dismiss him as a fin de siecle romantic. In fact so strongly do I feel that this is a total misunderstanding of his importance that I have recently written an essay "Argument For Richard Strauss" which will appear in one of our record maga- zines later this Winter.[2] They are devoting much of the magazine that month to the work of Richard Strauss. I believe, and my purpose in writing the article particularly, was to challenge the peculiar notion that so many people have of his last works which I, however much in the minority I may be, find his most beautiful (the Opera Capriccio, Metamorphosen for Strings etc.) If you would like to see the article just let me know and when the magazine is published I will send you a copy.

At the moment I am busy writing a television script on the music of Bach. Next month I will do a one hour program on television on Bach which will include the Cantata #54 and the Fifth Brandenburg Concerto on which I will also discuss his music for about twenty minutes.[3]

Do take the best care of yourself and let me hear from you when you have time.

Love,
Glenn

[1]Sergey Ivanovich Taneyev (1856-1915) was a prolific Russian composer.
[2]*High Fidelity*, Vol. 12, No. 3, March 1962.
[3]"Glenn Gould on Bach," broadcast on "CBC Sunday Concert," April 8, 1962.

TO ROY MALEY[1]   December 30th, 1961

Mr. Roy Maley,
c/o The Winnipeg Tribune,
Winnipeg, Manitoba

Dear Roy:
Thank you so much for your Christmas greetings and for sending me your reviews on the last recordings. I am so very happy that you like them, particu- larly the Beethoven, which, as you know, is a little controversial. I don't know what one has to do to combat the impossibly teutonic and unrelenting manner which is so often applied not only to the stern granitular side of Beethoven but to the contemplative side as well. Anyway, I am delighted that you enjoyed it.

I am very sorry that I missed seeing you in November but I look forward to February, and in the meantime, all the very best.

Glenn Gould

[1]Music critic for the *Winnipeg Tribune*.

TO LOUISE SIMONS[1]

January 19th, 1962

Miss Louise Simons,
Errington, British Columbia

Dear Miss Simons:

Thank you very much for your letter. I am delighted that you enjoyed the C.B.C. program.

Your question regarding contemporary music and the means of approaching it is not an easy one since it involves some necessary comparison with the way in which one learns any and all music. In my opinion, the only really successful way of learning a work, regardless of its period, is to do so quite away from the instrument – in other words, to study it in purely analytical terms first. Obviously these analytical terms will vary to some extent depending on the repertoire, and certainly one could not analyse a work by Schoenberg in quite the same way one would analyse a Beethoven sonata. But by and large, and certainly in all of the music from the sixteenth century to the present, it ought to be possible to find common grounds of contact in the structural relations in the work.

I realize that this does not help you in your specific problem very much, but you will find that the music of Honegger can be approached in much the same way that you would approach Beethoven or Brahms, and I think you will find, however difficult it may seem to be at first, a work learned in analytical terms and only secondly at the instrument will leave you permanently a stronger sense of its structure and its internal workings. I hope this is of some help.

Sincerely,
Glenn Gould

[1]A fan who wrote: "I am learning a composition by Honegger and am finding it quite difficult to memorize. Since you perform much of this type of music at concerts, what do you find to be the best methods for memorizing it?"

TO M.A. GROSS[1]

January 29th, 1962

Mr. M.A. Gross,
Toronto, Ontario

Dear Morris:

Enclosed please find the latest Summons.[2] I do feel that it would be a great mistake for Her Majesty's Government to persecute me on this matter, since there is little question that I serve as a valuable example to the younger generation of what not to do on the highways. Taking me temporarily out of circulation would not, it seems to me, serve her Majesty's cause and I feel this point ought to be brought home to Her.

By the way, I think we should consider writing to Mr. Miller at Guarantee Trust and making an official protest about the hot water taps in this apartment. As I may have told you, ever since I moved in here various guests have come in danger of being scalded due to the fact that the pressure in two of the three hot water taps is at once both ferocious and erratic. On various occasions I have mentioned this to the Superintendent who has dutifully taken a look and resolved all the attending problems by shaking his head. He claims that there is little that can be done, due to the fact that this apartment is at the top and that the system is a venerable one. I do feel however, that with the rent they collect they have an obligation to provide better service in this matter than they seem willing to do, and I feel that it should be brought directly to Mr. Millers' attention. You may ponder this at your leisure.

Best,
Glenn Gould

[1] In 1962 Morris A. Gross, Q.C., was Gould's lawyer from the legal firm of Minden, Gross, Grafstein and Greenstein of Toronto.
[2] Gould enjoyed driving, but his delight in singing at the wheel, and thinking about music at the same time, led to minor accidents and speeding tickets, and caused him to commit other traffic misdemeanours. At the time of this letter he was in danger of losing his license for a period of time – something that filled him with concern because he liked to visit the family cottage at Uptergrove, on Lake Simcoe, north of Toronto.

TO JOHN MAURER[1]

February 28, 1962

Dear John:

Thank you for your letter. I am afraid that your many questions of my childhood would involve me in a much too detailed recollection and so I hope you will forgive me if I must beg off replying to some of them.

53

I did, however, have an idol when I was a young man like yourself. Pianistically at least, my idol was Artur Schnabel[2] and he was so not because I necessarily admired his piano playing more than all others but simply because he seemed to me to be a person who used the piano as a means of conveying his great love for music rather than someone who simply saw it as a chance for personal display of some kind. And this, it seemed to me, was surely the proper perspective for the actuality of playing the piano – that it should become simply a vehicle which permits access to the whole fascinating world of music.

Now to your question about the Royal Conservatory of Music. (It was called the Toronto Conservatory in my day but has since been changed.) I am afraid that I cannot speak with any authority about it since I have not for at least ten years had any connection with it. Moreover, quite frankly, I think that there are perhaps many other institutions much closer to your home which are equally well established to serve you for your musical education. I cannot, in short, recommend it without some reservations.

Sincerely,

[1] A young fan.
[2] Austrian pianist and composer, Schnabel (1882-1951) became a naturalized American.

TO HUMPHREY BURTON

12 Sheppard Street
April 17, 1962

Mr. Humphrey Burton,
c/o The B.B.C.,
London, England.

Dear Humphrey:

Thank you very much for your letter of March 28th. I have mentioned to Mr. Homburger the fact that you will be on this continent towards the end of May, and we would both be most happy to talk over with you any ideas for television which you may have. I am, of course, very sorry you feel the format of our C.B.C. shows lies somewhere between your programme and straight music broadcasting, but I quite understand that a one-hour show of that kind cannot readily fit into a more documentary format. It seems to me, nevertheless, that it is a format which, at least in terms of our North American audience, has worked very well, although I agree that if one becomes too elaborate with sets, et al, it can prove a distraction rather than an assist to the viewer.

I am not, at the moment, planning any tour in Europe for next season, or indeed at the moment for any season. This is due to the fact that, as of two months ago, I decided that when next season is over, I shall give no more public concerts. Mind you, this is a plan I have been announcing every year since I was 18, and there is a part of my public here that does not take these pronouncements too seriously, but this time I think I really mean it.[1] One of the things I will not, however, give up is television, since I enjoy it far too much to lose contact with this fascinating medium. So, if we can work out a satisfactory arrangement, I am still interested in doing something for you, and, if we could meet at the end of May, we might come up with some ideas which might be mutually intriguing. Do let me hear your plans for coming over when they're final. Until then, all the best.[2]

Sincerely,

[1] Gould gave his last concert in Los Angeles on April 10, 1964.
[2] Gould finally collaborated with Humphrey Burton in 1966 in four television programs called "Conversations with Glenn Gould," co-productions of the BBC and PBS. Because Gould hated air travel, Burton was obliged to come from London, and the productions took place at the CBC studios in Toronto.

TO EDWYN HAMES

12 Sheppard Street
April 17, 1962

Mr. Edwyn Hames,
Conductor,
The South Bend Symphony Orchestra,
Hillsdale, Mich.

Dear Mr. Hames:

Thank you very much for your letter of April 10. I must admit, with some embarrassment, that I do not possess a metronome, and therefore I do not know if the indications noted in your letter are those which reflect my own performance with the New York Philharmonic.[1] I can say, however, that despite all the fuss and controversy attending it, the performance bore exactly the character and consequently the tempi which, to my mind, reflect the true measure of this work. Consequently, even though some of the tempi may have sounded rather arbitrary, I would like to do it in the same way for the South Bend performance.

It has always seemed to me that over the years generations of musicians have added a series of cliches to the basic conception of the romantic concerto interpretation, to the extent that a work such as the Brahms D Minor has tended to become notable less for organic unity than for a coalition of inequalities. It seems to me that, particularly in the outer movements, it is imperative to find tempi which, as much as possible, will support the inter-related thematic strands of the work, minimizing in some ways the sheer masculine-feminine contrast of themes in order to stress the organic connection between them.

In any event, although I am quite sure we will stir up as much controversy in South Bend as was the case in New York, I hope that we can approach it in this way and hence, although I cannot answer for the metronome markings you have set down, preserve the same spirit of rather somber dignity that I feel was created in the Philharmonic performance. I look forward to seeing you again and to working with you, and until then, with all good wishes.[2]

Sincerely,

[1] In this letter to Gould, Hames included metronome markings he had noted while listening to the radio broadcast of Gould's performance of the Brahms Piano Concerto No. 1 in D minor, Op. 15, with the New York Philharmonic. He asked Gould if they were approximately the tempi he would like to use with the South Bend Symphony Orchestra.
[2] The performance was cancelled, although Gould did play the Brahms D minor in Baltimore on October 9 and 10, 1962, and again in Denver on March 5, 1963.

TO HENRY RAYMONT[1]

GLENN GOULD
32 Southwood Drive
Toronto, Ontario
April 18th, 1962

Mr. Henry Raymont,
Cambridge, Massachusetts.

Dear Henry:

Thank you very much for your letter, which was, indeed, long overdue and for letting me know what has happened recently in your life. I am very pleased about the new academic bent and I am sure that you have a great deal to contribute in that direction. I am not at all sure, however, that I would agree with you about the participation of Canada in the C.A.S.,[2] but that is another story and one in which I hope we will have the chance to argue in person sometime.

It is rather lucky that, according to your telegram, you were unable to make it to New York since until I got the telegram I had not, in fact, seen your letter. It was properly delivered to me by the back stage people and I stuck it away in a pocket and forgot about it, and not until getting the wire did I realize that there had been a letter – at which time I remembered to dig it out. You also missed, as you probably know by now, the most scandalous performance to hit 57th Street in some years.[3] I hope very much, indeed, that you were able to hear the broadcast complete with Leonardo's lecture, because, despite all the wild accusations that have been flying about, the speech was completely charming; indeed, done with great generosity, and far from having precipitated a fued (as the newspapers suggest) we have never been better friends.

What really scandalized them, of course, was the tempi proportions of the first and last movements – not, I think, the slowness per se, although this, of course, is the first thing that is detectable and hence the first thing to object to if one has a mind to do so; but rather I should imagine the proportions that were held throughout each of these two movements. I have been gradually evolving a view of the 19th-concerto in the last couple of years which perhaps views this strange and wayward jerne with the eyes of someone who looked back having also known Schonberg – this is to say that I have begun to find, I think, a way of playing the middle and late 19th century repertoire in which the predominant characteristic will be the presence of organic unity and not the continual acknowledgment of the sort of coalition of inequalities which, it seems to me, underlies most interpretations of 19th century music. If this sounds fancy and a bit arbitrary, it is not really. All that I am doing is deliberately reducing the masculine and feminine contrast of theme-areas in favour of revealing the correspondences of structural material between thematic blocks, and, of course, one of the things which this approach requires are tempi – which, be they fast or slow, will be capable of applying with equal validity to all of the primary thematic functions of a movement. (Unless otherwise indicated in the score, of course). So it seems to me that what was really different and perhaps disturbing to most people about our performance was the fact that these proportions were held in some kind of minimally fluctuating line and not the basic determination of the tempo itself.

Mind you, Lenny does not by any means completely agree with me on this but, nonetheless, his own will to explore is sufficiently strong to make him undertake an experiment of this kind which, agreed or not, has validity; and undertake it he did with an immense goodwill. And so, that, in brief, is what lay behind the scandal – just for your private information.

Do you ever plan a trip to Canada?

All the best for now,
Glenn Gould

[1]Curator, Nieman Foundation for Journalism.
[2]Gould is referring to the O.A.S., the Organization of American States.

[3] Brahms Concerto No. 1 in D minor, Op. 15, was performed with the New York Philharmonic Orchestra, conducted by Leonard Bernstein, on April 6, 1962, causing a scandal. Bernstein spoke to the audience beforehand and dissociated himself from Gould's choice of tempi, which were extremely slow in the first and last movements. Gould was made the butt of Bernstein's humor even though later in life the conductor chose to remember the incident differently. However, while outwardly avoiding any sense of dispute with Bernstein, Gould certainly took umbrage at the remark of the critic Harold Schonberg who wrote in the *New York Times* that the pianist played the work slowly because he did not have sufficient technique to cope with its difficulties. Considering Gould's prodigious technique, such a remark was absurd.

TO HARRIET INGHAM[1]

32 Southwood Drive
Toronto 8, Canada
April 19th, 1962

Miss Harriet Ingham,
Toronto, Ontario.

Dear Miss Ingham:

Thank you very much for your letter – it was, indeed, very good of you to write to me and I am so happy that you enjoyed the Bach programme.

I still have very fond memories of the time spent in your English classes, not the least of which are my recollections of our many friendly and productive after-class discussions. Perhaps sometime later this spring or summer when I have a little more free time than at present you would like to come up and have tea at my apartment. At the moment, I am in town for only a couple of days between concert engagements but the later spring is always a very pleasant and quiet time for me, and I would be most happy if you could visit me and talk over old times.

I must take issue with you very seriously, though, on the question of whether or not in my talk I avoided the subject of religion as an influence in Bach's music. It seems to me that, on the contrary, fully half of that script was written with the idea of showing the musical parallel of a man of faith in an age that was becoming faithless. I did this in the early minutes of the script by attempting to draw comparisons between the fin de siecle position of Bach as a musical man who summed up all the thought of the several preceding generations in a world which was dominated by the galant theatricality of his sons and the generation which they represented. So, although it is true that I talked very little about the sources of the German reformation in Bach's music (after all, you know, we had a French version of this translated for the Province of Quebec as well), I did put, I think, a good deal of emphasis upon the nature of Bach as a spiritual man in a

58

world which was at that time becoming increasingly hostile to the sanctity of spirit.

Again – many thanks for your letter and all best wishes.

Yours sincerely,
Glenn Gould

[1]Gould's former high-school English teacher at Malvern Collegiate. The renowned Greek-Canadian soprano Teresa Stratas also attended Malvern Collegiate.

TO C.H. PERRAULT

April 19th, 1962

Mr. C. H. Perrault,
ST. HYACINTHE, Quebec.

Perrault:

Thank you very much for your letter. I am indeed sorry that I am so late in acknowledging it. I am afraid that due to the fact that the Art of Fugue recording was necessarily done in some haste, Columbia have already prepared the cover material. I have not seen the cover myself, though I do know that they were giving the dedication programme which contained the specifications. I have no way of knowing, however, whether they made use of it, but I certainly hope that they were able to.

The organ is a delight[1] and I think you will be very pleased with the recording though, through considerable oversight, we listened to all takes and did all of our editing in stereo with the result that when a monaural tape was run there are several moments in which, due to my lack of familiarity with the church and more specifically our eagerness to use stereo potential to the full by utilizing two manuals almost constantly, a slight time lag results between the manuals. Fortunately, this happens only once or twice and is really scarcely noticable in the stereo version in which the very separation and sense of distance is, if anything, an attraction; so I suggest therefore that you also do your listening to this recording in stereo.

The record is due for release at the end of next month and although I am sure it is now much too late to add any information to the cover, if you would like to write to the person in charge of cover material, the address is: Mr. David Johnstone, c/o Columbia Records, 799 Seventh Avenue, New York City.

All best wishes,

Sincerely,
Glenn Gould

[1]J.S. Bach's *Art of Fugue* BWV 1080, Vol. 1, Nos. 1-9, recorded at All Saints Church Kingsway in Toronto on a neo-Baroque style Casavant organ. (Columbia, released in 1962.)

TO CARL LITTLE[1]

June 18th, 1962

Mr. Carl Little,
c/o Canadian Broadcasting Corp.,
Toronto, Ontario.

Dear Carl:

Herewith the questions for Mr. Anhalt.[2] Some of them, as you will notice, are those which I have asked Copeland,[3] Parese,[4] etc., others are more specifically directed to his own work.

Please remind the Montreal producer to instruct the announcer, or whoever asks the questions, to let Istban speak in long uninterrupted paragraphs for each question.[5] There should be no conversation of any kind between Istban and the announcer.

All the best.

Sincerely,
Glenn Gould.

Enc.

QUESTIONS FOR MR. ANHALT.

1. What do you as a composer owe to Schonberg?
2. Do you feel in recent years that his influence is exerting itself more strongly upon your writing? Perhaps you would discuss the aspects of your Symphony[6] which derive from Schonberg.
3. Most of the generation of younger composers today seem to have been influenced by Webern more than by Schonberg. Some, indeed, feel that Schonberg was too traditional a composer in some respects – too Nineteenth-Century in origin to be of significance as an influence today. How do you feel about this?
4. Many people feel that Schonberg was of greater value as a theorist than as a composer. In your opinion is Schonberg, the theorist, well represented by Schonberg, the composer? In other words, do his works, particularly his later works, stand well by themselves apart from the theoretical formulations to which they gave occasion?
5. You have recently become interested in music by electronic means. Could you say in what way the disciplines which you have developed through your interest in serialism have affected your work in the electronic music and, more specifically, could you comment upon any aspect of the writing of Schonberg, or indeed of Webern (such as the spatial effect of certain techniques of serialism for instance) which have been particularly noticeable for their influence on electronic music?

6. Would you speculate as to what, in your opinion, will be the reputation of Schonberg in the year 2,000? Will he be primarily thought of as a theorist or as a composer and, if the latter, will his work have found a solid place in the repertoire?

[1] Pianist and organist, Carl Little was Associate Head (with John Roberts) of the CBC's Music Department in Toronto.
[2] Istvan Anhalt (b. 1919), Budapest-born Canadian composer and teacher. Gould was a great admirer of his music and included Anhalt's *Fantasia for Piano*, written in 1948, in his Canadian Centenary recording, which he called *Canadian Music in the 20th Century* (Columbia).
[3] Aaron Copland (1900-90), American composer, writer on music, pianist, conductor, and teacher.
[4] Edgar Varèse (1883-1965), French-born American composer.
[5] Anhalt's commentary was for Gould's first radio documentary, "Arnold Schoenberg: The Man Who Changed Music," broadcast on "CBC Wednesday Night" on August 8, 1962.
[6] *Symphony*, written in 1958 using composition techique based on serialism. The pitch material centers on a four-note group while other aspects are freely composed.

TO SCHUYLER CHAPIN

June 26, 1962

Mr. Schuyler Chapin,
c/o Columbia Records,
New York, New York.

Dear Schuyler:

Herewith, as I promised you, some thoughts on repertoire which you can ponder at your leisure.

Assuming that the project of the '48' is faithfully upheld by yours truly, it will, I imagine, occupy us for the next 2 to $2^1/2$ years. In regard to other repertoire recorded during that period, I imagine that a good deal will depend upon the manner in which you plan to release the '48'. If, as we now plan, they are made in six volumes of eight Preludes and Fugues each, would you release them individually or hold back the first three volumes until Book 1 is completed? If the former (i.e. the release of each volume independently), there will be no problem of a release for the fall months. If, however, you propose to release a triple-decker album consisting of the complete Book 1, it would certainly be optimistic to count on it for release earlier than, let us say, a year this coming Christmas (i.e. late fall 1963). If this were the case, we would certainly have to get busy immediately with releases for the interim period. So I set down her some thoughts as to what these releases might consist of.

1.) Partitas number 3 and 4 – these should definitely be done within the next year since we have long delayed the completion of the Partitas set. In view of the fact that numbers 5 and 6 were recorded only in monaural, does this preclude issuing a boxed edition of the six Partitas in the monaural version? In any event, the instrument should be a standard piano as previously agreed upon.

2.) Art of Fugue Volume 2 – if your recent unpleasantness with the Department of Internal Revenue has been adequately settled, it would be best certainly to do these on the same organ as Volume 1. If you anticipate great problems with the Customs, I could investigate an organ which the President of Casavant Freres has recently described to me. It is one of their 'new look' instruments, similar to, but rather smaller than the organ at All Saints Anglican. It does, however, have the advantage of being located in a community on Long Island – forget which one for the moment. I feel that this recording should be made not later than next winter (indeed it would be preferable if it could be done in the fall) so that the complete Art of Fugue could be assembled for the market by this time next year.

3.) When the Art of Fugue is safely tucked away, I think we might consider a further organ recording to consist of the Schonberg Variations on a Recitative and the Krenek Organ Sonata.[1] Both of these works have been recorded previously – the Schonberg on the Esoteric label and the Krenek on the label of the University of Oklahoma (whatever that is!). In any event, this is a project which we can afford to ponder since it must definitely wait for the completion of the Art of Fugue.

4.) Plans for the Strauss Year 1964 – I assume that you still favour recording the Burleske with Herr Doctor Leonardo[2] and I would only remind you about the scheduling problem. You will recall that my presence is required in Los Angeles three days after the Philharmonic concerts next season and that, consequently, since I am no longer patronizing the air lines, this would necessitate my leaving New York not later than Sunday evening. Therefore, I would not be able to attend a Monday recording session, nor even a Sunday evening one, since most Westbound trains leave in the late afternoon. Fortunately, we have no Sunday concert on the series next year. I would be in the West for approximately two weeks, but have considerable free time in the latter part of February. Do you think it would be foolish to postpone the recording for approximately three weeks after the performance? There is a further problem with this recording – what to put with it! Since the good Burger Strauss did not provide us with anything else involving solo piano and orchestra (unless you would care for the Parergon of the Sifonia Domestica – thank you, I didn't think so). We will be coupling with it chez Philharmonic, the Bach Concerto in G minor, but I feel that that would be a far more absurd combination than our recent Schonberg-Mozart, and really one which would have very little raison d'etre. I would suggest to you, therefore, that one possibility might, in some wise, depend upon my next adventure with C.B.C. television in which, as you know, I am going to endeavour to conduct from the key board excerpts from both Le Bourgeois Gentilhomme and the

Tanzmuzik nacht Couperin.³ Although the Couperin-music is not, by any means, one of my favourite pieces, it would, nonetheless, fill out a recording with something extremely substantial and could quite easily be done without a conductor. Bourgeois Gentilhomme, on the other hand, would be extremely difficult to do in that fashion, since only certain of its movements utilize the piano as a continuo. Let's leave this problem for the moment and pass on to a few other thoughts on Herr Richard.

5.) As you know, I would very much like to do the Violin Sonata. According to the only Schwann catalogue which I have handy (which is a year old and upon which all of these tabulations are based), the Violin Sonata is not represented in the recorded repertoire. I am sure this is inaccurate, because I distinctly remember that Leonide Kogan recorded it a few months ago. But, in any event, I gather that the old Heifetz recording is now extinct. This could be coupled with the Sonata for Cello and Piano Opus 6 which, quite frankly I don't know but which would, along with the Violin Sonata, give a good picture of the young Strauss. I firmly believe that the best person to play the Violin Sonata with me would be Oscar Shumsky who does it magnificently.⁴

6.) Lieder – assuming that you can think of a suitable accomplice for such a project, I would like to set down at least one volume of Schonberg lieder. I gather from your comments a few weeks ago that you felt it would be someone of considerable standing in the vocal community and, of course, the only one on your own roster who fits this description would be Eileen.⁵ With all respect, I do not really think of her primarily as a Lieder singer, though it might be worthwhile to try. My own preference among the older (i.e. middle-aged) ladies would be Madame Schwarzkopf,⁶ but I gather that you feel it would require a lot of effort to disentangle her from the arms of Herr Legge.⁷ One possibility, though, would be to suggest an exchange with Legge – i.e. one album for Columbia, one for E.M.I. I think he just might consider it. If neither of these work, there remains the possibility of Lois Marshall who would, I am sure, acquit herself nobly. I would, by the way, like to go further afield than Cecily et al and to include, along with the better known songs, such songs as the Ophelia-lieder which I am going to do on my television show in August.⁸

7.) If we could find a really interesting partner for a lieder album, I would also like to use the same person for an album of Schonberg-lieder. This could include, as its major offering, the Book of the Hanging Gardens Opus 15 which times to about 24 minutes and, hence, could occupy one side and be prefaced with a side which would include a collection of his early songs from Opus 2, 3 and 6.⁹ I think this could make a marvelous collection and a very generous sampling of Schonberg's years of transition.

8.) Finally, getting back to solo piano endeavours, I think it is time to put down, believe it or not, another collection of Mozart sonatas. I would suggest that two or three of the last sonatas would make a good combination particularly those in C minor (with or without the accompanying fantasy) and the one in B flat major which exists also as a violin sonata.[10]

I am sure, dear sir, that you will agree that even half of these projects will keep us properly occupied and out of mischief for the next year or two but, as you will see, a lot depends on just what your plans are for the release of the '48'.[11] I feel that if you want to delay the '48' until it is well underway, it will be necessary to put down one of the other projects fairly soon since it would certainly be best to hold all of the Strauss releases for 1964. I would suggest that the Schonberg-lieder album would be an appropriate release for next winter along with the remaining Partitas and the completion of the Art of Fugue.

I await your thoughts on these various and vital matters.

All the best,

Yours sincerely,
Glenn Gould

[1] This recording was not made.
[2] Leonard Bernstein. This recording proposal did not come to fruition.
[3] This television program was not produced. Instead, Gould devised an all Richard Strauss telecast which included Le Bourgeois Gentilhomme Suite, Opus 60. It was shown on October 15, 1962.
[4] This recording was not made, but Gould and Shumsky did perform the first movement of the Violin Sonata in E♭ major, Op. 18, for CBC-TV on "Festival/Richard Strauss: A Personal View," broadcast on October 15, 1962.
[5] Eileen Farrell.
[6] Gould recorded some Strauss lieder with German soprano Elisabeth Schwarzkopf (b. 1915) but no Schoenberg lieder. The Strauss lieder were released in 1980 for the Glenn Gould Silver Jubilee Album (CBS). They included the three Ophelia Songs, Op. 67.
[7] Walter Legge (1906-79), music administrator, writer, producer, and eminent British figure in the recording world; husband of Schwarzkopf.
[8] Lois Marshall (b. 1924), Canadian soprano, performed the Three Ophelia Songs, Op. 67, for the Strauss program on CBC-TV.
[9] Book of the Hanging Gardens, Op. 15, was sung by mezzo-soprano Helen Vanni (Columbia). Vanni also sang Op. 3, 6, 12, 14, 48, and Op. post., on Columbia. Ellen Faull sang Op. 2 on Columbia.
[10] The Mozart Sonata No. 14 in C minor, K 457, was recorded in 1973 and 1974, and released in 1975 (The Mozart Piano Sonatas, Vol. 5. CBC). The Sonata No. 16 in B♭ major, K 570, was produced in 1970 and 1974.
[11] The Well-Tempered Clavier, Books I and II were released between 1963 and 1971.

TO PETER OSTWALD[1]

June 29, 1962

Dr. Peter Ostwald,
San Francisco, California.

Dear Peter:

Just thought I would let you know that our interview has become a most valued contribution to the Schonberg documentary. We have tried to surround it with rather good company including Aaron Copland, Goddard Leiberson and Winthrop Sargent[2] all of them reminiscing to various degrees about experience with Schonberg or giving their views on his music. But I must say that, in some ways your interview has proven the most valuable of all, since it throws an especially human light on Schonberg. I am very grateful to have it.

There is one moment in Copland's interview in which he says something to the effect that "Schonberg was not really my kind of person – not the sort of person I would want to spend an evening with." He says this by way of indicating that he found Schonberg rather reluctant to absorb the views of others in conversation, but I am going to truncate his comment, I think, with that in which you begin "I spent an evening with Schonberg" – or words to that effect. In any case, between you and Mr. Copland, at this point there will be, I hope, a rather delicious dialogue which should provide, if not a clear picture of Schonberg in toto, at least an illuminating contrast of view.

Do give my best to Lise and, of course, best to you.

Sincerely,
Glenn Gould

[1]Dr. Peter Ostwald, a psychiatrist, was a friend of Gould's. A Schoenberg admirer, he had visited the composer in his home. Gould used a description of this visit in his first Schoenberg documentary in 1962.
[2]Music critic for *The New Yorker* magazine.

TO WINTHROP SARGENT   September 7, 1962

Mr. Winthrop Sargent,
c/o The New Yorker,
New York, New York.

Dear Mr. Sargent:

I am very sorry that it has taken me so long to write and thank you for your wonderful co-operation with the Schonberg program. It has finally been put together and given public airing and was, I think, quite successful. I believe that within the next week or so, the C.B.C. are going to forward to you a copy of the show and I do hope that you enjoy it.[1]

I felt that your own contribution was an extremely important one. First of all because it was such an articulately negative one and it indicated, I think, something of the range of the good opinion against, and it also managed to do this while preserving a very human tone which added a great deal to the validity of the portrait.[2]

I am not at all sure what Frau Schonberg's reaction is going to be. I expect that anything less than 100% enthusiasm is considered disloyalty in that quarter. But, nevertheless, I hope she will realize the responsibility which we had to dramatize all views on Schonberg.

Again many thanks for your help and all best wishes.

Sincerely,
Glenn Gould.

[1]"Arnold Schoenberg: The Man Who Changed Music" was aired on "CBC Wednesday Night" on August 8, 1962.
[2]Although Gould was trying to promote Schoenberg's music, he realized that his documentary would lack credibility and tension if there were no negative views. Because of this he conducted an interview containing approximately eighteen questions with Sargent, who felt essentially negative about the music of Schoenberg. He said that it had no emotional impact on him, and added it would not be of lasting value after the year 2000. He did agree that "the influence of the man is overwhelming."

TO MARGARET AVISON[1]

September 14, 1962

Miss Margaret Avison,
Toronto, Ontario.

Dear Miss Avison:

Thank you very much for your letter and for your many kind comments. I am delighted that the program of August 10th was meaningful to you, though I must admit that I feel with hindsight that, as a total structure, it did not work successfully. It seemed, afterwards, so obvious that that portion of an audience which might have greeted Schonberg or Alban Berg receptively would not feel similarly inclined toward William Walton or the early Hindemith – no matter if whimsically presented. And so it was! Nevertheless, I feel that it is important, every once in a while, to find out where the boundary of concert format lies at present – to find out just how far one can go without invading the domains of theatre or television and still present music in an intelligible fashion.

Once again, many thanks for your letter and all best wishes,

Sincerely,
Glenn Gould.

[1]One of Canada's finest poets, Margaret Avison wrote Gould a fan letter in 1962.

TO RALPH CORBETT[1]

September 14, 1962

Mr. Ralph Corbett,
Cincinnati, Ohio.

Dear Ralph:

Walter[2] told me of your conversation this week and of your request that the public lecture be broadened to include other aspects of the contemporary scene besides those specifically descriptive of Schonberg. I think that it should be possible to do this at least insofar as the title might be concerned and also by inference, scope and direction of the lecture. But I feel that there are so many lectures given which go off in all directions at once on the subject of contemporary music that I should like to prevent mine from being another of these. In other words, I would like to have a very strong point of view, a very specific angle of talk, as it were, and I feel that I could best do this by relating much of what I have to say to a sharp focus on one personality – in this case, Schonberg.

Nevertheless, your conversation with Walter, as he reported it to me, has given me a very good idea. I think it should be possible to discuss the specific achievements of Schonberg as reflected in, and in many other cases, directed by recent developments of those who nominally were influenced by him. Hence, the title and the theme of the lecture could concern itself, let us say, with the heritage of Schonberg – that is not the title, but you know what I mean – something like that.[3] I think that, in this way, it would provide the wider base which you are looking for and still maintain a concentrated point of view. And also since much of what has been done in the last ten or fifteen years could be thus directly compared with the direction in which Schonberg seemed to be going, it could provide, I believe, some strongly controversial points of view.

Walter did not make it very clear to me what you have in mind for the seminar with the public lecture and I shall write you again shortly with some questions in that regard.

Sincerely,
Glenn Gould.

---

[1]A friend who brought Gould to Cincinnati to give a lecture on Schoenberg as part of the Corbett Lecture Series on April 22, 1963.
[2]Walter Homburger.
[3]The title became *Arnold Schoenberg: A Perspective* and was published in a limited edition (Glenn Gould. *Arnold Schoenberg: A Perspective*. Cincinnati: University of Cincinnati, occasional papers No. 3, 1964).

TO BENJAMIN BRITTEN[1]   November 30, 1962

Mr. Benjamin Britten,
Suffolk, England.

Dear Mr. Britten:

I am writing to you on behalf of the Stratford (Ontario) Music Festival, of which I am now Co-director. We hope that we can persuade you in the near future to resume your association with us, since we remember with greatest pleasure your visit of 1956.

At the moment, and although I know the time is ridiculously short between now and next season's festival, I am attempting to put together a programme consisting entirely of world premieres or, at any rate, North American first performance of works for chamber combinations, vocal or instrumental. (One work which we expect to have on this programme is the first premiere of the completed version of Lukas Foss' "Echoi" for piano, clarinet, cello and percussion). Because the time is so short, I realize that it would be more or less out of the question to commission a work specifically for the programme, but I am writing to you with the thought that you might have on the drawing-board a chamber work of some kind for which the initial performance might not yet be scheduled.[2] If so, we would, needless to say, be greatly honoured by its presence on our programme and would certainly consult with you on all matters relating to its performance – choice of interpreters, etc. If there is the slightest possibility of this, I would appreciate it if you could let me know at your earliest convenience.

I was very sorry to read recently of the recurrence of your shoulder injury – as a long-time bursitis sufferer, I can sympathize.

Sincerely yours,
Glenn Gould.

[1]British composer, conductor, and pianist (1913-76).
[2]In his letter of February 21, 1963 Britten responded that he was "tied up with commitments" and that he preferred to try out his new works at the Aldeburgh Festival first. He did offer a new opera to the Stratford Festival for the following year "subsequent to a performance at Aldeburgh."

TO V. KRASTINS[1]   January 3, 1963

Mr. V. Krastins,
Riga, U.S.S.R.

Dear Mr. Krastins:

Thank you very much for your letter and for telling me about your most interesting project in Bach research.[2] I would certainly be delighted to be able to see your essays when they are finished.

I only wish that I could be of more direct help to you as regards my own writing on the subject, but unfortunately although I have managed to write a number of essays on various musical subjects, I have written nothing that specifically applies to the interpretation of Bach's keyboard works. Curiously, it has been suggested to me that I should write a book on this or a related subject and I may possibly do that in a few years: but I am, just at the moment, finishing a book of collected essays, none of which really deal with Bach or with Baroque music.[3] From time to time, I have given lectures on subjects relating to Bach and his period, sometimes concerning such matters as the archaic in Bach – the sense of what I suppose could be called historical retrogression – in other words the defiance of chronology that was implicit in his own development through the fact that towards the end of his life he was completely disinterested in the new music of his day and withdrew into that glorious contrapuntal reflection of past ages (as in Kunst der Fuge).

In other words, although I have lectured on subjects relating to Bach and his development, I am afraid that I have not written anything specifically concerning the keyboard literature. I have, of course, a good many theories about the performance of Bach at the piano, chiefly centering around the fact that I feel that if one is going to use the piano for Bach's music at all, one has to attempt to some degree to simulate the terraced registration of the harpsichord. While I am far from puritanical in this matter and do not believe in any case in carrying such theories to excess, I feel that the main progress in Bach interpretation which has occurred in the last generation or so, has been that so many people have been willing to attain the necessary clarity and delineation by sacrificing to some degree colouristic qualities of the piano.

I suppose that the logical extension of my attitude would be to simply play the works on the harpsichord and yet I cannot help feeling that in many ways the piano, with its range of sonority and the possibilities it provides for effects of registration which are quite within the plateau concept of Bach's music, but for purely mechanical reasons are impossible on the harpsichord, is a perfectly sensible alternate; and in so many ways the most practical keyboard instrument for the performance of his music. I do feel it requires a willingness to surrender what you might call the glamour qualities of the piano and this, it seems to me, happily is now being accepted more and more widely in the present generation of musicians.

I hope that this letter is of some help to you in assessing my own attitude toward Bach interpretation and I am only sorry that I did not have available the sort of essays which you have in mind. May I say once again how delighted I would be to receive any of your own essays on this subject.

Sincerely,
Glenn Gould.

¹Latvian-born pianist and post-graduate student at the Leningrad Conservatory.
²His project was "the interpretation of keyboard works by Bach in our century" and his intention was to use Busoni, Fischer, and Gould as examples of the "world's most brilliant exponents of tendencies in modern Bach-playing."
³The book was not published.

TO BENJAMIN BRITTEN   February 8, 1963

Mr. Benjamin Britten,
Suffolk, England.

Dear Mr. Britten:

Thank you very much for your reply to my earlier letter. I am indeed sorry that we were unable to present a work of yours at this summer's Festival but, if I may, I should like to try out your reactions on a slightly different proposal concerning next year's Festival (i.e. 1964) or even possibly the season after that.

We have for sometime been concerned about the fact that holding our concerts as we now do in the Festival Theatre proper, the limitations of the stage were such as to prevent us doing opera in that theatre. Nevertheless, the assets of the stage are also very obvious and last year we commissioned two ballets to be designed specially for the theatre. This has prompted us to consider the possibility of an original work of musical theatre specially written for our stage. Because of the special nature of the stage, it might not be remotely like proscenium opera and could, perhaps, involve elements of ballet, of mime, etc. But in any event, I suspect that given the right subject matter, the assets of the stage would outnumber its liabilities and that it could give occasion to a very exciting concept.

Now then, to the point – would you be available to accept a commission from the Festival for such a work? Does it strike you that such an idea is viable? I imagine that you remember the design of Tanya Moiseiwitsch's stage (slightly altered last year).¹

I do not think that there would be any need for such a work to occupy an entire evening's performance. In fact, a work of approximately three quarters of an hour to an hour's duration would be satisfactory if we would find an appropriate companion piece for it. The matter of librettist would be left entirely to your discretion and we would, of course, negotiate with the librettist separately. The Festival Board has authorized me to offer you the sum of $2,000.00.

I do hope that you will look favourably upon it and I look forward to hearing from you.

Sincerely,
Glenn Gould.

¹From the Stratford Festival program, 1962, ". . . the back area has been widened and opened up while the apron remains unchanged. The balcony has been raised eight inches, and four of the supporting pillars removed. Two hinged panels, providing extra entrances have been added."

*TO LOUIS BIANCOLLI*¹

May 27, 1963

Mr. Louis Biancolli,
New York, N.Y.

Dear Mr. Biancolli:

Thank you very much for your letter and for the three recordings. I have found them, to say the least, an engrossing experience and I am delighted to enclose a few remarks which may be of some use to you for the cover or the jacket notes.

I must confess that it has also been a rather disturbing experience for me in that I have suddenly been made aware by these recordings just how transitory are our values of performance and how dependent they are upon the analytical approach of the particular generation. I found that in these recordings, the desire to sectionalize, to play from the passion of the moment tended to jeopardize the larger structures just as it tended to lend great charm and whimsicality to the smaller ones. I thought that Grieg and Faure were exquisite, but I felt that the larger structures, the Chopin Ballade by Paderewski² etc. just did not seem of a piece and yet one must admit that these were the great pianists of their day and reflected the analytical concepts of that time and since that time is really not so far distant, is it possible that the integrationist, everything – hanging – togetherness views of our time are just as transitory? Will we sound just as odd 40 years from now?

I would suspect that part of the hard – to reconcile distinctions of taste that are involved here are the responsibility of the Schonbergoan type of molecular analysis in which every facet of a work has to prove itself of structural necessity and I suspect that people of my own generation have applied this kind of analysis to the music of all earlier times as well. I certainly think that it works in terms of the Renaissance or in terms of the baroque, but hearing a record like this makes me wonder just to what extent it is viable applied to late 19th century music. This is what I meant when I said that I have found the recording a disturbing experience.

The piano playing, as piano playing, is very often quite wonderful. There are some remarkable qualities for instance in Carraneo,[3] pianistically, though she strikes me as the most wilful of the lot in architectural concept. It occurs to me the sound is uniformly beautiful. Indeed, one particular surprise was the remarkable clarity of most of the playing – very little of it was of the over-pedalled sort that I, at least, had always associated with that generation. I would suggest, though, if they are to make another series of these recordings, the instrument used to accommodate the piano-roles might be chosen with an eye to a certain archaic mellowness. It seems to me that a piano of approximately the same vintage as the roles themselves would enhance the nostalgia of these recordings and assuming it was kept in good condition, without losing anything in the clarity and lucidity of the sound available. Something along the lines of the turn of the century Chickering for instance would be ideal for this project, I would think.

As you can imagine from these remarks, these recordings have opened up so many areas for comment I have found it difficult to condense all of this into a couple of sentences which might be of use to you on the jacket. However, I hope that the enclosed will be suitable in that regard. I would be delighted if we could sometime chat at greater length about this. But, in the meantime, I thank you once again for allowing me to hear these recordings and for introducing me to an area of performance which I had never before been able to investigate to any great extent. With warmest regards and all best wishes,

Sincerely,
Glenn Gould.

[1] A fan, Biancolli wrote music reviews for the *New York World Telegraph and Sun*. He was at one time the program annotator for the New York Philharmonic Orchestra.
[2] Ignacy Paderewski (1860-1941), Polish pianist and composer.
[3] (Maria) Teresa Carreno (1853-1917) Venezuelan pianist.

TO B.H. HAGGIN[1]

10 St. Clair Ave. West
November 16, 1964

Mr. B.H. Haggin,
c/o The Hudson Review,
New York, N.Y.

Dear Mr. Haggin:
Thank you so much for sending along Music Observed and the Autumn issue of the Hudson Review.[2] The latter I would have seen in any case, since I am a long time enthusiast of that quarterly. I was delighted, needless to say, with the

amount of space that you devoted to my argument of the Sonata.[3] Naturally, it would be better still if you agreed with everything I said. But, never mind, a few well placed dots and dashes will make it read without any reservation whatsoever.

Music Observed is a delight! Your writing is always most beautiful to read and it is very good to be able to have access to your thoughts of several decades compiled in this way. I do feel though that you should sometime do a long piece – not necessarily a book but a fairly lengthy essay at the least – explaining why you feel as you do about certain matters to which you refer parenthetically with such frequency. Most particularly I think of your many references to Bach as being a composer of "dull" music or words to that effect. Mind you, I have nothing whatever against your having a bias of this kind. I am firmly convinced that a good solid mental block is the source of creativity. I have plenty of them as you know – practically everything of Mozart and the Opus 60 environs of Beethoven[4] – to this day, I cannot listen to the Violin Concerto with any real pleasure, certainly not as top drawer Beethoven. But I realize that most everyone else feels differently and therefore the onus is upon me to prove otherwise.

It may well be that you have indeed written such a piece in regard to Bach at sometime. You have written a great deal and I don't pretend to be familiar with everything you have put down. But I do feel that a bias of this kind directed against someone who, for most of us, is the most overwhelming composer who ever lived, is deserving of more explanation than you give it.

Then too, you proclaim it at a time when the whole neo-Baroque craze (which I, of course, find a bit exaggerated, as with all such crazes) makes a view of this kind seem slightly out of fashion. So much the better for that – as far as I am concerned. But I do feel that you owe us a real explanation of the why and wherefore of your relations with J.S.B., after which, as far as I am concerned, you can go back to all the parenthetic assumptions that you want to about him.

Again thank you for the book, and with all best wishes,

Sincerely,
Glenn Gould.

[1]American author and music critic.
[2]B.H. Haggin, *Music Observed* (New York: Oxford University Press, 1964) and the *Hudson Review*, Vol. XVII, No. 3, Autumn 1964.
[3]Haggin devoted twenty-one lines to Gould's argument regarding the Beethoven Sonata No. 30, Op. 109, E major. A key statement was that "Gould carried his interest in the structural harmonic element of the music to the point of regarding it as primary and as more important than the thematic melodic element."
[4]Symphony No. 4, Op.66, in B♭.

TO WILLIAM GLENESK

110 St. Clair Ave. W.
January 10, 1965

Reverend William Glenesk,
Spencer Memorial Presbyterian Church,
Brooklyn, New York.

Dear Bill –

Thank you for your letter. I was delighted to hear of your acquisition of an organ and, needless to say, I have followed your activities in the various news media.

I am afraid that my organ playing days are behind me, however. As you know, I did record the first half of the Art of Fugue a couple of years ago and I did this on a rather special instrument – a new Casavant, neo-baroque in design, and an instrument that greatly appealed to me.[1] But even with all that in its favor, I found the consequences of the session a bit disturbing in that for several weeks thereafter, I had enormous problems with my never too dormant shoulder trouble and consequently, the whole experience was a bit costly in terms of piano playing. The reason is quite simple – the whole sense of tactile relation to an organ is totally different from that of a piano and all of the correlative forces involved have to be geared up accordingly. I very much envy people who can stray back and forth from one instrument to another with a minimum of effort but I am afraid that I cannot operate in quite such cavalier fashion. So, except for finishing the Art of Fugue at some future date which can be suitably removed from piano playing for some several weeks, I am determined to do no organ concerts in the foreseeable future.[2]

All best wishes,

Sincerely,
Glenn Gould.

[1] *Art of the Fugue*, BWV 1080, Vol. 1, Nos. 1-9 (Columbia).
[2] Gould never completed recording the *Art of the Fugue*.

TO SILVIA KIND

110 St. Clair Ave. W.
January 10, 1965

Miss Sylvia Kind,
West Berlin.

Dear Sylvia:

What marvellous news that you are coming again in '66. I called Greta[1] to tell her but she was out last night and I know that when she does hear, she will be as pleased as I am. I think it is not at all too soon for you to think in terms of getting the very best manager for your next tour. You mentioned to me that Mr. Seaman was quite interested and I should think that with any good manager you would have very much less difficulty in making the necessary arrangements. So do keep me aware of your plans and of the possible dates when you might be out.

I feel very ashamed of myself that I have not written long ago to thank you for your marvellous Bach autograph[2] which I am very proud to have, and to tell you how sorry I was that you were not well at that time. I know, however, that with your incredible resilience and vitality, it would not be too long before you were completely better.

I so very much enjoyed reading your Hindemith tribute which was full of wonderful warmth and nostalgia. I did not attempt to do anything with it in terms of University publication here because in the few months after his death, there was so much written and said about him in all of our journals here. Had I had it some months before, it would certainly have been easy to find a place for it, but I did feel that the Hindemith articles had been appearing in such abundance, it had better be left for a more propitious time.

Tonight, on the radio, I am giving a one and a half hour documentary about the recording industry and its effect upon lives of modern man.[3] This is already taped so I can say with some assurance that it is a rather fascinating program, I think. What I did manage to do was to examine from the standpoint of the composer, of the performer and most of all of the audience, the effect that records have on our listening, and to do this with interview material taken from conversations with a number of friends as well as a good deal of my own narration and all of this accompanied by many excerpts from recordings which seem to me in one way or another the more important. One of these, from which I am playing several minutes, is your recording with Fricsay of the Petite Symphonie Concertante,[4] and I selected it because of its incredible balance of the three solo instruments, something which, as I point out in the script, would be virtually unobtainable in a concert hall and could only be done with such perfection before the microphone. In any case in preparing the show I listened again, as I have done so many times before, to that recording and, as always was overwhelmed with the achievement of it. You really must do more recording!

All the very best and do let me hear from you,

Love
Glenn.

[1]Greta Kraus.
[2]The National Library of Canada does not hold a Bach autograph facsimile in relation to this letter.
[3]"CBC Sunday Night," "Dialogues on the Prospects of Recording" broadcast on January 10, 1965. One of his most important broadcasts, the program was written and narrated by Gould. In it he propounded his view that the public concert would disappear after the passage of a century and that the future of music lay in the electronic media. In particular Gould made a case for recordings

being the "very reality of music." He went on to examine various dimensions of the making of recordings as well as the roles of the composer, performer, musicologist, producer, engineer, and the listener, the latter being central to his arguments. The broadcast was turned into an article for *High Fidelity*, Vol. 16, No. 4, April 1966.
⁴*Petite symphonie concertante, for harp, harpsichord, piano, and string orchestra* with the RIAS Symphony Orchestra, conducted by Ferenc Fricsay. Recorded in Europe by Deutsche Grammophon. Issued by Decca. (Silvia Kind was the harpsichord soloist.)

TO MARSHALL McLUHAN

110 St. Clair Ave.W.
January 24, 1965

Professor Marshall McLuhan,
Centre for Culture and Technology,
University of Toronto,
Toronto, Ontario.

Dear Marshall:

Thank you so much for your letter. I am delighted that the show pleased you and I must thank you again for the enormous contribution that you made toward its success.[1]

A complete script, as a matter of fact, four different versions of the complete script are extant which include the interview material as well as my narrative comments, and I would be delighted to send a copy of any or all of these versions to you. The script from which we worked was necessarily deprived of about twenty-five minutes of what I thought to be among the more pertinent comments but which were taken out to meet the exigencies of radio time, and I should think that if excerpts were to be published there would be no reason to hold too precisely to that material which was, in fact, broadcast.

I have promised to write one or more articles on recording as it effects the performer and composer for High Fidelity Magazine[2] and while I plan to base these pieces largely upon my narrative comments from the script, I see nothing to prevent excerpts being reproduced elsewhere. Indeed, I would be most pleased to have you make use of them if you should like to, and if you will serve as editor and anthologizer, or whatever, I shall be flattered in the bargain.

Do give me a call when you get back from England and we can discuss it further.

All the very best,

Sincerely,
Glenn Gould.

[1]McLuhan (1911-80) had been interviewed by Gould for "Dialogues on the Prospects of Recording."
[2]"The Prospects of Recording." *High Fidelity*, Vol. 16, No. 4, April 1966.

TO KITTY GVOZDEVA   February 15, 1965

Madame Kitty Gvozdeva,
c/o Leningrad Conservatory of Music,
Leningrad, U.S.S.R.

Dear Kitty:

I am terribly ashamed of myself that I did not reply sooner to your greetings at
the New Year, but late though it is, my very best to you for 1965.
The last year has been quite eventful for me. I've written a great deal for one
thing – many lectures and magazine articles of one kind or another, and my first
book – a small one and on Schoenberg, so you won't approve![1] And it's given me
the urge to publish more. This last year has also crystallized in a way my feelings
about travelling and concert giving, of which I have already told you a good deal.
But having found the kind of productivity that is possible when I can be more or
less rooted to one place and be in a position to spend a lot of time thinking and
writing, I simply cannot conceive of going back to that awful, transient life
which, as you know, I never did enjoy. But I have, however, been able to do much
more recording than in earlier years and I am asking Mr. Homburger to send you
some of the new records. I will send two of each so that you can, if you wish to,
give one to the Conservatory Library. The next big recording project which will
take me fully ten years, since it has to overlap with the continuing series of Bach's
works, is recording all of the Beethoven Sonatas. We have just started this and the
first record in the series is to be released this Spring.[2]
We have been virtually invaded by your Russian performers in Toronto in the
last few months. Gilels was here a few weeks ago; Kogan was here a couple of
months ago, and Richter in the early fall. I didn't hear any of the concerts, since
when I am at home, I spend most of my time in the country, but I did see Richter
play on television – absolutely miraculously!
Do let me hear from you. With all best wishes,

Affectionately,
Glenn Gould.

P.S. I do hope you remain free of the Flu. We have been reading that almost
everyone in Leningrad seems to have it. So do take good care of yourself.

---

[1]*Arnold Schoenberg: A Perspective* (Cincinnati: University of Cincinnati, 1964).
[2]Beethoven Sonatas No. 5 in C minor, Op. 10, No. 1; No. 6 in F major, Op. 10, No. 2; and No. 7 in D
major, Op. 10, No. 3, were recorded in 1964 and released in 1965 (Columbia). Gould did not live to
complete recording all thirty-two of Beethoven's piano sonatas.

TO YEHUDI MENUHIN[1]

July 27, 1965

Mr. Yehudi Menuhin,
London, England.

Dear Yehudi:

Thank you for your letter. I am very much looking forward to seeing you in October and, of course, to working with you. I have done a bit of thinking about our program and the form which it might take and have had one or two talks with Eric Till, the producer. However, we certainly have not adhered to any hard and fast notions of its structure and I hope that you will feel absolutely free to reject any or all of the suggestions that I make herewith.

The idea with which we began is that it would be important to think of the program as being built out of a conversation which could occur on camera between the two of us. The conversation should, I think, be absolutely informal, no script or teleprompter or anything like that. The most obvious subject for such a conversation would have something to do with the relation of the violin and piano in chamber music repertoire and the logical expansion of this would be to find works that make some special comment upon this dialogue.

The work that comes most immediately to mind is Schonberg's Fantasy. I remember that we talked about it the year before last and that you did express some interest in it. It is a 'natural' for such a program since it was conceived as a violin solo to which a piano obligato was later added and, as such, it might provide us with a perfect jumping off place for such a discussion. The only thing against it is that for its length (8 or 9 minutes), it would perhaps require an inordinate amount of rehearsal and since your time is so limited and since we would have to rehearse perhaps two other longer works, I am a bit reluctant about the Schonberg on that score. But on no other. It would be a fine talking point for the program.

Assuming then that this were to be our subject, another further possibility would be to consider the Mozart B. Flat Sonata, the one that is K.570 in its piano version and for which I forget the Kochel number in the violin piano form.

Assuming that the performance time of the Mozart plus Schonberg was approximately 25 minutes and that our conversation probably in two or three segments would be anywhere between 8 and 12 minutes. If the program were to begin with Mozart and continue with Schonberg, this last could perhaps be a Beethoven or Brahms Sonata, though it could be almost anything else with equal justification. (If it were Beethoven, my own preference would turn toward the C. Minor or the G. Major, Op.96.)

If, on the other hand, you feel that the Schonberg would be more nuisance than it is worth, various other possibilities open up. Mr. Till is a little shy of including more than one contemporary work on the program, but if we did not do Schonberg then certainly the contemporary work could be a Prokofiev

Sonata or something of that kind. I would suggest the Strauss Op.18 for which, with the exception of the slow movement, I have a very real affection, but I did once use the first movement of it on a program as illustration of the early Strauss. However, if you would like to do it, we do not need to rule it out at this point. And needless to say, I would be most happy to play a Bach Sonata with you.

So I leave it with you and await your reactions. You should keep in mind that we require between 45 and 50 minutes music, though if we were to do works such as Schonberg's which are more or less unfamiliar, examples would be quite in order and in that way much less actual music could be scheduled and a bit more time given to illustrations.[2]

Do let me hear from you when you get a chance and please give my best to Diana and, of course, the very best to you.

Sincerely,

[1]American violinist (b. 1906), Menuhin was one of Gould's idols. He had long wanted to collaborate with Menuhin, and one of his greatest disappointments was that commercial recordings never resulted from their encounters.
[2]The final program choice consisted of: Schoenberg's *Phantasy* for violin and piano, Op. 47; Bach's Sonata No. 4 in C minor for violin and harpsichord, BWV 1017; and the Beethoven Violin Sonata No. 10 in G major, Op. 96. It was broadcast on CBC-TV's "Festival" on May 18, 1966. Menuhin was frankly puzzled by the music of Schoenberg, but Gould's understanding and enthusiasm for this composer won him over at least on this occasion.

TO SHIRLEY FLEMING

August 31, 1965

Miss Shirley Fleming,
c/o High Fidelity Magazine,
New York City, N.Y.

Dear Miss Fleming:

Herewith L'Esprit De Jeunesse which has been an extraordinary nuisance.[1]

Last week sitting in a chalet in the Laurentians, I had what seemed at the time the brilliant idea of doing the whole piece in a more or less consistent metre. The CBC had just asked me to write for them a mockumentary for radio – a sort of Arctic 'Under Milkwood'[2] – and I was so taken with this idea that I decided to get in some poetic practice. Anyway – it must have been the altitude – because when I got back to Lake Ontario level and began inserting into the first draft Miss Lamontagne's quotes and other such diversions, it no longer seemed much a stroke of genious, as a matter of fact I got motion sickness reading it.

So for the last couple of days, I have been deliberately sabotaging my own metrical minefields and a heartbreaking task it is. There is one sentence which, as you will see, remains in its original state like a paleozoic ridge in a pre-cambrian topography – the one about Carl Czerny. And that, if you can believe it, was the way the whole blasted thing read two or three days ago.

I have indicated by double parenthesis on page 3 a cut of half a page or so which will not be missed, but if you use it, would you please make sure that the sentence which follows is part of the same paragraph as that which preceded it. I would also ask that you preserve the Continental spelling of Chaikovsky and the accented rendering of Deckere for Miss Lamontagne's quotes, and that you check the spelling of Mr. Spector's name which I have no means to look up here. All the best,

Sincerely
Glenn Gould.

¹"L'Esprit de jeunesse, et de corps, et d'art" published in *High Fidelity*, Vol. 15, No. 13, December 1965. This article about the National Youth Orchestra of Canada was written by Gould under the pseudonym Dr. Herbert Von Hochmeister.
²Poem by Dylan Thomas. Gould was referring to his documentary "The Idea of North."

TO KITTY GVOZDEVA   September 6, 1965

Madame Kitty Gvozdeva,
c/o Leningrad Conservatory of Music,
Leningrad, U.S.S.R.

Dear Kitty:

The fault, I am afraid, rests with me and not with the Post Office. I wish I could blame the Post Office but to be honest, after writing you in the Winter, I completely forgot to ask Mr. Homburger to mail the records to you. I do apologize and assure you that they are leaving this week.

The Villa Pushkin sounds marvellous – I wish I could see it – and I do hope you are having a wonderful vacation. Believe it or not, I took a trip this Summer myself to the lower reaches of the Canadian Arctic. Ever since I can remember, I have been fascinated with geographic studies, etc., of the Arctic and I finally determined to see a small part of it for myself this year. In sum, next to visiting the Soviet Union, it was perhaps the most fascinating two weeks I have ever spent. By your standards, I was not really at any time very far North; in fact, I was never quite as far North as the latitude of Leningrad. But the Canadian Arctic and the Russian Arctic are two very different tracts and a general rule the tree line, that is to say the most northerly growth of trees, is in the Canadian Arctic about

500 miles to the South of the equivalent line in the Soviet Union. This means that one does not really have to go too many hundreds of miles to the North in order to reach some very extraordinary and desolate country.

Consequently, I went to Hudson's Bay to a point just a few miles above the most Northerly growth of forest in that area and ended up at Fort Churchill which is for the moment the most northern point to which you can take a train in Canada. (There is a very short rail line in the Yukon Territories which is considerably farther to the North but which connects only to the sea, so it really doesn't count.) In any event, this train, although it has one car with sleeping accommodations, is not really intended for tourists. Everyone seemed to think I was just slightly mad to be on it in the first place – and practically every member of its crew turned out to be fabulously gifted as a raconteur in the way that people who have experienced great isolation tend to be. And so for approximately 1000 miles and for two nights and a day (each way), I was able to see an aspect of Canada with which very few people concern themselves. And I have come away from it with an enthusiasm for the North which may even get me through another Winter of city living which, as you know, I loathe.

Before I conclude about the Arctic, I should tell you that a delegation from the Soviet Union is at the moment in Canada, visiting various towns of the North by way of an exchange for a visit paid to the Russian Arctic last Spring by some Ministers from our Government. These latter, according to the papers, came home enormously impressed with Norilsk, etc., of which the equivalent development simply does not exist in Canada's North as yet.

Next Summer, if all goes well, I hope to take a trip to Alaska which is, of course, a good deal farther North than my route of this Summer but also a good deal more habitable.[1]

The movie about which you read was made specifically for television, though it was made on film and not videotape, so that it has sometime been shown in theatres as well. It is a very simple movie, really, of one hour's duration divided into two thirty-minute segments, the first of which was filmed in the country and the second mostly in New York city at a recording session. If I remember correctly, the title of the two thirty-minute segments are respectively: "Glenn Gould – Off the Record" and "Glenn Gould – On the Record." The movie was made by the National Film board of Canada whose offices are in Montreal and if I can be of any help in getting a copy for you to use at the Conservatory, or in any other way, please let me know. I am sure that the National Film Board would be delighted to be able to show it in the Soviet Union. You must realize, however, that there is an enormous amount of talk in it which would require translation. I know that it was shown on television a year or so ago in the Netherlands but I have no idea whether they used sub-titles or simply ran it with the assumption that a certain percentage of their audience would be able to understand English.

Please do forgive me for forgetting about the records. I hope they arrive in good condition and that you enjoy them.

All the very best,

Sincerely,

P.S. I will also send you a copy of the Schonberg book which is really just a preparatory sketch for a longer work which I have been commissioned to write next year.[2]

[1]Gould travelled by train as far North as Churchill, Manitoba, but never made his trip to Alaska.
[2]Gould did not write a major book on Schoenberg.

TO HUMPHREY BURTON

September 18, 1965

Mr. Humphrey Burton,
BBC Television,
London, England.

Dear Humphrey

Thank you very much for your letter. It arrived yesterday and early next week I shall consult with George Young[1] as to studio availability in late Winter.

Could I persuade you to abandon your executive quarters ever so briefly and recapture those glorious days when H. Burton, compere extraordinaire, was the Third Programme's answer to Mike Wallace?[2] Here's what I have in mind: Roland Gelatt, the Editor of High Fidelity – to which magazine I have contributed on an irregular basis in recent months, occasionally under my own name but more frequently, believe it or not, as Herbert Von Hochmeister, my preferred alias of the moment (the above information is classified) – has invited me to become a sort of guest editor-of-the-month next March at which time the magazine observes its 15th anniversary. The space customarily set aside for free-lance essays will be given over to an in-depth (I hope) consideration of the Prospects of Recording – that's the title. I am working on a long – very long by magazine standards – 15,000 words approximately – article, in which I will try to evaluate the present state of the industry and attempt a few guesses about its future. Supplementing this, I plan to tape-record interviews with some 15 to 20 people whose experience of music is especially bound up with the making of recordings – people like Stokowski, Copland, Robert Craft, Milton Babbitt,[3] George Marek,[4] Goddard Leiberson, Walter Legge, etc. Extracts from the views expressed by each of them will be packaged in margin boxes sprinkled throughout my essay. The interview-guests are not being chosen because their views necessarily confirm my own convictions about the inherent superiority of canned music – indeed, all challenges are gratefully received. However, it is, I think, important that they should – (a) all submit to a basic set of questions from which I can draw cross-referenced replies: i.e., "Mr. Rubinstein, Mr. Serkin has stated that he does not regard recording as an adequate replacement of live concerts. How do you feel about this?" – I do not plan to interview Serkin but you see what I mean; and (b) that they should each be able to discuss in some detail an area of involvement not duplicated by any of the other guests: i.e., Babbitt, tape and computer research; Stokowski, acoustic experimentation, etc.

Now then, first of all, could I involve you in an interview with yourself – in which, in addition to some basic thoughts about past and future recording, you would deal quite specifically with the role of recording in television.[5] You could explore it from whichever angles seemed most productive – music as sound track; video-tape cartridge recording – i.e., recordings produced with a visual component for home consumption; environmental similarity between the recording studio and the television studio – audience factor, etc. Really there are so many angles that it could be a whole other essay quite by itself. It can be as factual or as speculative as you choose to make it and needless to say, whatever method of interrogation you want to adopt with yourself is fine by me. In the interview which I will conduct, my questions will be edited out and a digest of the most striking or infuriating, or thought-provoking comments from each of the guests will spring spontaneously from the merge.

We hope to have in addition to yourself and Herr Dr. Legge, one or two other U.K. opinions – John Culshaw, most definitely, and perhaps one more. I very much want to relate some portion of these viewpoints to subjects who are not professional musicians but with whom, as laymen, the reader will be able to identify to some degree. We have thought of two names in this category – Lord Harewood, not really a layman I agree, and, believe it or not, one Edward Heath, who is, I understand, given to perusing Hansard against a stereo backdrop. This may be shooting a bit high, though a friend of mine in New York, Schuyler Chapin, has offered to act as go-between. In any event, either Heath or Harewood would make splendid interview subjects, I should think. I am fairly sure that Harewood would be amenable to it since in some recent correspondence re an invitation to Edinburgh (which, of course, I declined) he seemed a most pleasant sort.[6]

Anyway, my second question is – would you be willing to sit down with Culshaw and either Harewood or Heath and collect their opinions for us? Needless to say, we would approach them directly on behalf of the magazine and set it up at your and their convenience – the only stipulation being that we would need this material not later than the second half of November. Then you could simply mail us the tape of the three interviews and we would have it transcribed in New York.

Walter Legge will be in New York in November, so I can handle that interview myself. I do hope you will agree to participate in both parts of this Project. It is most important that we make the scope of the interviews and the choice of the interview subjects as impressively catholic as we can.

Do let me hear from you. All the best,

Sincerely,
Glenn Gould.

P.S. I would be most interested in hearing from you re any additional guest-types you might think appropriate – anyone who looms large on the U.K. recording scene.

cc: Mr. Roland Gelatt.

[1]CBC staff member.
[2]American television journalist.
[3]Milton Babbitt (b. 1916), American composer.
[4]George Marek (1902-87), Austrian-born American writer on music.
[5]Burton agreed to participate.
[6]Harewood was interviewed.

TO THE EDITOR, DAILY STAR

Letter to the Editor:
 Being on a dissertation on
 the news that's print to fit.

103 Avenue Road,
Toronto 4, Ontario
October 30, 1965

The Editor,
Daily Star,
Toronto, Ontario

Dear Sir:

I find myself vastly entertained by the temper tantrum with which your literary adjudicator, Robert Fulford, responds to Time magazine's current evaluation of the life and works of a fellow Welshman, Dylan Thomas.[1] Time calls Thomas "immature" and Fulford will have none of it. "A Book Review by some anonymous hack," puffs he, and asks Time "How mature are you?" Mature enough, I think, to hire the sort of 'anonymous hack' who can weekly contribute to a miracle of responsible, accurate and eloquent journalism. So much for the maturity of Time!

As to Dylan's, I should think Time's comment fair enough. Psychology has taught us that the concept of the alienated artist is not peculiar to the romantic novel, but is, rather, a continuing social phenomenon and that maturity and genius are, on occasion, mutually exclusive facts of life. Maturity qua the artist involves some control of temperament consistent with whatever tempo of existence circumstances force him to endure. And by this yardstick, the boozing, wenching, brawling, cussing, belligerently, self-destroying Dylan doesn't quality.

But, actually, I have no quarrel with Mr. Fulford. On the contrary, having read his column for some years now, I am quite prepared to concede him to be the one responsible staffer on the Star's entertainment pages, and, as such, to allow him an occasional critical gaff and, indeed, a spiritual haven on the New Republic, if such be his desire. I simply question whether as a journalist who turns up free-lance in innumerable minority quarterlies, he could not have dropped his Time-bomb elsewhere and spared us the hypocrisy of its appearance in the columns of a newspaper nationally celebrated for intemperate, inaccurate and inelegant reporting.

Yours truly,
Cornelius Dees.[2]

---

[1]*Time Magazine*, Vol. 86, No. 18, October 29, 1965.
[2]Cornelius Dees was Gould's physiotherapist. Gould was clearly irritated by Robert Fulford's comments in the *Time* article. However, as Fulford was a childhood friend, Gould was reluctant to write to the *Toronto Star* using his own name.

TO DENNIS BRAITHWAITE[1]

12 Sheppard Street
November 29, 1965

Mr. Dennis Braithwaite,
Globe and Mail,
Toronto, Ontario.

Dear Mr. Braithwaite:

This is a bit overdue but I do want to thank you very much for the more than kind comments in your column a few weeks back. I do agree with you – disinterestedly, I hope – about the role which music should play in television and I am delighted that you pointed out that, on this continent at least, television has not as yet come to terms with musical programming.

It is very hard to say if, or when, this bias will disappear, though I should imagine that the video-tape cartridge which seems certain to become involved with commercial recording may have a very great deal to do with whatever breakthrough is in store for music as television fare. As a matter of fact, I am, at the moment, writing a rather large scale essay for High Fidelity about the effect of recordings on our future and have compiled interviews with quite a few people involved in the industry in whose prognosis of the future the visual component looms large.

I am sure that, in the words of our mutual friend, Professor McLuhan, the 'feedback' of such a consumer demand arising in recording would necessarily stimulate new kinds of programming via television. In recording, of course, it could be an incredible nuisance – imagine having to cut, to black, every time one wanted to edit some tape!

The show with Yehudi Menuhin[2] was a great joy to make and I hope that, when screened, it will justify your enthusiasm.

Sincerely,
Glenn Gould.

[1]Toronto journalist.
[2]CBC-TV's "Festival," broadcast on May 18, 1966. Gould and Menuhin discussed each piece prior to its performance. J.S. Bach's Sonata for Violin and Harpsichord No. 4, in C minor, BWV 1017; Beethoven's Violin Sonata in G major, Op. 96, No. 10; Schoenberg's *Phantasy* for violin and piano, Op. 47.

TO THE EDITOR, DAILY STAR

Draft
April 11, 1966

The Editor,
Montreal Star,
Montreal, Quebec.

Dear Sir:

I am afraid that your music critic, Mr. Eric McLean, has once again dug in his heels and shied away from the implications of the twentieth century. In his column (April 2), Mr. McLean takes me to task for the "subjectivity" of my views re. The Future of Recorded Music and the obsolescence of the concert hall as set down in the current issue of High Fidelity Magazine. Now, even as I stand back to admire the unimpeachable critical objectivity with which Mr. McLean argues for the retention of reviewable public performances, I protest that in terming my arguments subjective, he does me too much credit. For indeed, these observations are not my private preserve; however, they may serve to confirm my own disinclination toward the anachronistic traditions of concert-giving and concert-going. They are nowadays fundamental to the musical experience of the Western world and as such, without any help from me, lead a life of their own.

The main thrust of Mr. McLean's rebuttal is concerned with the fact that I "glossed over" and "touched only lightly" upon the listener's role or, as Mr. McLean insists, lack of it, where recorded music is concerned. In fact fully $1/3$ – the last third of my essay was devoted, in almost obsessive detail to putting down that tired lament about listener deprivation which Mr. McLean chooses to revive. Thus he seriously contends that a number of audiences stuffed into Row L at Place des Arts,[1] periodically nudged awake to flap his blistered palms in mandatory approval, is more participant, more engaged with musical experience than when, at home, manipulating the already sophisticated, yet still comparatively primitive playback equipment which modern technology places at his disposal. He makes choices, exercises options, which heretofore were reserved as interpretive and, yes, even critical prerogatives.

Since Mr. McLean insists that I glossed over these vital questions, I can only assume that either he was not paying attention or that, inspired by my description of the listener's new-found editorial control, he made his own spliced-point totally aware through my essay.

Yours truly
Glenn Gould

[1]Montreal concert hall.

TO DIANA MENUHIN

April 25, 1966

Mrs. Yehudi Menuhin,
London, England.

Dear Lady Diana,

Somehow in the depths of my dour hieland heart, I feared it would come to this! With most grave apprehension have I anticipated that day when riotous living and multi-residential dwelling would catch up with you. But, braced against the event as one may be, one can scarcely minimize the shock with which these castrophies confront us. And imagine, if you will, my consternation last week when upon rifling through the New York Times and endeavouring to divert my glance from any item panned by Homer Sibelius, I encountered a modest dispatch telling of Sir Yehudi's fiftieth birthday celebrations this week and – oh, the humiliation of it – that upon that occasion the good burghers of London would hold a benefit performance for him.

A benefit! My dear, I am one with you in your embarrassment. But what a comfort it must be for you to know that men of goodwill will rally round in this your hour of adversity. And you, in turn, must not allow foolish pride to impede your acceptance of these benefactions. Indeed, I would direct your thoughts toward a phrase which has contributed to my comfort in many moments of stress and strain – a simple, homespun, hieland phrase, "Behind every silver lining there's a cloud."

For my part, I would ask that you direct Sir Yehudi's attention to three morsels of good news which may, each in its own way, serve to alleviate your distress:

(1) Remind him please that he promised to see what could be done about revising his EMI contract in such a manner as to permit us to make one or more recordings for Columbia in the not too distant future;

(2) I recently taped four programs for Humphrey Burton[1] and he tells me that the BBC will most likely purchase the TV show which Yehudi and I made last year;[2] and

(3) The Gould prospecting and stock counselling service is always at your disposal.[3]

One thing more, dear Lady Diana: I have chosen not to comment directly upon Sir Yehudi's elevation to the Knighthood because frankly, my nose is out of joint. I read of this extraordinary happening – a happening which under any other circumstances I should be compelled to say was long overdue, mightily deserved, and one of the few cogent arguments for the retention of the British Crown – in the pages of the New York Times not 48 hours after you had departed from these shores last November, and after we had spoken by telephone, and it is my unshakeable conviction that anything Homer Sibelius[4] can know about on Monday, I can know about on Sunday!

With much love to you both,

Sincerely
G. Herbert Gould
Treasurer and Principle Beneficiary,
Knightly Musicians' Benevolent Fund.

---

[1]"Conversations with Glenn Gould," a four-part program on Bach, Beethoven, Richard Strauss, and Arnold Schoenberg, produced by BBC in 1966 at the CBC's Toronto studios.
[2]Television program recorded with Menuhin in Toronto on April 18, 1966.
[3]Gould took pride in keeping in touch with stock market reports and watching his own investments.
[4]A Gould pseudonym.

TO JOHN HAGUE[1]   11/5/66

Mr. John Hague,
Birmingham, England.

Dear Mr. Hague:

Under that venerable crest and motto, "Never accomplish today what can best be put off 'till tomorrow," the Gould family has flourished for generations, and I must now take my place among the formidable ranks of my procrastinating forefathers. It is indeed no fault of her Majesty's mails that you have not received the W.T.C.,[2] etc.

Apologies are useless at this late date but let me assure you that the first book which is now released in a three record set is going out to you right away as is a two record set of Schonberg which has just been released in North America this month,[3] and also a copy of last month's High Fidelity Magazine which you may not have seen.[4]

You may find it rather difficult to get me off your television screen next fall, since I have just made four forty minute programs for BBC-2[5] – which were produced here in Toronto, with the immense help of Humphrey Burton, who came out from London for a ten-day period last March. I gather that they are to be shown in the early fall and will perhaps be preceded by a one-hour program which was made here in Toronto last fall with Yehudi Menuhin and on which we did the C minor Sonata of Bach, G. major Opus 96 of Beethoven, and the Fantasy of Schonberg.[6] Needless to say, I am enormously pleased about all this because with my reluctance to concertize abroad, it offers the best sort of introduction to England, I think. The forty minute programs were in the form of lectures cum conversations with Humphrey and, of course, all quite liberally illustrated with examples, and were, I think, more fun to make and, all in all, more satisfying than any television I've ever done.

I do look forward to hearing from you and again apologies for the really inexcusable delay.

Sincerely,
Glenn Gould.

---

[1]A friend.
[2]J.S. Bach, *The Well-Tempered Clavier*, Book I: Nos. 1-8, BWV 846-853 (Columbia).
[3]Schoenberg, *The Complete Music for Solo Piano* and *Complete Songs for Voice and Piano*, Vol. 1, 1966 (Columbia).
[4]"The Prospects of Recording," *High Fidelity*, Vol. 16, No. 4, April 1966.
[5]"Conversations with Glenn Gould" (1966).
[6]Aired on CBC-TV's "Festival," May 18, 1966.

TO GODDARD LIEBERSON

May 14, 1966

Mr. Goddard Lieberson,
c/o Columbia Records,
New York, N.Y.

Dear Goddard:

I should long ago have written to thank you for your participation in the High Fidelity project.[1] I was very grateful indeed for the time you set aside for it (not to mention the marvellous lunch), and the material that you gave me made a tremendous contribution toward what I profoundly hope was the success of the article.

It seems to me that at lunch that day, we spoke at some length about the strange views of Professor McLuhan and that I promised to send you some sampling of his work. I have now interviewed McLuhan twice – for High Fidelity and for the CBC – and have between times got to know him rather well. He remains for me a subject both fascinating and frustrating and his writings – an extraordinary mixture of wackiness with brilliant perceptions. I had the feeling, however, that he has in many rather significant ways put his finger on some of the central issues of our time, and notwithstanding all the cafe society cult that is now growing up around him in the U.S., he remains, I think, an intriguing and important figure.

I am sending along the "Gutenburg Galaxy"[2] which, from my point of view, is his best book and as soon as it becomes available again – its between printings at the moment – "Understanding Media,"[3] which is his latest one. I hope you find something of interest in them.[4]

All very best wishes,

Sincerely,
Glenn Gould.

[1]"The Prospects of Recording," April 1966.
[2]Marshall McLuhan. *The Gutenberg Galaxy* (Toronto: University of Toronto Press, 1962).
[3]Marshall McLuhan. *Understanding Media* (New York: McGraw-Hill, 1964).
[4]In a 1972 conversation with John Roberts Gould commented that McLuhan did not communicate by answering questions but was more like a medium, and added, "I'm perhaps somehow closer to the 'message'."

TO LEOPOLD STOKOWSKI

May 25, 1966

Mr. Leopold Stokowski,
New York, N.Y.

Dear Maestro:

Our "Emperor"[1] has just reached me in its final form and I must say I am very proud of it. It was a great joy to be able to work with you.[2]

I was speaking earlier this week to Franz Kraemer who is Executive Producer of a series of CBC TV programs collectively called 'Festival'. For each of the past several seasons, I have video-taped programmes which appear on the Festival Series and which have involved solo performances as well as chamber music and, on occasion, something with orchestra. Mr. Kraemer asked whether I thought that you might be well disposed toward TV in general, and this series in particular, and whether you might be willing to conduct a programme which could be taped at some point during the next year. He suggested to me that his own preference was for a programme which could be done with an orchestra of fifty pieces or less and volunteered that he would be particularly happy with an all-Mozart programme – i.e. something on the lines of a symphony, a piano concerto and perhaps an overture to begin.[3]

The programme need not, however, necessarily include Mozart at all – it could, with forces of that size, be concerned with Beethoven or, in fact, contemporary music or a combination of all three. The reduced size of the orchestra is advantageous not only fiscally but accoustically as well, since the best TV studio in Toronto, like most others of its kind, was designed specifically for the spoken word and tends to be rather dry, where a large orchestra is involved, but quite acceptable for a smaller group.

Performances on this series are not necessarily treated with the formality of a concert. A certain amount of experiment is often involved with the concept behind a particular program. In the past two years Hermann Scherchen and Karl Boehm have taken part in this series in programmes which featured substantial segments of rehearsal prior to the actual performance (in Boehm's case it was the Beethoven Seventh Symphony and in Scherchen's "Die Kunst der Fuge"). Last week they showed a programme which I taped last Fall with Menuhin and on which we did Bach and Beethoven Sonatas and the Schonberg Violin "Fantasy," prior to which we engaged in a vigorous argument as to its merits (I was pro).

All of this is simply to say that these programmes are sufficiently flexible that one can, in fact, try new ideas while making them. They can be as formal or as informal as you want them to be and in that context Mr. Kraemer's suggestion of a Mozart programme simply serves as a rough outline for a form which could be as adventurous or as straightforward as you would want it to be.

As far as I know there is no particular deadline as to when this would need to be taped, though it would be intended for showing during the calendar year 1967 and I rather imagine they would prefer to tape during the winter or spring months.

Perhaps when you have time you could give me your reactions to this idea. Indeed, I would be most interested in your reactions to music on TV in general, because since I do a lot of TV programmes nowadays, I am always most curious about the views of those who have had a good deal of experience with the medium as to its potential for music programming.

Very best wishes for your European tour this summer and, at your convenience, I look forward to hearing from you.

Sincerely,
Glenn Gould.

[1]Beethoven's Concerto No. 5 in E♭ major, Op. 73, the *Emperor*, with Stokowski conducting the
American Symphony Orchestra (Columbia) recorded in 1966.
[2]Gould had a profound admiration for Leopold Stokowski as a musician and as a pioneer in the
advancement of music and technology through his early radio and recording projects.
[3]Nothing came of the proposed television program.

TO JOHN McCLURE

Apt. 902, 110 St. Clair Ave.W.
June 11, 1966

Mr. John McClure
Columbia Records,
New York, N.Y.

Chere Maitre:

Many thanks for the Australian clippings. Its good to know that CBS International is really operating these days.

I do very much hope that you and Adrienne will be able to join me for dinner
next week and the purpose of this letter is to permit you to prepare your defences
against a proposal with which I intend once again to accost you.

You will remember that on one or two occasions some months back, I
endeavoured to enlist your enthusiasm for a "Legacy Type" spoof in which I
would be presented in recital at Whitehorse, Yukon Territories; Yellowknife,
Northwest Territories; or some other such romantic spot. When I brought up
this worthy project on previous occasions, it was as an adjunct to our Centennial
plans,[1] and I had in mind at that time a *real* recital in a *real* Arctic or sub-Arctic
outpost. Indeed, Nicky Goldschmidt of the Centennial Commission in Ottawa
took the idea so seriously that, had I not been dissuaded from my own Operation
Yukon this month, he and I were to meet at Whitehorse during the Commission's hearings there and scout the possibility of an acoustically suitable lodge,
church basement, trapper's cabin, etc.

Now right from the start, it was apparent to me that there were very grave
obstacles to be overcome – my piano's susceptibility to an asthmatic attack in
permafrost conditions being not the least of them. A still more serious one,
however, was the notable lack of enthusiasm which I detect on your part, Cher
Maitre, and I raise the matter again and with utmost formality, not only in order

that you may have time to marshall your most strenuous objections to this project, but also that you may realize that I meant it all along.

What I propose to you now retains the original idea with but one significant modification – to wit: that we fake the whole event studio-wise – cuts rather close to home doesn't it? It seems to me that here is an opportunity to spoof in a delicious way the whole absurd contradiction of the recorded public recital (Sviatoslav at Sofia, etc.),[2] and, in addition, do a send-up on the profuse documentation of the Legacy Series.

We could concoct an irreproachably chronological recital format consisting exclusively of pieces that I would be unlikely to record as part of any more sober project. For instance:

– some Scarlatti
– the 32 Variations in C minor of Beethoven
  (heaven spare us Wanda's wrath!)[3]
– some Mendelssohn's Songs without Words
– the Prokofiev Sonata No.7

How's that for the all-time safe, intellect-proof, Ibbs and Tillett[4] debut special? It would, of course, be recorded to the best of our ability with perhaps just a few conspicuous clinkers left in to give it credence (this last is optional). Then we would over-dub the splutters, sneezes, and sighs of the noisiest damn audience since Neville Chamberlain was shouted down in the House. Depending on the locale ostensibly selected for it, this sound track should include one or more disruptive canines (there might even be a role for a disgruntled bluejay assassin to sound an alarm on the old "22"). And all of this over-tracking would, needless to say, be in and of itself a work of art, obtrusively filtering through the music which, as you will note in my suggested program, should be notable for its absence of contrapuntal idioms.

Above all, it would afford us the opportunity to commission a series of brilliant and perceptive and entirely irrelevant essays dealing with the vegetation, geology, history of settlement and sociological analysis of the region selected. I would suggest that a real live geologist might be invited to give a perfectly deadpan essay – I have contacts at the Department of Northern Affairs in Ottawa and I am sure I know of at least one superb with the works therein and would be well qualified to do a sociological study. And we can be sure, of course, that Dr. Von Hochmeister[5] would have an essay available. Above all, I should think it important to produce some eloquent and very square Holiday-Mag. style pictures of, let us say, Tuktoyaktuk at Dusk, which would be as unrelievedly navy blue as Rauschenberg's Opus 1. We might also have a hearty Welkommen from His Worship the Mayor, who could be photographed, by contrast, in broad daylight upon a waste of tundra and standing beside a neatly lettered sign which reads "Industrial Sites Available."

I realize, dear sir, that this all sounds quite mad, but I suggest to you that it is from such madness that the Hoffnung concerts and the Baroque Beatles Book grew, and I feel that we must talk about it further, because if this does not turn out to be the sleeper of 1967, I will stake you and Adrienne to half-a-dozen T-bones at the Automat of your choice.[6]
All the best for now,

Sincerely,
Glenn Gould.

cc. Mr Andrew Kazdin (same add.)

[1]The centenary of Canada (1867).
[2]Gould is probably referring to Sviatoslav Richter's concert recording of Moussorgsky's *Pictures at an Exhibition*.
[3]Wanda Landowska (1879-1959), Polish-born harpsichordist and leading figure in the twentieth-century revival of the harpsichord. Stenographer's error; Gould meant this reference to apply to "some Scarlatti", above.
[4]British concert agency that represented performing musicians.
[5]Dr. Herbert von Hochmeister was a Gould alias.
[6]This project was something Gould badly wanted to undertake; however, Columbia Records was not interested.

TO HUMPHREY BURTON[1]

June 27, 1966
(dictated June 25)

Mr. Humphrey Burton,
BBC Television,
London, England.

Dear Humphrey:
Have just seen, with Franz, "The Golden Ring".[2] It's a masterpiece! You have captured in the most faithful way the atmosphere of a recording studio and since next week (27th) will be my first session in five weeks (which is along abstinence for me) it made me terribly eager to get back before and behind the microphones.
I particularly loved the Dr. Strangelove-type shots of the console and I thought that Culshaw[3] was wonderfully spontaneous and relaxed. But my favorite character was the electrician's helper who, at about eight minutes into the film, was shown on two occasions crawling under a bank of ampexes and saying "Not getting anything yet, 'enry." I don't know how intentional that was but it seemed to me like a running gag from early Alec Guinness and I somehow kept hoping that, as we came down the home stretch, he would make yet another appearance

in the same spot and with the same line – sort of a Burtonian version of "Ready when you are Mr. DeMille."

Two questions: I had a letter from a friend in Birmingham who assured me that some or all of our programmes are scheduled for BBC-2 beginning the end of June and continuing through July.[4] Is this true or are we still set for September? Also, were you or your sales force able to make headway with Curtis-Davis?[5] If we can nudge things along from this end, please let us know. In any event, I still hope you will find it feasible to let me screen one or two or our programmes for CBC in New York. I realize that all sorts of tariff complications can arise when one moves films from country to country, but would it not be possible to gain some sort of restricted entry permit, if the films were classified 'for audition purposes' only?

All the best for now. Do let me know what you are up to.

Sincerely,
Glenn.

[1]BBC television producer and director.
[2]"The Golden Ring" was a one-hour television documentary produced by Humphrey Burton for the BBC about the audio recording of Wagner's operatic cycle *Der Ring des Nibelungen*, conducted by Georg Solti, and produced for the Decca Record Company by John Culshaw.
[3]John Culshaw, recording and television director (1924-80).
[4]"Conversations with Glenn Gould" (1966).
[5]Curtis W. Davis of PBS.

TO DIANA MENUHIN   July 30, 1966

Mrs. Yehudi Menuhin
London, England.

Dear Diana:

Your letter was terribly welcome – all twelve illegible pages of it. I had been pining away for want of news from you and set to work deciphering it with a vengeance. But the news was not of the best. You must take better care of yourself. I know that this is easier said than done, but do please try to get a good rest this Summer.

Now then, as you know, when not trekking through the wilds of Arctic Canada, I contribute occasional articles to High Fidelity Magazine and a week or so ago, I received a call from one of the editors who told me that next December upon the cover of the Musical America Annual (a subsidiary of High Fidelity), they intend to enshrine Sir Yehudi as "Musician of the Year."[1] This is one of our quaint North

American customs intended to distract attention from Her Majesty's New Year's list. In any event, who do you think has been asked to compose the dedicatory foreword? Correct! And I was wondering whether you would feel inclined to supply me with any choice morsels of Menuhiniana. These would not need to be attributed directly to you unless you so desire, though I should prefer not to introduce them with – "As a feminine admirer recently remarked. . . ." They could, in fact, cut as wide a swath through Yehudi's leben und werken as you might wish – Bath, Gstaad touring, sitar accompanying, the Menuhin dynastic impulse, etc. I suppose what I am really asking is for a collection of your inimitably bristling bon mots which I can drop into my foreword as context dictates.

The only problem is, I need them soon – like next week. It seems idiotic to have an August deadline for a magazine that will appear in December but that's all part of our super-efficient North American production-line way of life.

Do please let me have your scratchings, if you feel so inclined and, in the meantime, all the very best,

Sincerely,

¹"Yehudi Menuhin: Musician of the Year: Some Thoughts" in *High Fidelity/Musical America*, Vol. 16, No. 13, December 15, 1966.

TO ROBERT ALTSCHULER   September 14, 1966
Air Mail – Registered
Mr. Robert Altschuler,
Columbia Records,
New York, N.Y.

Dear Bob:

Herewith my contribution to Cosmopolitan.¹ I didn't know whether you wanted a capsule comment to accompany each of the choices, so in that event, I dashed off one more or less suitable to each.

All the best,

Yours very truly,

GOULD'S PREFERRED

1. The Symphonies of Hans Werner Henze – DGG.

The season's most impressive and most generous retrospective.

2. Bach: The Brandenburg Concertos; Herbert Von Karajan – DGG.

Karajan sometimes reminds me of the late Dimitri Mitropoulos because of his seemingly grudging concessions to baroque scholarship. Thus, on these discs, impeccable phrasing, unarguable tempi but far too many strings, too distant cembalo. Yet, even in its fuzzy way, rather wonderful.

3. Chopin: Sonata No.3; Robert Casadesus – Columbia.

I find that I can live quite nicely without Frederic Francois' Sonatas, but I've always felt that if one is to do them, one should surely do them straight. And this is the straightest, and best, performance of the B minor Sonata I've ever heard.[2]

4. Ruggles[3]: Suntreaders – Columbia.

I haven't yet been able to bring myself to sign the 'Ives for Mount Rushmore' petition, for despite his remarkably inventive mind, I've always been put off by the sheer garrulousness of his manner. But, on the other hand, I find myself completely won over by the pointedly laconic language of his Yankee contemporary, Carl Ruggles.

* * * * *

GLENN GOULD
September 14, 1966.

[1]*Cosmopolitan Magazine.*
[2]Gould's comment that if the Chopin sonatas are to be undertaken "one should surely do them straight" is interesting in that his own performance of the Sonata No. 3 in B minor, Op. 58, in a radio recital on "CBC Thursday Night," broadcast on July 23, 1970, was anything but "straight."
[3]Charles Ruggles (1876-1971), American composer.

TO LEON FLEISHER[1]   November 14, 1966

Mr. Leon Fleischer,
Baltimore, Maryland,
U.S.A.

Dear Leon,
    Many congratulations on the arrival of Julian Ross and, of course, even more of them to Ricki!
    I have tried to pick up your orthopaedic trail from time to time and I gather

that things are beginning to seem much more hopeful. As you know, no one is in a better position to realize what you have been going through this last year or two than I, even though my own experience with this sort of malaise is by comparison limited both as to duration and, I expect, severity.[2] I do hope, more than I can say, that all will be well soon because I feel very strongly that you are one of the very few original performers and, as such, far too valuable a person to absent the scene for long.

I was down visiting our friend, Dr. Stein, in Philadelphia, about a month ago because I threw my left leg out of whack, but since I gather that you had moved on to other orthopaedic counsel, I thought it best not to ask him for an up-to-date report on your case.[3]

If you have time and feel like it, do please drop me a line and let me know how things are going. All very best to you both,

Sincerely,
Glenn.

[1]Leon Fleisher (b. 1928), American pianist and conductor.
[2]Gould is referring to Fleisher's right hand, which became disabled in 1965, and to his own shoulder injury.
[3]Dr. Stein treated Gould's shoulder injury as well.

TO MARTIN SOHN-RETHEL[1]   November 14, 1966

Mr. Martin Sohn-Rethel,
Birmingham, England.

Dear Mr. Sohn-Rethel:

Thank you very much for your letter and for your kind words about our program on Schonberg.[2] I regret that I do not know Adorno's Citation[3] but I have encountered a number of quotations from Schonberg's essays in which the composer expressed similar sentiments and I do believe that he was entirely justified in anticipating a certain dichotomy as between the intuitive grasp of his style and objective verification of his method.

This question of objectifying the musical experience is relative, I think, to all kinds of music – I believe I mentioned something of the kind in another of the BBC programs dealing with Beethoven[4] – but undoubtedly it comes to the fore very particularly when one examines important and still somewhat illusive trends in contemporary music. It seems to me that one of the major barriers which has stood between Schonberg and the wider audience, which I do believe he deserves, and I feel certain that it is only a question of time until that barrier will be permanently lowered.

Again thanks very much for your letter.

Yours sincerely,
Glenn Gould.

¹A fan.
²"Conversations with Glenn Gould" (1966). The fourth and last telecast in this series dealt with the music of Schoenberg.
³This publication was not part of Gould's personal library; however his copy of Theodor W. Adorno's *Prisms* was heavily annotated.
⁴Second program in the series "Conversations with Glenn Gould."

TO SARA McANENY¹   February 19, 1967

Mrs. Sara McAneny
Nashville, Tennessee.

Dear Mrs. McAneny,

Thank you so much for your delightful letter. I very much appreciate your writing to me and I was, of course, most happy to read of your enthusiasm for my recordings.

This question of key and key-association is a rather elusive one. (I don't think its an odd question, by the way, for I think about it a good deal myself.) As you know, many composers in the latter part of the 19th century developed a veritable mystique of key identities through attributing specific characteristics to various tonal regions and, consequently, key-association played a significant part in the composing attitude of the period.

It also related in some sense to the color spectrum, and Alexander Scriabin was only one artist whose imagination was stimulated by that particular link. Surely, its no accident that E flat major seems always to have represented a heroic stance for Richard Strauss, as perhaps for Beethoven, and that C minor in Beethoven, Brahms and Bruckner, is somehow associated with epic statements.

Anyway, this is just to say that I do know what you mean and that, although I have never thought about a 'favorite' key as such, I would have to confess that insofar as I think tonally, a rather high percentage of motivic ideas have tended to present themselves to me either in the key of my Spring Quartette (F minor) or some close relative thereof – A flat major, perhaps.

I am not really sure what all that means. I suppose if one thinks of the F minor works of Bach, they present a rather dour facade on the whole – but, in any case,

I should certainly think that anyone who experienced a preference for B flat major as you do is unquestionably possessed of a more cheerful disposition.[2]
With all best wishes,

Sincerely,
Glenn Gould.

[1]A fan.
[2]The matter of key and key-association was one that Gould thought about constantly. He frequently played key-association guessing games with people. "If you were a key what one would you be? Let us guess." If someone guessed him as C major, Gould did not take it as a compliment.

TO JUDITH TAITT-WERENFELD[1]   April 12, 1967
Miss Judith Taitt-Werenfeld,
Montreal, Quebec.

Dear Miss Taitt-Werenfeld:
I am afraid your signature was just a bit on the illegible side, so if I have misspelled your name, do please forgive me.
Thank you very much indeed for your kind comments about the CBC television program.[2] It was a great joy to make and I am very pleased indeed to have so enthusiastic a reaction.
The probability of a recital in Montreal is, I am afraid, rather remote. I haven't given recitals for several years now – found that whole way of life rather distasteful – and would be most reluctant to go back to it.
Your question about 'gesticulations' is a rather difficult one. I would indeed like to think that they represent a kind of intensifying relation to music that you very generously suggested. But its hard to know, since I have never been able to play the piano without gesturing semaphorically toward an imaginary horde of sidemen. I suspect that it has to do with a desire to externalize, not the music or even one's relation to it, but perhaps the responsibility for it. That sounds rather strange, I know, but I have thought a good deal about this question and, as of the moment, it is the only relevant answer I can arrive at.
Again many thanks for your note. With all best wishes.

Sincerely,
Glenn Gould.

[1]A fan.
[2]Gould is probably referring to the CBC-TV "Festival" program entitled "To Every Man His Own Bach," a musical conversation with Gould, broadcast on March 29, 1967.

TO ILSE THOMPSON[1]   April 24, 1967

Mrs. Ilse M. Thompson,
Maple, Ontario.

Dear Mrs. Thompson,

Thank you very much for your letter and for telling me of your interest in our "Festival" programme.

I realize that what I had to say in conversation with Mr. Burton was, indeed, rather contentious, though I can honestly say that although some of my comments were necessarily speculative, they were no more than projections into the future of certain circumstances affecting the musical life of the present day, which already seem to me to make recorded music a more cogent and rewarding experience than the public concert.[2] I did not, of course, mean to suggest that my recording of a particular Bach Fugue, which I discussed at some length, was in any sense *the* performance of that particular work. I do feel, however, that so far as my notions about Bach at a particular period in my life are concerned, it was *the* performance. And I don't think that the degree to which that performance was indebted to the facilities of the medium of recording in any way compromises or invalidates that fact.

As I suggested to Mr. Burton, the real virtue of the recording process is not in its inherent perfectionism but in the after-thought control by which one can operate upon the raw material of performance. For me, the best of all possible worlds would be one in which the art of performance supplied raw material only and the process of assembling or reconstructing the work occupied the major portion of the performer's activity.

Again thank you very much for your letter and with all best wishes,

Sincerely,
Glenn Gould.

[1] A fan.
[2] "To Every Man His Own Bach."

TO DEBBIE BARKER[1]   May 22, 1967

Miss Debbie Barker,
Delhi, Ontario.

Dear Debbie,

Thank you very much for your letter and for including me in the book which you are compiling at your school.

Your question as to whether Bach has always been my favorite composer is a very interesting one and one which is not so easy to answer. There is a school of thought which holds that whichever composer you are studying or playing at a particular time ought to be, for that moment at least, your favorite, and just as many actors will tell you that their present role is the one to which they are most devoted.

At the same time, I think that if I were required to spend the rest of my life on a desert island, and to listen or play the music of any one composer during all that time, that composer would almost certainly be Bach. I really can't think of any other music which is so all-encompassing, which moves me so deeply and so consistently, and which, to use a rather imprecise word, is valuable beyond all of its skill and brilliance for something more meaningful than that – its humanity.

All best wishes for your project at school and for your own future.

Yours sincerely,
Glenn Gould.

¹A fan.

TO WILLI REICH   May 24, 1967

Dr. Willi Reich,
Zurich, Switzerland.

Dear Dr. Reich:

Thank you very much for your letter. Indeed, your name is well known to me through your magnificent biography of Alban Berg.¹

The radio documentary which was referred to on page 19 of my Schoenberg essay was prepared for the Canadian Broadcasting Corporation in 1962.² At that time, I interviewed a number of people who had either known Schoenberg well, or had arrived at some very definite position in regard to his work.³ At the end of each of these interviews which were conducted with a tape recorder, I did indeed ask each of the guests the same question, "What will happen to Schoenberg in the year 2000?" The problem was that not all of the answers were equally instructive or, for that matter, amusing, and I retained in the final script for the broadcast only a cross-section of comments which seemed to me indicative of the divergent opinions about Schoenberg. They were, in any case, chosen more for their pointedly argumentative character than for any profound grasp of prognostication.

I am explaining all this simply because, careless though it may seem, I no longer possess the original transcripts of the interviews from which these final excerpts derive. And, as you will see from the enclosed copy, which I have asked my Secretary to prepare for you, in many cases the results were conditioned by the previous comments of the speakers, i.e. Mr. Sargent, who is hardly a champion of contemporary music, was simply expressing the extent of his own displeasure with the whole phenomena of which Schoenberg forms a part. In any case, you will, I hope, understand that the technique involved was one which attempted to present Schoenberg's life to a radio audience by means of a fairly lively debate and hence the somewhat contentious aspect of several of the remarks quoted was justified by that context.

I look forward with great interest to your Schoenberg biography[4] and remain with best wishes,

Sincerely,
Glenn Gould.

Encl.
cc. c/o Mr. William Goodman, Harcourt,
Brace & World 757 – 3rd Ave., N.Y. (10017) Plse Frwd.

(As I was not quite certain of your Zurich address, I am taking the liberty of sending a copy of this letter to Mr. Wm.Goodman, of Harcourt, Brace & World, New York City – for forwarding to you.)

Istvan Anhalt (Canadian Composer):
The image of Schoenberg in the year 2000 will to a great extent depend upon the (subsequent) developments in the art of music. It seems to me, however, a good guess that several of his works will stand up to the test of time and through them he will continue to represent an important stratum of an important musical period for a long time to come. Or, perhaps I should say, that his musical voice will be recognized in the year 2000 as a manifestation of a singularly turbulent period of human history in Central Europe.

Winthrop Sargent (Music Critic, New York Magazine):
I don't think the year 2000 will hold very much for Schoenberg. I don't think that Schoenberg's popularity has increased to any extent even over the last thirty years. There are people who like it; there are people who play it, but the general public have never taken much interest in it for the reason, I think, that it does not convey anything much to them. In fact, I would guess that the Schoenberg style is finished, that it offers no future potentiality of any real value.

Aaron Copland:
I find it difficult to imagine exactly what the fate of the pieces will be. Its difficult to know how sympathetic people will be to that curious atmosphere which we connect with (the) Vienna of a certain period and a certain school.

That music is inconceivably without the life that those men lived in those days – the sense of terror, the sense of being lonely, the sense of being completely different from the classical tradition and yet feeling so strongly that they belonged in it and were the natural result of it. All that makes, from my standpoint, a rather tortured musical expression, and while its a very powerful musical expression, it nevertheless (continues) to seem tortured. Now whether the big public will find it less and less tortured – it would seem normal because that's what always has happened in the past – I don't know. Certainly, when I listen to Wozzeck now, when I think of Wozzeck thirty-five years ago, when I first heard of Stokowski do it, it seems like a different piece. It seems much more continuous, much more accessible to everyone and its very possible that the same may happen to Schoenberg's pieces. But not to everything! I doubt whether the Woodwind Quintet will ever seem like a jolly little piece one would want to put on before breakfast every day.

Mrs. Gertrude Schoenberg:
I hope that he will be recognized as a whole. But even now you can see that not every work of Beethoven is played, and, in fact, people dare, little critics dare, to write in the paper "This is a weak work of Beethoven," which every time gives me a cold shower. It is not easy to follow Schoenberg.

Glenn Gould
May 24, 1967

[1] Willi Reich, *Alban Berg*. Translated by Cornelius Cardew (New York: Harcourt, Brace & World, 1965).
[2] "Arnold Schoenberg: The Man Who Changed Music."
[3] Gould interviewed Gertrud Schoenberg, Aaron Copland, Goddard Lieberson, Peter Ostwald, Istvan Anhalt, and Winthrop Sargent. For the questions see Gould's letter to Carl Little, June 18, 1962.
[4] Willi Reich, *Arnold Schönberg oder der Konservative Revolutionar* (Munchen: Deutscher Taschenbuch Verlag, 1974).

TO JAMES LOTZ[1]

September 1, 1967

Professor James Lotz,
c/o St. Paul's University,
Ottawa, Ontario.

Dear Professor Lotz:
I wonder if I could tempt you to participate in a documentary project which I have agreed to undertake for CBC dealing with the Canadian North? The

program will be produced by Janet Somerville; will consist largely of tape-recorded interview material, and is tentatively entitled, "The Idea of North".

Although we are free to range over any and all aspects of Arctic endeavour, I am anxious to avoid both the "that thar grizzly back on the trail' anecdotal approach, which has been worn to a cliche by many such documentaries, and the Norilskian scientific frontierism, which would necessitate an in-depth study quite beyond the scope of this particular program.

What I would most like to do is to examine the effects of solitude and isolation upon those who have lived in the Arctic or Sub-Arctic. In some subtle way, the latitudinal factor does seem to have a modifying influence upon character, although I have no editorial axe to grind in the matter and am quite prepared to find some characters unmodified. I think, though, that by counterpointing several such experiences of the North, it should be possible to put together a rather interesting, and, hopefully, original program, and I do hope that you will agree to take part.

If possible, I would like to wrap up the interviews by the end of October, though, in fact, the program is not scheduled until December, and if you could advise me as to your schedule, I will arrange a trip to Ottawa accordingly.

Yours sincerely,
Glenn Gould.

¹An anthropologist, Lotz appeared in Gould's radio documentary "The Idea of North."

TO FLOYD CHALMERS¹   March 16, 1968.

Mr. Floyd Chalmers,
c/o MacLean-Hunter Publishing Co. Ltd.,
Toronto, Ontario.

Dear Floyd,
Many thanks for your letter and once again let me say how very much I appreciate your interest and your most kind offer. I am afraid, however, that at the risk of doing a Morley Callaghan,² I must confess that I am not altogether happy about the particular kind of stratification implicit in the Order of Canada. I know that some systemization is necessary in any program of that kind but I can't help feeling that there is something unnecessarily divisive within that system as it is presently constituted. I do feel – and I hope you won't think I am

just being ornery or eccentric or whatever – that I would prefer not to have my name submitted to the committee.[3]
    With all best wishes,

Sincerely,
Glenn Gould

[1]Chairman of MacLean Hunter Ltd. and one of Canada's most generous philanthropists in the field of the arts.
[2]Canadian author (1903-1990), known for his novels and short stories, who had created a controversy by refusing one of the lower levels of the Order of Canada.
[3]Gould would undoubtedly have received the highest level of the Order of Canada but he continued to refuse the attempts of friends and well-wishers to bring his name forward. He insisted that the accomplishments of his life might not be as important as those of Canadians who were being offered lower levels of the Order.

TO JOHN CULSHAW

cc Ron Wilford
June 22nd, 1968.

Mr. John Culshaw,
Television Centre, (Music Division)
British Broadcasting Corporation,
LONDON, England.

Dear John,
    Ron Wilford forwarded your letter and suggested that I get in touch directly. I must say that I'm looking forward to working with you very much indeed, and I would like to know even in roughest outline the sort of television-music that you'd like to be involved with so that we can perhaps come up with something a bit off the beaten track. Do you, for instance, want programs embodying 'a great quantity of thinking' as was said for Dr. Donne; do you want more or less unembroidered recital formats, or perhaps elements of both which might be manipulated so as to use the medium more indigenously than is often the case, at least on this side of the Atlantic.
    If the conventional recital item is what you had in mind, as I think Ronald proposed already, I would very much like to think about the Liszt Transcription of Beethoven's Sixth. It is by far the best of the Liszt realizations – quite a miracle really – and it could have the added merit of providing a somewhat off-beat contribution to the Beethoven year.[1] However, its running time is well over 50 minutes – I did it just last week on a CBC radio program and turned in the least

con motoed andante in history – consequently assuming a one-hour format, there would not be a great deal of time left for any sort of talk about Liszt, Beethoven, or their mutual enterprises.[2] However, I am not sure that there's all that much to be said about Liszt the transcriber, that hasn't already been said via the interminable comments of Mr. Harold Schoenberg and his undoubted British counterparts. Perhaps rather a discussion, if there is one, and if we have a span greater than one hour available, of sufficient latitude as to include the whole nation of musical revisionism, would be appropriate, in which case, the examples would not have to come necessarily, certainly not exclusively, from the symphony itself, and thus the better surprises which Liszt has in store would not lose their edge prematurely.

At some point during the next year or so, I would like to try devising scripts primarily in video terms. I made a rather half-hearted attempt in this direction on a program for PBL[3] in New York last spring and am going to attempt to 'Take 2' for them next winter. How it's going to work out or indeed what it's going to be about I'm not quite sure as yet, but the problem, I should think, is to find a way of writing and/or improvising television material so that the end product doesn't sound or look as though the video-track had been arbitrarily added to a radio lecture-concert.

I have a feeling that unless one can capture the intimacy a good interlocutor like our friend H.B.[4] almost automatically assures by his presence one should perhaps forsake the tried and true notions about taking to a camera, earnestly but without pontification etc. On the PBL show, for instance, I created an alter ego for myself in the form of a slightly retarded English academic who contradicted me quite frequently on a screen within a screen.

Needless to say, this sort of undertaking would necessitate a very sympathetic director, a good deal more studio (and perhaps extra-location) allotment than the conventional program, but it just might make a dent in television's reluctant coming-to-terms with music.

Last winter, I produced a program for CBC Radio which was called 'The Idea of North' and which had to do ostensibly with life in the remoter parts of our upper latitudes. In fact, though, it was really an exercise in the techniques of radio, or rather, techniques which seem to me strikingly obvious and shockingly neglected. Two, three, or four characters spoke simultaneously in different sound perspectives and emerged, considering that this wasn't stereo, with remarkable clarity. (I'm about to try another venture of the same sort, on Newfoundland, and this time bringing stereo to bear as well).[5] Anyway, it seems to me that it should be possible to use television as fragmentarily as that, and to offer, for example, a quorum of opinion, even from the comment of one person. It would mean, in addition to the above-mentioned considerations, the right sort of topic, obviously – a multi-faceted, interpretative concept of one work, for instance – but that is off the top of my head and I won't be held to account for it.

Some such venture, though, ought to be tried on television, it seems to me, and even if it comes to nought, I would like to have your reaction.

All the best,

Sincerely,
Glenn Gould.

¹In a telecast in the series "Telescope," "Variations on Glenn Gould," use was made of Gould's recording of the first movement of the Beethoven Symphony No. 6 in F major, Op. 86 as a background to a program that profiled Gould as a pianist and nature-loving recluse (broadcast on April 10, 1969). Gould gave considerable thought to recording all the Liszt transcriptions of the Beethoven symphonies. It was a project that never developed beyond Symphony No. 5, plus one movement of Symphony No. 6.
²Radio recital for "CBC Tuesday Night," broadcast on June 11, 1968. Gould also spoke of Liszt as the transcriber for piano of Beethoven's symphonies.
³For "P.B.L." read "P.B.S."
⁴Humphrey Burton.
⁵"The Latecomers," the second of the documentaries known as "The Solitude Trilogy," was commissioned by CBC Radio and inaugurated the stereo facilities at CBC FM, Ottawa, on November 12, 1969.

TO B.H. HAGGIN

September 21, 1968

Mr. B.H. Haggin,
Cambridge, Mass.,
U.S.A.

Dear Mr. Haggin,

Thank you very much for your letter.¹ The P.B.L. show (which I will be happy to screen for you if Messrs. CBC and P.B.L.² oblige) contained, I dare say, a certain degree of exaggeration. As I've come to think more about the whole process of editing and its structural ramifications especially through some rather interesting experiments in radio documentary which I'd very much like to tell you about and/or play for you, I've realized that it's most difficult (though not impossible and that's what one should aim for, obviously) to make a convincing statement about Mozart sonatas or Arctic Canada or indeed anything whatsoever while eliminating all snappy lines and abrasive cuts. It should however be possible and to this extent the P.B.L. show which was written, taped and edited in nine days (contractual problems had imperiled it previously) suffered to a degree from that lack of distance and perspective which can help a program realize its own structural rhythm.

Nonetheless much (most?) of what I said I meant, and I was careful I think to confine the less appreciative remarks to Mozart's concerto writing and to be (relatively) enthusiastic about the sonata output. Indeed, I have just been recording Kochels 309 and 284[3] which latter piece is, for the moment at least, my favourite of all Mozart's keyboard works – an incredibly imaginative opus – and the sonata project in general has been a joyous task.

I haven't a score with me so I am going to side-step your more specific questions until we meet. I must say, however, since most of them involve to some degree the relation of melodic and accompanimental textures, this particular segregation of the attention is, I'm afraid, a concept which I have never been able to share. I don't think that it's just the long exposure to baroque entanglements that makes me unsympathetic but rather that the whole idea of a melodic attribute as distinguished from the component parts of a harmonic environment has always seemed to me anti-structural and even, dare I say it, undemocratic. It does seem to me the more singable, likeable and memorable the tune one encounters the less likely it is that that particular melodic strain will require any special emphasis other than the careful delineation of its profile and that consequently one should then be entirely free to expose the harmonic texture whether contrapuntal or not. Far from saluting this concept as an abstract theory which may well have been the case when we first spoke, I feel more than ever convinced about it now that I've actually committed approximately two thirds of the sonatas to the 'can'.

All best wishes,

Sincerely,
Glenn Gould

[1]In his letter of September 2, 1968 Haggin asks, indeed challenges, Gould's remarks about the music of Mozart.
[2]For "P.B.L." read "P.B.S."
[3]Recorded in 1968, the Mozart Sonata No. 6 in D major, K 284, the Sonata No. 7 in C major, K 309 and Mozart Sonata No. 9 in D major, K 311; released in The Mozart Piano Sonatas, Vol. II, in 1969.

TO WIVELIA HYLLNER[1]

c/o National Music Department,
C.B.C., 354 Jarvis Street,
Toronto 5, Ontario.
September 25th, 1968

Miss Wivelia Hyllner,
Malmo, Sweden.

Dear Miss Hyllner,

Thank you for your letter of July 26th and for your kind comments about the television programs.

It is, of course, quite true that a great deal of Bach's music, having been conceived with the organ in mind, absolutely requires that instrument in order to be realized effectively. On the other hand, that very large percentage of Bach's work which was written for the harpsichord or clavichord can be realized, I think, on the contemporary piano without too much loss of clarity or historical identity. I do believe that it is largely a question of the performer's attitude, and that if you keep in mind the performance circumstances which influenced Bach – not least the fact that•he often exhibited a lofty disdain for all aspects of instrumentation and wrote works such as the 'Kunst der Fuge' for which no instrumental specification is included and which can be plausibly rendered on the organ, the harpsichord, by a string quartet or indeed a full string orchestra – then I think it is not improper to consider the contemporary piano as a perfectly viable instrument for the performance of such music.

Again, many thanks for your letter.

Sincerely,
Glenn Gould.

¹A fan.

TO PAUL MYERS

December 29th, 1968

Mr. Paul Myers,
c/o C.B.S. Records,
LONDON, England.

Dear Paul:

It was good to hear from you at Christmas and, when you have the time, I look forward to a detailed account of your impressions of London, 1968. I am not too surprised that you miss North America. We are a likeable lot on this side of the water and I do hope that you can be persuaded to return for occasional forays into the Canadian and/or American Broadcast field.

The Newfoundland project, by the way, poses a considerable quandary just at the moment. The C.B.C. in its wisdom, has declined to sanction the conversion of F.M. stereo for next Fall and since this project was conceived with stereo very much in mind, I really cant decide whether we should proceed with it as a monaural operation, play a waiting game and hope that sanity as well as more generous fiscal planning will prevail in Ottawa, or scrap it altogether. The latter course would be agonizing because the interview material is, I think, very good indeed and because, with its concentration on the abandonment of the outport villages which is the current cause celebre of Newfoundland politics it has, no matter how we might eventually amplify and generalize this theme as was done with the motive of isolation in 'Idea of North' an inevitable topicality which might be less apparent several years hence.[1]

We could of course, proceed with it as a stereo operation and simply hope that a monaural dub would afford a reasonable approximation of our original intentions and remain a reasonably valid experience until the finished product could be broadcast in its, by then no doubt, outdated stereophony. This would have the advantage of offering us some badly needed stereo experience but also the disadvantage that many effects would probably appear as major miscalculations so far as monaural presentation is concerned.

In any event, some decision as to its future will have to be made within the next month or so and I would hope that by that time I can let you know whether there is any chance at all of stereoizing it (if that is what we decide to do) in Toronto, and thereby taking advantage of your offer to join us as technical producer. Needless to say however, if the local interest in F.M. stereo remains at its present negligible level, it is most unlikely that C.B.C. itself will acquire equipment sufficient to the task within the coming months and should we opt for a stereo version the latter portion of the operation would then have to be transferred either to New York or to one of the local independent studios. In any case, if we do decide that Opus 2 necessitates stereo and will go lacking a future if prepared monaurally, I still very much hope that you can see your way clear to join us in the latter stages of its preparation.

My own schedule for the coming spring and summer has undergone a major and welcome metamorphosis in that Herr Dr. von Karajan has, to the surprise and delight of us all, expressed some interest in transferring the film-making originally scheduled for Berlin to, would you believe it, Toronto.[2] This is by no means a definite as yet – he is flying up in February to have a look at local facilities – but if he could be so persuaded, and it was his idea, I, needless to say, as the least confident Trans-Atlantic traveller in history, would be delighted. His reasons for the switch are rather complicated though they have principally to do, as I understand it, with the termination of his Bata film contract and the development of a more flexible attitude in regard to the facilities which might be made available to him in North America during the fairly frequent off-weeks of his Met. schedule these next few years. I am not at all sure that he will find the local facilities satisfactory especially since he insists upon 35 Mill. colour and the studio norm in these parts is 16. Nevertheless, the C.B.C. is prepared, I think, to extend the welcome mat and we are all very curious to see what result the exploratory mission in February will produce.

Since this project was, of course, the main event of my planned European sojourn, that trip is, at least for the moment, postponed. I dont think there is much point in your holding studio time in London during May or June since I doubt very much that even if von K's reaction to the local facilities proves unenthusiastic, the Berlin project could be revived before Fall at the earliest. I think that for the moment, we will go ahead with some Bach Concertos in New York next month[3] since they werent on the London agenda in any case and, if the trip should be indefinitely delayed, I'll try to persuade John McClure[4] that we should, at the very least, re-do the Beethoven Second with a pick-up group in New York later in the year.[5]

I am sending along, under separate cover, a copy of the current issue of Saturday Night in which I set down a few thoughts about Walter Carlos and the Moog.[6] We also devoted 40 minutes of a 90 minute Radio Magazine show which I produced last month to a consideration of the theological and sociological implications of the Moog and in which two interviews – one featuring Gene Lees with Walter Carlos and the other between Janet Somerville and the French-Canadian poet-essayist Jean Le Moyne were counterpointed with I think, rather remarkable results.[7] The whole programme dealt with various aspects of auto-mation but this final portion was a delight to work on, and as soon as I can arrange for an extra dub I am going to send it along.

All the best for now,

Sincerely,
GLENN GOULD.

[1]"The Latecomers."
[2]The film with Herbert von Karajan was not made.
[3]Recorded in 1969: Bach Concerto No. 2 in E major, BWV 1053; Bach Concerto No. 4 in A major, BWV 1055, with Vladimir Golschmann conducting the Columbia Symphony Orchestra (Columbia).
[4]John McClure, Music Director of Columbia Masterworks.
[5]Gould had performed the Beethoven Concerto No. 2 in B♭ major, Op. 19, in Stockholm, October 1958, with Georg Ludwig Jochum conducting the Swedish Radio Symphony Orchestra at the Musical Academy in Stockholm; he did not record it in New York.
[6]"The Record of the Decade . . . Is Bach Played on, of All Things, a Moog Synthesizer?" in *Saturday Night*, Vol. 83, no. 12, December 1968.
[7]CBC Radio, November 10, 1968, "Sunday Supplement," a news magazine and public affairs program, which on this occasion was hosted and co-produced by Gould.

TO LEOPOLD STOKOWSKI

Glenn Gould
110 St. Clair Avenue West
Toronto 7, Canada
January 13th 1969.

Mr. Leopold Stokowski,
NEW YORK.

Dear Maestro Stokowski,

The Canadian Broadcasting Corporation have invited me to prepare and produce a radio documentary about you and your work, and I thought that, before officially accepting, I should find out whether or not you would in fact be intrigued by such a project and able to spare me a bit of time, either at your apartment in New York or at the C.B.C's New York studios for an interview.

Radio, fortunately, is still alive and well in Canada and in recent years I have spent a fair amount of time trying to assess the potential of the medium, and particularly of the documentary form. About a year ago, I produced a one-hour documentary dealing with life in Arctic Canada but designed ostensibly for the urban F.M. listener, and which was, I think, in many ways, a great success.[1] We were determined to avoid all the 'that thar grizzly back on the trail' approach which has usually been taken for granted in programmes of this sort, and by using some rather elaborate audio techniques (two or three conversations coun-terpointed in such a way as to minimise the static quality inherent in most interview-derived documentaries, for instance (approach the qualities of drama). Techniques of the same kind also worked very well in a programme about the theological implications of technology which I produced this past November but, barring a documentary on Schoenberg, written in 1962,[2] yours will be the first full-length programme I have attempted dealing with a musical personality.

In any event, all of this preamble is simply to indicate that I would not want to settle for anything like the sort of chronological-biographical essay for which, since one hears so much of it on radio, a law of diminishing returns prevails. I would like to create a mood-piece in which, avoiding as many didactic elements as possible, we could suggest, the aesthetic ideals which have been prevalent throughout your career. In order to do this, I would like to attempt a compot in which excerpts from your discography could be counter-pointed with the mate-rial derived from our interview session (my habit in the past by the way, has been to edit our my own questions and interjections and preserve a monologue-like continuity) and I expect that the editing and audio-mixing will necessitate at least two weeks of studio time at some point prior to its tentative air-date next fall.[3]

Because of other commitments, I won't be able to get to work on it until this summer, but since I recall that you usually spend the late spring and summer months in Europe, I could be available for the interview sequence at your convenience during the next few months. (We need not, by the way, limit ourselves to one such session only; it might be profitable to set aside a second date and having perhaps studied the transcript from the first interview, supple-ment some answers accordingly). Assuming then, that you do share something of my enthusiasm for the project, I would very much appreciate it if you could let me know whether any particular period of the winter or spring would be preferable. I usually record in New York at least once a month and I can perhaps schedule a studio session on the same visit.

All the best for now. I look forward to hearing from you.

Sincerely,
GLENN GOULD.

C.C. John Roberts
C.C. Carl Little.

[1] "The Idea of North."
[2] "Arnold Schoenberg: The Man Who Changed Music" was broadcast on CBC radio on August 8, 1962.
[3] "Stokowski: A Portrait for Radio" was broadcast on "CBC Tuesday Night" on February 2, 1971.

TO RONALD WILFORD[1]

January 26th, 1969.

Mr. Ronald Wilford,
c/o Columbia Artists Management,
NEW YORK, N.Y.

Dear Ronald,

Although I expect to be on the phone with you before this arrives in New York or even, given the not infrequent breakdown in my dictation – thru-mailing production line, before it gets sent off, I thought it might be useful to set down my reactions to Mr. Glotz' latest proposal re London, May 6th.

1. There is simply no way in which the 'Emperor' Concerto, or for that matter any other work of substance, can be recorded and filmed in one day. Assuming that von K.[2] remains adamant re sync techniques, a period of not less than two days would be required for audio alone. Not necessarily full days, though I can't imagine rehearsing and recording such a work in less than nine hours which, applying North American studio-rate provisions (15 minutes per 3 hour session) would be par for the union course and while these provisions will not necessarily apply to the more accommodating attitudes of the British and/or German locals, six hours on any given day pretty well defines the upper limits of my productivity.

I am less familiar with the requirements for sync filming – though a few times I've been involved with that process (repairs for mile-boom shadows and other video lapses) have certainly conditioned me to expect a generous allowance for re-takes. The problem of a convincing sync treatment is perhaps less serious when one deals with an orchestra sans soloist and can take refuge in vague tutti shots etc. but unless one cuts all kinds of stylistic corners – i.e. shots through the piano, overhead coverage etc. – there is just no recommendable shortcut when dealing with a keyboard. Consequently my guess is that we could hardly expect

114

to film a forty-five minute concerto using this method in less than two days – probably more than six hours per since fatigue in the usual sense, would not be a factor – and I suspect I'm being optimistic. A relevant statistic perhaps would be the schedule applicable for the taping of a 1 hour sonata recital with Menuhin in 1965 (20 hours in the studio, counting crew breaks, on two successive days) or last year's taping of two concertos – both of them (Bach G minor and Strauss Burleske) short ones with a total running time not in excess of the 'Emperor' (12 hours of studio time again counting crew breaks) and these, apart from the lapses mentioned above, did not employ sync procedures.

2. I can only gather Mr. Glotz' letter that the 'Emperor' project has been re-assigned to London on May 6th in lieu of John Culshaw's earlier proposal. As you know, I wrote John, endeavoured to persuade him that even the more improvisatory format which he had in mind could not properly be executed with only one day in the studio and suggested with all due respect to his quite possibly superior facilities that, simply by virtue of its relaxed and improvisatory intent, it would require a much more leisurely schedule.

3. If I understand Mr. Glotz' reference to a project for 1969-70 correctly, he has in mind something very like the Culshaw proposal which having been pre-empted by the 'Emperor' could then take place in Toronto during the winter. Indeed, I still think it should take place here though it would perhaps be a mistake to discount the availability of the MET studios in Boston, but either way Karajan would still have to approve the use of those facilities and perhaps survey them in advance.

4. The – you'll pardon the expression 'Art of Glenn Gould' is now set for a 22 week run on radio beginning the third week of May.[3] I okayed this after it became reasonably certain than von K would be able to work in Toronto and, even though we do hope to have several programmes in the can before the series starts, this does mean that, with the addition of the NET films,[4] the Newfoundland documentary[5] (tentative studio schedule June and July), and a documentary on Stokowski[6] (that one's new) which has been pencilled in for October, I will not be able to undertake anything else prior to November or December when von K. was, as I understood it, able to work in North America.

Hope this helps a bit.
All the best for now,
Sincerely,
GLENN GOULD.

[1]Gould's agent after he withdrew from the concert stage, Wilford was concerned with promoting and developing Gould's career in the mass media.
[2]Herbert von Karajan.

³CBC Radio aired "The Art of Glenn Gould" from May 20, 1969 to October 7, 1969 – 21 programs in all.
⁴"Stokowski: A Portrait for Radio." It was recorded at the same time as a NET film.
⁵Entitled "The Latecomers."
⁶"Stokowski: A Portrait for Radio."

TO PETER HERMAN ADLER[1]   July 6th 1969.

Mr. Peter Herman Adler,
c/o National Education Television,
NEW YORK CITY.

Dear Peter:

Many thanks for your note, for the Saturday Review article[2] (which I thought was a remarkably clear expose of the problems and potentialities of the medium), and apologies for the delayed reply. Indeed, I do hope that we can get together very soon in New York though, since I'm presently locked into a C.B.C. schedule which involves a weekly radio show plus one hundred and sixty-eight (repeat, 168) hours of editing on a documentary-drama about Newfoundland between now and the first week of August, I doubt very much that I can manage to get any recording done chez C.B.S. until the latter half of that month.

Although you will perhaps be in Maine just then, we must get together to compare notes as soon as your Fall schedule is under way. The Fugue show[3] is now entirely in the can, although the real work begins in August when we get around to editing it, but I think that, judging by the fairly prolific number of takes with which we attempted to cover our harmonic traces (the organ, harpsichord, and piano textures are going to be woven together into one tapestry much of the way) we have at least the nucleus of a very promising program.

Have you, by any chance, seen the Bata film on which von Karajan does the Beethoven Sixth. I know you were much less enthusiastic about the Fifth Symphony than I was but I do hope you can get a chance to take a look at this one which was aired in Toronto a few weeks ago because it represents one of the two or three most remarkable film experiences I've ever had. It's prefaced by a not particularly distinguished-musically or visually-performance of the B minor Bach Suite but the 'Pastorale' was, to my mind, simply overwhelming and I've asked for a private screening at C.B.C. because I can't quite believe my eyes. Do try to see it if you can.

All the best for now,
Sincerely,

¹Czech-born American conductor, in 1969 Adler was Musical Director of the Baltimore Symphony Orchestra and Musical and Artistic Director of NET (National Educational Television).

²The article, by Richard L. Tobin, was entitled "Why Radio Is Here to Stay" and refuted the idea that television would put radio out of business (*Saturday Review*, July 9, 1966, p. 47).
³"The Art of Glenn Gould," Take Nineteen. *Art of the Fugue*, BWV 1080 was heard along with a discussion between Gould and Ken Haslam regarding the fugues of Bach, Mozart, Bartok, Verdi, Buxtehude, and Beethoven.

TO RONALD WILFORD

Glenn Gould
110 St. Clair Avenue West
Toronto 7, Canada
August 10th, 1969

Mr. Ronald Wilford,
Columbia Artists' Management,
NEW YORK CITY.

Dear Ronald:

I'm sending along, under separate cover 3 dubs (7½ IPS mono) of the weekly radio series upon which, as you well know, we have lavished a good deal of attention this spring and summer. The series runs for twenty-two weeks in all – it goes off the air on October 12th – and since there is no such thing as a tried-and-true format upon which we have relied from week to week, the dubs that I'm sending along are no more than randomely representative of the series as a whole. Even though, in its FM incarnation, a full hour of material is required, the real length of the programme is approximately 56 minutes 30 seconds to accommodate Am scheduling and, in each case, a pad of approximately 3 minutes duration is appended for the FM audience.[1] As I believe I mentioned to you some time ago re the QXR proposal, it would be exceedingly difficult to reduce most of these programmes by even three or four minutes since, with one or two exceptions, the 56 minute limit has been allowed to condition our sense of form as pertaining to the programme, and I simply do not believe that it would be possible to achieve any semblance of coherence if we were to sacrifice either three or four minutes of voice-track material or, where applicable, an equivalent amount of music. In short, I think that these programmes have been conceived in such a way as to necessitate their being heard in toto and without any deletions beyond the 56 minute limit. (If by the way, you should have any choice in the matter, I would much prefer that the 56 minute version be utilized rather than its sixty-minute counterpart, since, in the latter version the inevitable 'pad' is at best an unobstrusive bit of fill, either perpetuating the mood of the pro-gramme which has preceded it, or, in some way linked with the announcer's promo for that of the week to come. The 56 minute version, of course, is particularly useful in those broadcast formats such as that of CBC – AM where a three-or-four minute hourly newscast is the rule.

The programme is, in a sense, nothing but a disguised discography – approximately half of my current Schwann representations are included (along with a few deletions) but, since each of the programmes tend to find a thematic raison d'etre, the overall effect, I hope, is that the catalogue is used in order to substantiate points made, or attitudes struck within a particular programme, rather than simply exploited because it happens to be readily available. The ratio of talk to music varies from programme to programme – the script which I'm writing at the moment, Take 13, being the shortest by far – approximately 3 minutes – while on one or two occasions, something close to 40 minutes has been devoted to conversation and/or interview material. Many of the interviews have been devoted to relatively unexplored or, at any rate, under-examined musical matters – i.e. the interview with the Psychiatrist Doctor Joseph Stephens, which takes a look at the psychology of concerto playing – and concerto-writing, and thereby gives me the opportunity to make a few pronouncements which, I do believe, the world had been in need for these many years. Some programmes, on the other hand, are intended to be 'entertaining' in a somewhat surreal way – for instance the combination of Claude Rains and Petula Clark and hence, Richard Strauss and Tony Hatch, which I've also included in the present (Care) package, and in a few programmes such as Take 8, the Homage to Schnabel' in which Claude Franke's comments and reminiscences were book-ended with my own recollections of that gentleman's influence upon me circa my thirteenth year, we've managed to combine both qualities.

Certain of the programmes, of course, incorporate documentary material which has been prepared for other occasions, and which is included here, not only as a sampler of our better radio efforts from days gone by, but in an attempt to avoid having the programmes seem persistently indebted to the phonograph. Thus, Anti-Alea (a programme about the chances-for-chance in music), the Le Moyne-Carlos dialogue, which examined the theological ramifications of technology, and of course 'Idea of North' (which on this occasion is being treated as a one and a half hour special,) the half-hour prologue being devoted to an examination of its process, and to some notions about what radio ought to be and do, which, I think, it implicitly conveys.

In this respect however, it is, I think, important to make clear to whichever outlets might be interested in this series, that a programme such as 'North'[2] or its successor project 'The Latecomers' which is about Newfoundland, are quite separate from, and not to be confused with, the much less elaborate treatment accorded to the weekly series as such. In other words, it would be unfair to sell the weekly series as though it contained twenty-two programmes upon which the sort of attention we gave to 'North' (approximately 150 hours of editing) or are giving to the Newfoundland programme (336 hours scheduled thus far has been expended). It does not of course, and with a weekly allotment of approximately eight hours for voice-tracking, editing and mixing, it obviously cannot. It has, however, I think, maintained a remarkably high standard, and I hope that the dubs which I'm sending along, underseparate cover, will whet your appetite for more.

All the best for now,
Sincerely,
GLENN GOULD.

P.S. I'm enclosing some review and publicity material which may be of use.

[1]Entitled "The Art of Glenn Gould," this series began on May 20, 1969 and concluded on October 7 of the same year. As Gould said, it was a "disguised discography" but with some rebroadcasts of programs produced for CBC Radio, such as "Anti-Alea," "The Idea of North" and "Conference at Port Chilkoot." "The Art of Glenn Gould" was designed for the CBC English-language FM network. The latter was established in 1964 as a means of providing a cultural service that paid special attention to music. It became the CBC-FM stereo network in 1975.
[2]"The Idea of North."

TO JOHN ROBERTS

November 11th, 1969.

Mr. John Roberts,
Canadian Broadcasting Corp.,
TORONTO, Ontario.

Dear John:

Just to make it official, I'll be happy to record for the E.B.U.[1] early in, or indeed prior to, the Season '71-72. Actually, I can foresee no scheduling problems at all and if they would prefer to have the tape in their hands during, say, the Spring of '71, I'm sure we could arrange that as well.

As I told you on the telephone the other day, I'm pleasantly surprised with Studio 'G' and among all the local facilities we have investigated it has, I think, given us the best results to date. I can imagine also that we could improve on those results if the instrument in question were my own from New York rather than the Parliament Street Steinway which, however, is remarkable for its age.

Needless to say, I would prefer to do the E.B.O.[2] concert in New York, if you feel it's tactically possible, since in that way we could obtain the optimum accoustic result and at the same time not expose C.D. 318 to travel fatigue. But, assuming

Studio 'G' is not altered substantially in the near future, I'm really quite confident of continued good results in that location.

All the best for now,

Sincerely,
Glenn Gould.

¹European Broadcasting Union.
²Read E.B.U. for E.B.O.

TO DMITRI SHOSTAKOVICH¹   February 7, 1970

Mr. Dimintri Shostakovitch,
c/o Embassy of the Union of
    Soviet Socialist Republics,
Ottawa, Ontario.

Dear Mr. Shostakovitch:

Thank you very much for your letter and for the kind invitation to be your guest during the Tschaikovsky competition next June in Moscow. I am afraid I must regretfully decline since my schedule during the coming year prohibits any extensive travel arrangements, but I very much appreciate your generous offer of hospitality.²

Sincerely yours,
Glenn Gould

¹Soviet composer (1906-1975).
²This was simply a polite reply. Gould disapproved of competitions and had ceased flying long beforehand.

TO PAUL MYERS¹   February 12, 1970

Mr. Paul Myers,
C.B.S. Records,
London, England.

Dear Paul:

Many thanks for your note and for sending along that intriguing bit of Beethoveniana.² Are you sure Joyce Cary didn't make up its author, however? He sounds (reads) like a musical variant of the Gully Jimson legend. My first mistake, of course, was expecting the 'Hammerklavier' variations to have something to do with the 'Hammerklavier' sonata. There may, of course, actually be a few concealed permutations relative to Op. 106 but I gather his real intention

120

was to create a sort of 'in memoriam' to the late Beethoven rhythmic spirit, and to let the melodic chips fall where they may.

Did I ever play you the several symphonies which Ludwig Diehn of Washington D.C. wrote in the style of Bruckner, and privately recorded? (I know I told you about him because I made reference to his work in the 1965 radio documentary on recordings in which you took part.) In any case the present work is a fascinating bit of esoterica and I do thank you for it.

'North'[3] is indeed under way! Judy[4] has completed all of the official shooting, though she wants to redo several episodes, and I have thus far seen approximately seven hours worth of rushes. The material, especially the black-and-white footage shot on the train to Hudson's Bay and intended to be intercut with the colour material obtained in Ottawa, Toronto and Fort Churchill, is, I think, absolutely remarkable. It reminds me, in its restrained and even understated way, of the Bresson 'Diary of a Country Priest', circa 1950.[5] The more amazing thing, in view of the various bureaucratic road-blocks which have been put in her way locally, is that she managed to get it done at all. Some portion of the Churchill material was sabotaged by edge-fog which may have been due to climatic conditions or one or more faulty filters but even there the spirit is absolutely faithful, I think, to the audio original and, with any luck it is going to make a quite remarkable film.

The latest reports on you via Andy[6] are that you plan to remain, for the time being, in London. I am glad only because I couldn't really see you being happy in N.Y.C. but I do wish it were possible for you to come to Canada, if only for a working visit.

Newfoundland came off extremely well, I think, although it was very frustrating to have nothing more sophisticated than a four-track available (we had two of them but, of course, real synchronization was impossible). In any case, it was an extremely useful rough-dress for the kind of stereophony I'd like to try if the C.B.C. will just break down and acquire a sixteen-track unit. Needless to say, with anti-inflation trends all around us, there is no sign of that at the moment.

Do keep in touch. All best wishes.

Sincerely,
Glenn Gould.

[1]Producer, formerly with Columbia Records in New York.
[2]This refers to a score, *Variations on the Hammerklavier*, composed by a former colleague of Myers. While anything but a masterpiece, the work was sent to Gould for his amusement, together with some reminiscences of the composer who had been a delightful but eccentric colleague during the fifties in Salisbury (now Harare) in what is today Zimbabwe.
[3]Television version of the radio documentary "The Idea of North."
[4]Judith Perlman, American television producer.
[5]Robert Bresson's film was based on Georges Bernanos's novel *The Diary of a Country Priest*.
[6]Andrew Kazdin, who produced more than forty Gould recordings for Columbia over a period of fifteen years. He is the author of *Glenn Gould at Work: Creative Lying* (New York: E.P. Dutton, 1989).

TO WILLIAM STEVENSON[1]   March 5th, 1970

Mr. William Stevenson,
Willowdale, Ontario.

Dear Mr. Stevenson:

Thank you very much for your letter of February 19th and for the most
touching memoir about Albert Schweitzer.

I do remember that at the time of his death in 1965, I was asked by CBC Radio
to provide a brief assessment of his life and musical times[2] and that in the script I
mentioned a visit some years before to the New York office of a rather typical and
typically pressured Madison Avenue-type executive. It was quite late in the
afternoon, though his working day, I gathered, was far from done and in the
background, muzak-style, was Schweitzer's recording of the Bach G minor
fugue. The exec in question explained that, given the circumstances of a life in
New York City – with which he had a 'love-hate' relationship, the tranquillity of
spirit which is built into every note that Schweitzer played, was somehow the
only appropriate antidote.

I imagine that in many ways, Schweitzer represented a similar antidotal experience for many of us (he certainly did for me) and for that reason, I'm particularly
moved by your recollections of his life at Lambarene.

Sincerely,
Glenn Gould

[1]A fan.
[2]This program was not produced.

TO ELIZABETH McKAY[1]   March 5th, 1970

Miss Elizabeth McKay,
Downsview, Ontario.

Dear Miss McKay:

Thank you very much for your letter of February 20th and for your kind
comments about the 'Well-Tempered Listener'.[2] As you surmise, we did indeed
attempt to compose the programme in such a way as to make it, in and of itself,
an organic structure, to avoid telegraphing the various illustrative episodes (the
recital portion excepted, of course) and to treat them as though they were in fact
a spontaneous complement to the basso continuo provided by our conversation.[3]

I'm really too close to the programme at this juncture to assess with any clarity
the degree of its effectiveness, but I would like to think of it as the inauguration of

122

a new kind of musical television and I do very much appreciate your thoughtfulness in writing.

All best wishes,

Sincerely,
Glenn Gould

¹A fan.
²Television program broadcast by CBC on February 18, 1970.
³For "telegraphing" read "telescoping."

TO AUGUSTUS PERRY¹

354 Jarvis Street,
Toronto 5, Ontario
April 17th, 1970

Mr. Augustus Perry,
New York, N.Y.

Dear Mr. Perry:

Thank you very much for your letter, for your kind comments about our radio-series and my apologies for the belated reply.

In regard to your question re baroque interpretation, I'm afraid that I really do not know of any shortcut other than the necessarily mechanical one which you describe by which one can more readily assimilate that particular repertoire. However, it does seem to me that, in that music, the intellectual aspiration of the composers (Bach being the obvious example) and the tactile considerations demanded for the realization of their works are, if not one and the same, at least intimately linked, and that consequently the strand-by-strand dissection of a Bach fugue, for instance, is not merely rewarding for its tactile efficacy, but is, in fact, indicative of the real nature of that music which is, of course, a multi-linear experience.

I had occasion last year to record several of Bach's fugues experimentally – wearing earphones, performing one voice at a time only. The experiment which, in view of the deficiencies of ensemble that inevitably resulted, will not, of course, be made public, was intended purely as an in-house demonstration at Columbia Records of the possibilities for a quadraphonic sound-system – i.e. each voice was recorded on a separate tape track and emanated from a different speaker (one at each corner of the room). For me, however, the real benefit of this never-to-be-released recording was that it offered conclusive proof of the appropriateness of the one-voice-at-a-time approach to Bach. I have rarely been able to enjoy so clear a perspective on the fugues in question and I do believe that some modification of that principle remains the most rewarding approach to the keyboard music of Bach.

All best wishes,

Sincerely,
Glenn Gould.

¹A fan.

TO LEOPOLD STOKOWSKI

354 Jarvis Street
Toronto, Ontario
August 17, 1970

Mr. Leopold Stokowski
NEW YORK, N.Y., U.S.A.

Dear Maestro Stokowski,

I'm happy to be able to tell you that the radio documentary about you, upon which, as you know, I have been working for many months, is at last completed. It is not as yet scheduled for broadcast though I understand tentative plans include its use as one of the inaugural programmes for a new FM stereo network which the CBC will, if all goes well, inaugurate next spring.¹

In accordance with the plan which I outlined in my original letter to you about this project, the only voice heard from throughout (barring a four-minute introduction of my own) is yours. The interview which you granted me last winter was extremely rewarding in terms of the material which derived from it and it does, I think, manage to produce an effect at once relaxed and concentrated.

As background for your comments there is a continuous and, I hope, seamless musical texture consisting of fragments drawn from works which you have recorded through the years. None of the works are, of course, heard in their entirety and they all are treated, in cinematic terms, to an extended dissolve so that a consistent harmonic climate prevails throughout the musical background. You might be interested to know that the primary selections are: Verklarte Nacht, (approximately the first eight minutes worth), about one-half of the second movement from our recording of the 'Emperor' Concerto, a portion of the first movement of the Brahms' Serenade, the entire first movement of the Ives Fourth Symphony, approximately seven minutes from the first movement of the Shostakovitch Symphony No.11, a brief segment from the 'Swan of Tuonela',² several minutes from 'Francesca da Rimini',³ approximately one-half of the 'Saturn' movement from 'The Planets',⁴ and the last two minutes from 'The Poem of Ecstacy'.⁵ In addition, there is also a segment which reflects your early interest in the technology of recording and for which, with the help of an archivist at CBC I was able to locate a number of 78 r.p.m. recordings made with the Philadelphia Orchestra. I certainly hope that I shall soon have the opportunity to play the tape for you.

In the meantime, however, I should like to mention that Mr. Jim Gonzalves of the CBC Publications Department will shortly be writing to you in regard to it. Mr. Gonzalves' department occasionally makes available in disc form and, of course, on a non-profit basis, programmes which are felt to possess unusual merit so that they can be used by educational institutions etc. for the enhanvement of various learning systems. He is extremely enthusiastic about this partic- ular programme and would like to ask you permission to reproduce it in that form.[6]

I trust that you are having a good summer – well away from New York, I assume – and I shall look forward to seeing you at your convenience next season.

All best wishes,

Sincerely,
Glenn Gould

cc: Mr. Jim Gonzalves
CBC Publications Dept.

[1]"Stokowski: A Portrait for Radio."
[2]By Jean Sibelius.
[3]By Peter Ilyich Tchaikovsky.
[4]By Gustav Holst.
[5]By Aleksandr Scriabin.
[6]The Stokowski documentary was never issued as a disc.

TO PAUL HOLLIS-ELLERY[1]

354 Jarvis Street
Toronto, Ontario
October 17, 1970

Mr. Paul Hollis-Ellery
TE AROHA, North Island
New Zealand

Dear Mr. Hollis-Ellery,

Thank you very much for your letter and my sincere apologies for the delayed reply. I'm delighted to learn that my interpretations of the 'Well-Tempered Clavier' have been of interest to you but I'm sorry to hear that the Prelude and Fugue No.36 is not yet available in New Zealand. We have, in fact, the first forty on release in North America and plan to complete the set during the current season.[2]

In regard to the Fantasia in C Minor: I'm afraid I've never played this particular work and I really would be most reluctant to even hazard a guess as to an appropriate tempo for it.[3] In any event, I do agree with you that the essential matter in Bach and, for that matter, in all music really is, as you put it so well, 'one's own discrimination'. As you know, many of my tempi in the W.T.C. are rather unorthodox and, although none of these were designed in order to create a spectacular effect or for any inherent shock value (more often than not indeed, I was relatively unaware of the 'traditional' method of performance for the particular work) I really do not think that it is possible to impose a 'one and only' concept in regard to such works which should ideally give rise to so many diverse points of view.[4]

Again, many thanks for your letter and all best wishes for your examination.

Sincerely,
Glenn Gould

[1]A fan.
[2]Recorded in 1969 and 1971. *The Well-Tempered Clavier*, Book II: Nos. 17-24, BWV 886-893 (Columbia).
[3]Gould did record the J.S. Bach Fantasia in C minor, BWV 919 in 1980. According to the Music Division of the National Library of Canada, Gould also recorded Bach's Fantasia in D minor, BWV 903, and his Fantasia in C minor, BWV 906. These performances will be issued in the future.
[4]Gould tended to not listen to recordings of the standard repertoire by other pianists. In this respect his performances have a certain innocence.

TO ANDREW KAZDIN

354 Jarvis Street
Toronto, Ontario
November 21, 1970

Mr. Andrew Kazdin
c/o CBS Records
New York, N.Y.

Dear Andy,

Herewith, as I promised some weeks back, a few thoughts about the future.[1] In view of the extraordinary response engendered by my latest missile to the Accounting Department in which I utilised the systematic, point-by-point ennunciation of all of the major issues therein at stake, I thought I'd adopt the same method for this letter. Here goes:

CLASSIFICATION "A" – MATERIAL ALREADY COMMISSIONED TO THE 'CAN'

1. Mr. Schoenberg's complete lieder (barring Opus 12 No.2) – i.e. Six Songs

Opus 3; Eight Songs Opus 6; One Song Opus 12; Three Songs Opus 48; Two Songs Opus Posth.

The above items were recorded between 1964 and 1970.

2. Hindemith Sonatas Nos. 1 and 3 (1966).

3. Mozart Sonatas K.310, 311, 330, 331, 332, 333 and 545. These works were recorded between 1965 and 1970.

4. Mozart Fantasia in C. Minor K.475 (1966).

5. Beethoven Sonatas Opus 31 No.2; Opus 31 No.3; Opus 78. (1966-68)

6. C.P.E. Bach 'A Prussian Sonata' (can't remember which one) 1968.

7. Scarlatti – Two Sonatas (1968)

8. Pentland-Ombres (1967)

9. William Byrd and Orlando Gibbons – Five pieces by the former and, I believe five by the latter as well (1967-68).

10. Scriabin Sonata No. 5 (1970)

Looking back over this list my general conclusions are that there's a hell of a lot of work represented by it, much of it is already at least half a decade old and that, if we intend to make use of it on release, we should certainly think about doing so in the near future. As you know, several of the items have been edited already – the Mozart Sonata K.332 and at least one movement of K.331, for instance – and a great many of the others, including all of the Schoenberg lieder, are ready for editing by virtue of the fact that all takes have now been chosen, still others, such as those represented by items 6, 7 and 8 which were originally designed for the dual purpose of enriching our 'cans' and facilitating the broadcast efforts of Messrs. CBC have already been prepared for the CBC and a surefire editing plan exists on their behalf.

As you know, there are several records represented by the ten items listed above which I'm particularly anxious to see in circulation. I do think that the Schoenberg assembly is one of our more significant efforts and should certainly be foisted on the public as soon as possible. To this end it would be helpful if we could decide on baritone soloist for Opus 12 No.2 in lieu of Donald Gramm for whom the Tessitura is not ideally suited. As you know, Mr. Thompson at CAMI recommends Tom Krause and I'm sure this would be an excellent idea. If, for any reason, his involvement is not deemed advisable or essential I'm quite sure we can find someone on the local scene, particularly the baritone Maurice Brown, to record it with us in Toronto. I do know that Mr. Brown is venturing into these parts (he's now resident in Germany) during January and if there were any thought of having him do it at that time I think probably we should attempt to make contact in the immediate future. All in all, the Schoenberg project is one which I've been particularly proud to be associated with and I do think that, even if the multi-record sets of his works have been abandoned, this particular disc should be made available as soon as possible.

Another record that I'm very enthusiastic about, as I know you are, is represented by item 9 – the Byrd-Gibbons collection. Although I no longer recall the exact timing for any of these selections, my impression is that a reasonable average would involve something in the neighbourhood of three minutes per selection and that consequently we are a little bit on the short side in relation to this material as a disc. In the early spring of 1971 I will be recording a broadcast for the European Broadcasting Union and including on it two sets of variations – Grounds, more accurately – by William Byrd, both of which are at once of a length appropriate to fill out the disc and of sufficient virtuousic impulse to give it a necessary piece d'resistance. It would be a simple matter to re-record the Byrd variations during one of our Toronto sessions and we would then be in possession, I think, of a rather remarkable and altogether off-beat disc.

Items 3 and 4 – the Mozart Sonatas and Fantasia – bring us, of course, to one of our more major endeavours and one which I will deal with more fully in classification B (upcoming). It is, however, perhaps worthwhile to recall that editing has been completed on K.332, that the first movement, at least, of 331 was similarly put together some four or five years back, and that I am now in a position to 'pick and choose' from the available material in relation of K.330, 333 and 310. The '18th Century Drawing-Room' sonata, K.545, is obviously not destined for the next volume in our Mozart series so we should, I think confine ourselves to the consideration of Kochels 310 through 333. As I mentioned on the 'phone the other day, it would be virtually impossible to include those five sonatas within one 60-minute disc, though I suppose it might be done with a little luck and a cavalier disregard for tonal depreciation toward the end of each side. I imagine, however, that you would prefer a four-sonata assortment, if possible, and two possible solutions are available. We could either bypass, for the time being, K.310 and concentrate on the four consecutively Kocheled sonatas or alternately include 310 and drop, for this release, K.331, which may well cause us a bit of editing angst. Five years can certainly play tricks with one's memory but I do seem to recall that there were one or more tempo mismatches in the second movement of 331 and that when, on a tentative basis, we attempted to put it together back in 1965, we were fairly resolved at that time to go back into the studio and make appropriate covers for it. This would be a bit awkward nowadays since the character of CD 318 has changed considerably in the intervening years and, at the very least, we may have to consider the entire second movement as an appendage to some future session. Either way, the couplings of 310, 330, 332 and 333 or of 330, 331, 332 and 333 will give us a fairly generous Volume 3 for our Mozart series.

In regard to item 5 – the Beethoven sonatas – we are already in possession of material sufficient for a disc as between Opus 31 No.2 and Opus 31 No.3. The timing on both sonatas is in the neighbourhood of 20 minutes and it might even be a bit awkward to add to them the appropriate companion piece, Opus 32 No.1, which, although I've never played it, is of equal length (it would also make a less than felicitous side-break necessary). I do believe, however, that if the side-break problem is not considered too disadvantageous we should try to record Opus 31 No.1 since it would then make a suitable companion disc for our three Sonatas, Opus 10, released in 1965.

I'm not really sure what we can do with Opus 78 although the obvious compiling would involve Opus 81, 90 and 101. It would, I suppose, be possible to include it along with several other of the miscellaneous items found in items 6, 7 and 8 (well, maybe not 8) in some sort of recital potpourri. I don't know whether any market exists for a disc of that kind these days and whether its feasible to even think in terms of a recital miscellany at all but it would be nice to find some way in which such, as I recall, very well recorded items as the Scarlatti brace and the Phillip Emmanuel Bach sonata could be included without having to go to the considerable trouble of providing them with numerous companion pieces of a similar genre. I do recall that Peter Munvies had mentioned at one time his enthusiasm for a project involving the six 'Prussian' sonatas of C.P.E. and we could certainly record a dozen or so Scarlatti sonatas to accompany the two already in the can, but there might just be a way of combining both these items, at least, with other 18th century works, both on the off-beat in terms of repertoire appeal, so as to provide a veritable history of the developing keyboard sonata as, in a sense, a complement to our various Mozart and Beethoven sonata projects. We've never really discussed this idea at all and I would particularly appreciate your comments on it.

The Scriabin Sonata No. 5 brings us, of course, to that other major sequential idea with which we've been involved in the planning stages for some time and I'll delay my comments on it for a paragraph or so until we get to the next classification.

CLASSIFICATION "B' – FUTURE REQUIREMENTS FOR PROJECTS ALREADY UNDER WAY

1. Mozart Sonatas K.570, 576 and 457 (believe it or not, we're that close to the end of the Mozart project).

1A. Mozart Fantasias – K.394, K.396 and K.397. I'm proceeding on the assumption here that it would be advantageous to have the four Fantasias, one of which, K.475, is designed as a complement to the C Minor Sonata included within the project. This is by no means an essential item but it might in the long run help us to fill out more equitably the almost inevitable 5th disc of the Mozart series. Assuming, for example, that K.330 through 333 would be on one disc (volume 3 in the series) volume 4 will then need to consist of K.310, K.570, K.576 and K.545. All of these, with the exception of 545, which is perhaps not more than 8 minutes in length, are longer-than-average Mozart sonatas and I would guess at this point that a reasonable estimate for the length of that disc would involve something in the order of 14-minutes allotment for K.310 and 16-18 minute allotments for 570 and 576. In any event, and certainly with the addition of 545, it would be virtually impossible to include within volume 4 the Sonata in C Minor which is perhaps the largest in scale of the 17 and certainly one in any case which, according to the composer's own plan, demands the inclusion of the Fantasia in C Minor as a preface. If that Fantasia (see item 4 in category A) were utilised in this fashion, the result would be approximately 30-32 minutes of music on one side of the disc and it occurs to me that the most appropriate complement would be to append on the flip side the three remaining Mozart Fantasias, one of which, K.394, was, of course, originally recorded in mono in 1957 or '58 but which should certainly be redone in stereo for the project. In sum, then, the Mozart project is really very near completion – only three major Sonatas and (if you approve the format I've just outlined) three relatively brief Fantasias remain to be done.

2. Bach Fugues Volume 2 (W.T.C. Nos.17 to 24).Since this is the project which you are most anxious to have under wraps at the present time, I need not belabour any point in relation to it. As I mentioned over the 'phone the other day, I see no reason to prevent our accomplishing it in the course of perhaps four or five three-hour sessions and, even at the risk of doing so with rented equipment, I would be most pleased if this would be accomplished in Toronto.

3. Bach Concertos Nos.1 and 6. Before too much more time has elapsed we should really get back to the Bach Concerto series and wrap up the set with the two outstanding concertos. Is there, do you think, any chance that instead of working in New York we could manage to do these in Cleveland? I realise, of course, that your visits there are complicated by the fact that you must take along mobile equipment and mobile personnel and consequently that you are understandably resolved to get maximum value for the mileage involved and, where possible, to make use of the Cleveland Orchestra more or less in toto. Nevertheless, if it suited your convenience, I would be perfectly happy to drive over there on one or two occasions and append a Bach concerto to any session for which you have already begun to lay plans. I realise, of course, that this would be in addition to the possible sessions with Ancerl now under discussion.

4. Scriabin Sonatas – I feel that we should get on with this project as soon as possible even though it can not, perhaps, take precedence over the rather more

pressing matters listed immediately above. We should certainly try to find the disc which will involve Sonata 5, already in the 'can', and we should probably do so with either the Sonata No.4 or Sonata No.6, both of which are relatively brief and would, along with No.5, constitute one side of the disc. On the flip side for that one I would recommend, as I believe I suggested to Tom in a conversation some months back, that we consider either the First or the Second sonatas, both of which are in his reflected-glory-of-Chopin style, and both of which are considerably longer than any of their later counterparts. In this way, at such time as we get around to doing others of the later sonatas, we could again append two such to one of the early three including perhaps the performance of No.3 originally issued with the Prokofiev sonata, and consequently maintain as much stylistic diversity as the Scriabin canon permits.

CLASSIFICATION "C" – PROJECTS WHICH SHOULD BE CONSIDERED FOR THE FUTURE

1. Bach English Suites – there are six of them and they're every bit as attractive and important as the Partitas. We really should have gotten started with that set long ago.

2. French Suites plus the Overture in the French Style. The same comments as are relevant to the English Suites apply here.

3. Beethoven Sonatas – Opus 2. With luck we could fit all three onto one disc. I say with luck because they're a good deal longer than many of the later Beethoven sonatas (Opus 2 No.3 is at least 25 minutes) but it could be done and I think it should be done.

4. Beethoven 'Hammerklavier' Sonata – Having just recorded this for CBC I'm prepared to do it whenever you feel so inclined. It is not, I must add, one of my favourite pieces but it is a landmark and I think sooner or later we should attempt it.

Here endeth the repertoire list – past, present and future. I want to emphasize 'repertoire' list as opposed to other projects musical and extra-musical which we may, and I firmly believe, should be, in the process of devising. As you know, I don't think it's sufficient to assume that the activity of recording is exclusively at the service of music and musicians, I think that there are a great many things that we should think about as vehicles for recording which might run the risk of being only of interest to those who deliberately seek out arcane experiences but which, on the other hand, might just reflect a maturing of the record-making process as well. We've talked abut them before and they can be the subject of a further memorandum as time goes by but I really would like to feel that we could regard our repertoire activities, no matter how conscientiously outlined and prepared, as only one portion – albeit a very important one – of our total record-making activity.

Now that it's all down before you perhaps you can give me some idea as to your own views on the various priorities which these projects should be accorded and we can map out a release plan for the next couple of years accordingly.

All best,

Sincerely,
Glenn Gould

¹The letter is an example of the detailed planning process that went into Gould's recordings.

TO CARL LITTLE

354 Jarvis Street
Toronto, Ontario
December 5, 1970

Mr. Carl Little
CBC, Toronto

Dear Carl,

As you know, the fourth and last of our current recital projects is due to be recorded in the near future. We haven't really talked about the make-up of this programme but I would like to suggest an all-Bach recital (we haven't had one on his series since October '67) which would comprise one of the English Suites, one of the French Suites and the Italian Concerto.¹ I would also like to find a suitable interview guest – perhaps a musicologist – who could ramble on for ten minutes or so about aspects of nationalism as reflected by the 18th century artist in general and Bach in particular.² I think the idea is a fairly attractive one and that, one paper at least, the three works should make an interesting compot.

The Italian Concerto, of course, was recorded for CBC³ in 1959 as a flip-side filler for the disc which otherwise featured Partitas Nos.1 and 2.⁴ When the two-record set incorporating all of the Partitas under one cover was released some years later,⁵ however, this disc was withdrawn and, to date at least, the Italian Concerto has not been re-packaged or re-issued.⁴ Its inclusion, therefore, should not violate the spirit of our agreement re previously recorded material but, if you'd prefer to avoid it on this occasion, we could contrast the 'French' and 'English' items with a brace of very 'German' fugues.

I assume that this programme, unlike our previous efforts under the present contract, will be intended for the FM stereo facilities and that, consequently, we should plan to record in that mode. Having just completed a successful test at Eaton Auditorium,⁶ I would like to propose that, if Gordon⁷ can find a few extra dollars in the budget, we try to tape the recital in that hall. Of course, I don't know what scheduling plans you have for the programme but I would hope that we can get to it in the next couple of months so that I can clear the decks for the EBU recital which has been promised from spring. If you approve the idea of Eaton Auditorium in principle I'll have a chat with Mr. McLairnin in the auditorium office (I have to round up some dates on behalf of CBS, in any case) and, when I have some idea of their commitments and yours, we can perhaps map out a schedule accordingly.

All the best,

Glenn Gould

[1]Broadcast by CBC Radio on September 24, 1971: "Musicscope," on Bach's English Suite No. 2 in A minor, BWV 807; French Suites No. 5 in G major, BWV 816 and No. 6 in E major, BWV 817.
[2]Gould interviewed Hans Eichner of the University of Toronto on the influences of French culture on Germany in Bach's time.
[3]For CBC read CBS.
[4]In 1959 Gould recorded the Bach Partita No. 1 in B♭ major, BWV 825; in 1959, the Bach Partita No. 2 in C minor, BWV 826 and the Italian Concerto in F major, BWV 971 (released in 1960 by Columbia).
[5]The complete partitas were released by Columbia in 1966.
[6]A concert hall on the seventh floor of Eaton's College Street department store, now closed, used on a regular basis by Gould as a recording studio from 1970 to 1977.
[7]Gordon Rosch in the CBC Music Department, Toronto, was responsible for budget matters.

TO WENDY BUTLER

354 Jarvis Street
Toronto 116,
January 5, 1971

Wendy Butler
CBC

Dear Wendy:

Herewith, as I promised, some thoughts about Stokowski.

The programme, as you know, marks my second attempt at stereo-radio and offers, in many respects, a simpler and more direct (though, I hope, not less entertaining) utilization of the media than its immediate predecessor, 'The Latecomers'. The programme – an examination of outport life in Newfoundland – afforded virtually unlimited opportunities for vocal counterpoint in view of the fact that 14 characters were involved. In the Stokowski programme on the other hand, the maestro's voice alone leads us through the hour. (I suppose if we count the 'rehearsal-scene' and the 'folk-song sequence' there are other voices but, for all intents and purposes, Stokowski is both subject and narrator.)

Fortunately, the material that I derived during the two brief interviews I had with him (December 1969) was an embarrassment of riches in terms of quality (Stokowski is an exceptionally articulate old party, thinks paragraphically, edits himself en route, and signals the end of each answer by giving an up-beat cue to his interviewer) though it is somewhat limited as to quantity since the camera crew in attendance managed to blow the fuses in Stokowski's apartment on an average of once every ten minutes. (As you know, NET were filming their own documentary about him at the same time, a short sequence from our interview is included as a scene in that film, and a good many of our better lines serve as voice-over material).

Stokowski himself seemed impervious to the commotion. On many occasions, having been interrupted by the curses of the camera-crew, he would pause for five to ten minutes – however long it took for the fuses to be replaced – serve us tea, comment on the height of the water in the reservoir – his 5th Avenue apartment has a superb view of Central Park and if you've got to live in N.Y. that's the view to have – then, pick up where he left off, doubling back a word or two so that we could edit in the new material, and proceed with his original thesis, whatever it happened to be.

He is, of course, as we all know, the old stager par excellence. A lot of things that he says appear to be rather carefully calculated as to their probable effect upon his interlocutor. In part, this is because the appreciation of intimate dialogue, which is second nature to most people of our generation when caught out in an interview situation, was by no means taken for granted in Stokowski's day – the artist, then, was presumed to be the grandiloquent spokesman for a somewhat arcane craft and it behooved him to pronounce judgments rather than to engage in dialogue.

Something of this 'from on high' quality permeates Stokowski's interview manner, it's true, but, interestingly enough, does so only when he addresses himself specifically to the subject of music. In that area, one does not argue with him, one does not contest a point – one is up against an attitude every bit as monolithic, every bit as disinclined toward a genuine exchange of opinion as that of, say, Marshal McLuhan. And yet, away from the area of music, and again like McLuhan, Stokowski is a genuinely humble human being. His testimony is constantly subjected to subtle parenthetic qualifications and he seems incessantly involved in the search for moral correlatives of his aesthetic undertakings. Since, moreover this is the most dangerous but ultimately most crucial activity in which an artist can engage, he is understandably cautious in regard to the explorations it entails. The net result, obviously, is nothing like a conventional conversational style. It has, in effect, a quality of Old-Testament verse-making – an Ecclesiastes-like collation of thoughts and reflections about the musical situation, the human situation and, inevitably, the human situation within the musical situation. Stokowski, in my view, is an extraordinary and extraordinarily moving personality and I hope that something of his remarkable kindness and generosity of spirit as well as his relentless dedication to art comes through in this programme.

Just a word about the techniques employed: there are 26 separate musical items involved (singly or in combination) as background for Stokowski's comments. All of the orchestral items are conducted by him (there are, to be sure, two cadenzas, from Schonberg's Concerto, Opus 42 – my own recording with Robert Craft – but not one note of orchestral texture occurs in relation to either and the inclusion seemed a fitting one since Stokowski premiered many of Schonberg's later works.) But I emphasize *orchestral* works since, as you know, there is one sequence in which I grafted a number of folk-song segments – Rumanian, Yugoslavian, Scottish, English, Italian, American – to a superstructure provided by the first movement of the Shostakovitch Symphony No. 11. The other major Stokowski recordings included are:

Verklarte Nacht – Schonberg
Beethoven – 'Emperor' Concerto
Brahms – Serenade No. 1
Ives – Symphony No. 4
Tchaikowsky – 'Francesca da Rimini'
Holst – 'The Planets'
'The Poem of Ecstacy' by Scriabin.
Hopes this helps.

All best,
Glenn Gould

TO GILLES POTVIN[1]

February 25, 1971.

M. Gilles Potvin,
MONTREAL, P.Q.

Dear Gilles:

Herewith 'Radio as Music'.[2] It is perhaps ever so slightly longer than you bargained for but I hope that you like it as much as, if I may modestly say so, I do.

There will obviously be some need to explain the circumstances of the conversation which served as raw-material for this piece – as I mentioned in a previous letter John Jessop[3] is preparing a thesis based on my radio-documentary techniques – and I expect the logical way around the problem would be to include a prefatory paragraph (perhaps in a different type-face) which will make clear the nature of Jessop's involvement. It should, ideally, be in the form of an 'editor's note' but if you would like me to draft a line or two which will set out the facts and which can still be styled 'editor's note', just let me know. In your last letter you mentioned the onerous question of fee. As you know, I contribute fairly frequently to a number of American magazines and periodicals – most recently, 'Look'[4] – and I have long since given up trying to effect any sensible correlation between the pay-scale offered for articles by major publications south of the border with that available here at home. Consequently, I think the simplest way around the matter would be to place no unusual demands upon your budget whatsoever, but, in lieu of that, I must make two very specific requests: First of all, I would like to retain all rights in regard to future re-prints of "Radio as Music," both for Canada and other countries. I can assure you that I have no intention of offering it again, at least not in its present form, within Canada, but I would like to see it re-printed abroad. The second request, and this is one which I have had written into my contracts with 'Look' and other magazines, is that there must be no cuts and no changes whatsoever in the article, including changes of punctuation, without consultation. The punctuation clause is not a caprice on my part, by any means – it is particularly important in relation to an article of this kind which must preserve the integrity of its conversational flow. I would ask you to verify these two requests in a letter to me and inform your proof-readers et al accordingly.

Lorne Tulk is at work on the two sketches that I mentioned as embellishment to the article and expects to have them ready by the first of next week. One details the prologue to "The Idea of North," will be predominantly left-right, and could perhaps best occupy something like one-half or one-third page. The second sketch is a rather more detailed layout for the epilogue to "The Latecomers." It contains a great deal of information, is set out with a second-hand time-log down the left margin and consequently could easily occupy something close to a full page. The ideal spot for it, by the way, all other things being equal, would be in relation to pages 17 and 18 of the text. In any case I will have the sketches off to you within the next few days.

All best wishes.

Sincerely,
Glenn Gould

cc. J. Roberts

---

[1]Montreal-born producer for Radio Canada International until 1988, Potvin was also music critic for *Le Devoir* and *La Presse*.
[2]"Radio As Music: Glenn Gould in Conversation with John Jessop," *The Canadian Music Book*, Spring/Summer 1971.
[3]In 1971 John Jessop was a student at the Ryerson Institute of Technology in Toronto.
[4]"Rubinstein Interview" in *Look*, Vol. 35, no. 5, March 9, 1971.

Glenn Gould with dog, c. 1937. National Library of Canada.

Glenn Gould at the piano. CBC Photo.

◂ *Glenn Gould in CBC studio, Toronto. CBC Photo.*

Glenn Gould's Steinway piano in the living room of his apartment, Toronto, January 1983. National Library of Canada.

TO SUSAN EDWARDS[1]

Miss Susan Edwards,
CBC Toronto

Dear Miss Edwards,

Thank you very much for your note and for the invitation to nominate my favourite local eating spots and specialities therein. I'm afraid that you've simply turned to the wrong person for this assignment – I'm quite the opposite of a gourmet, almost totally indifferent to food, in fact, and at such time as the entire experience of nourishment-taking can be synthesized by a convenient tablet, I'll be among the very first to avoid all restaurants like the plague.

Good luck with the programme. Sorry I can't be of more help.

Sincerely,

[1] A fan.

TO LEE BROWN[1]

April 5, 1971

Mr. Lee Brown,
Music Department,
Ferguson Junior High School,
Arlington, Texas
U.S.A.

Dear Mr. Brown,

Thank you very much for your letter. I'm afraid that my somewhat delayed reply may have already compromised your class project but I am, in any case, sending along the photo you requested. I regret, however, that I cannot supply you with a press-book – unless you are willing to settle for one at least 10 years out of date – for the simple reason that when I decided to forsake the concert stage some years back and focus my attention instead on making records and producing radio and television programmes, the press-book, which is an indispensable item for concert performers, became excess baggage for me.

Your question about composers of the 'romantic' era interests me a good deal. I suppose that of those composers who represent the later manifestations of romanticism the one who means the most to me is Wagner. At the same time, however, I have always felt that among the earlier generation of 'romantic' composers – Chopin, Schumann, Schubert, et al – the most sadly underestimated is Felix Mendelssohn.[2] As you know, Mendlessohn's music has gone in and out of vogue with some regularity (very much 'in' for the English Victorians, for instance; very much 'out' for many people today who find it rather 'square' and perhaps a bit cautious) but, in my opinion, the precision of craft which Mendles-sohn exhibits – especially in his orchestral music – is equalled by few compos-ers in the 19th century and that craft, moreover, is put at the service of an extraordinarily touching, neo-devotional attitude which I find particularly alluring.

All best wishes for your project and once again my apologies for the delayed reply.

Yours sincerely,
Glenn Gould

¹A fan.
²Gould included some of Mendelssohn's *Songs Without Words* in a radio recital broadcast on "CBC Thursday Night" in July, 1970. At one point he contemplated recording Mendelssohn's six Prel-udes and Fugues, Op. 35.

TO RICHARD JOHNSTON¹   April 5, 1971

Professor Richard Johnson,
c/o University of Calgary,
CALGARY,
Alberta

Dear Dick,

John Roberts mentioned to me a few weeks back that he had been talking to you re a documentary on the general theme 'Canada West'. I did not respond at the time because no ideas were immediately forthcoming in relation to that topic but I am writing now because I do believe that I've finally hit on something that is at once congenial to me and which, at least geographically, relates to the area involved.

The program would concern itselv with the Mennonites, Hutterites and, if possible, the Doukhobour culture. All three groups interest me a good deal and since each, of course, demonstrates a different approach to the theme of community-in-isolation which served as underpinning for both 'The Idea of North' and 'The Latecomers' – my program about Newfoundland – this program would be, at once, a worthy challenge and a logical continuation of my previous documentary-dramas.²

It would also, I suspect, be a rather formidable assignment. I would not anticipate any difficulty in gaining access to articulate Mennonites – indeed, the whole point of their 'progress' (if that's what it is) is that they've successfully merged their notions of spiritual and physical isolation with a fairly broad working knowledge of the world outside. During the past week or so, while I've been hatching this project, I've also run down a few leads on a couple of relatively voluble Hutterites, and I'm sure that, with a bit of investigation, we can turn up a more substantial roster.

The problem, clearly, would be the Doukhobours. I have no idea whether these people are accessible to anyone from the 'outside' or whether, indeed, the presence of anyone who might be thought to represent the media – no matter how well disposed – would be regarded as a threat and a nuisance. It might, in fact, be necessary to confine ourselves to a two-shot (Mennonite Hutterite – still a lot of contrast) but in the meantime I can make a few enquiries as to whether or not an accessible Doukhobour exists.[3]

Basically, I would want the program to treat this particular subject (subjects?) much as 'North' and 'The Latecomers' treated the subject matter with which they were concerned. I would want it to develop a seemingly specific theme and to explore its universal ramifications accordingly. It would also, I hope, extend the techniques which were involved with the making of 'North' and 'The Latecomers'. The latter program was, of course, an exercise in a particularly elaborate stereophony ('North' was exclusively monaural) and although my great temptation at the moment is to get involved with a quadraphonic experiment, there are a few more tricks I would like to try before bidding farewell to conventional stereo.

John was not clear as to whether you anticipated a major musical involvement in the program in view of the fact that it would be prepared in part for the Canadian Music Council but, of course, while there are any number of possibilities in this regard, deriving particularly from the Mennonite tradition, it would not be a 'musical' program except to the extent that, in my view, the treatment of the human voice as an element of texture should, indeed, always be approached in a musical way. (I have, by the way, prepared a rather lengthy essay for the CMC journal – volume 2 – with the reasonably provocative title 'Radio as Music' and I would hope that this program would help to substantiate the arguments therein.)

The major problem at the moment is one of time. I understand that the conference will take place approximately one year from right now and, although I could go west and gather up the raw interview material this summer, the fine-editing, 8-tracking and mixing of the sort of program which we're talking about normally requires a period of 3 to 6 months. I have lately acquired my own 2-track equipment and am now in a position to prepare all of the fine-editing material at home, but the 8-tracking stage is a problem and necessitates the co-operation of Messrs. CBC and access (probably in the post-midnight hours) to a studio which is in almost constant use during the day at present. At the moment, in fact, I am more or less committed to begin work on my next major documentary for CBC radio and since this is scheduled for 8-tracking during January and February of next year the fine-editing stage will have to be gone through during the last 3 months or so of 1971. Since this is a program which I've budgeted at approximately 400 studio hours and since the project which I'm proposing to you would take at least that amount of time (excluding the actual interviews per se) it would be virtually impossible for me to complete both assignments prior to April 1972. It is certainly possible, of course, that CBC would agree to a postponement of the other project but, in view of our requirements for the 8-track machine, their involvement would be essential in any case in regard to the MHD (as it shall here-in-after be termed) project.

The other solution perhaps would be to try and devise MHD, again in collaboration with CBC, for some other activity which you may be planning at the University of Calgary within the next year or two. The advantage would be that I can then hold to the present schedule and not overload the already strained plant facilities here.

In any case, do let me know what you think about the idea and whether it in any way relates to the theme of 'Canada West' which, as I recall, we first discussed several years back.

All best for now,
Sincerely,
Glenn Gould

[1]Richard Johnston, a professor, composer, editor, critic, and a former Dean of the Faculty of Fine Arts at the University of Calgary. Johnston's lively interest in folk music and the cultures of minorities in western Canada was of interest to Gould.
[2]Gould's ideas developed into a radio documentary called "The Quiet in the Land," broadcast by the CBC on March 25, 1977.
[3]The project dealt only with Mennonites.

TO HANS RICHARD STRACKE[1]   April 6, 1971
Herr Hans Richard Stracke,
CBS Schallplatten Gmbh.,
Frankfurt-Main,
GERMANY.

Dear Herr Stracke,

Thank you very much for your letter of March 1. I am enclosing a copy of a note which I sent to Earl Price in regard to our project and which will, I'm sure, in most respects, at least, be self-explanatory. Perhaps I should explain, however, that the 'Ustinovization' to which I refer pertains to a promo which I prepared recently for CBC in relation to the North American release of the '48'.[2] They suggested a collection of spoken set-pieces in which Mr. Biggs, Mr. Kipnis, Mr. Ormandy, etc. – all of whom participate in the current month's release – would contribute some thoughts about the music of JSB.

Since I know that that sort of thing can get unduly solemn and since I couldn't be sure about the territory covered by my colleagues, I decided to avoid any hint of duplication. Taking a cue from our Beethoven-Lizst cover[3] which you translated so masterfully, I decided to interview myself and, playing one part at a time, create as a panel Sir Humphrey Price-Davies, Herr Klopweisser (the celebrated poet, as you'll recall) and the distinguished young American virtuouso, Theodore Slutz,[4] who has perhaps not crossed your path as yet in Germany.

Having produced separate tapes for each of the cast members of the panel, I then presented my own responses to their questions and, after editing them all together, mixed in a bit of the B-Flat Minor fugue, volume 2, (which all four were purportedly listening to during the latter stages of our discussion). It turned out very well indeed, and perhaps Earl Price can arrange to get you a copy, but what I meant to imply by the reference in his letter was that I was not about to try any similar comedic fireworks for the German version.

As things stand at present, I suspect that I can prepare the script during May and have it edited and mixed with musical examples during June. As I indicated in my letter to Earl, my own equipment (which we now use for all our CBS sessions in Toronto) is more than sufficient, and the only expenditure involved will be the hiring of a technician to operate it. In any event, I will keep you posted as I make my first timorous plunge into the German language and will hope to get the result to you by the end of June.

All best wishes,
Sincerely,
Glenn Gould

[1]A German friend who worked for CBS in Frankfurt.
[2]J.S. Bach, *The Well-Tempered Clavier* (CBS).
[3]Beethoven Symphony No. 5 in C minor, Op. 67 (piano transcription by Franz Liszt) (Columbia).
[4]Gould pseudonyms.

TO JANE FRIEDMAN   April 10, 1971

Miss Jane Friedman,
CBS Records,
NEW YORK, N.Y.,
U.S.A.

Dear Jane,

Herewith, as I promised, a breakdown of the repertoire for our coming sessions:

1) Next week on April 18 and 19, we will be doing 'Hughe Ashton's Grownde' and 'Sellinger's Rownde' of William Byrd, and the 'Variations in the Italian Style' by Bach. Both works, as I mentioned on the phone, are part of a project for the European Broadcasting Union[1] from which program (Byrd, Bach, Beethoven, Webern, Bizet) Andy suggested that the works of greatest interest and/or most utility re CBS would be Byrd, Bach and Bizet. In any case, the Byrd will round out our Byrd-Gibbons collection (although I must re-evaluate the Gibbons material since I seem to recall that one of his fantasias – recorded approximately three years back – was left without its appropriate inserts) and 'Sellinger's Rownde', in particular, should provide the piece de resistance of that disc. The Bach variations will, I think, come in handy since, as we proceed through the English suites, we're going to need some side-fill material of the sort provided in our partita discs by the 'Italian Concerto', the 'Toccata in E minor', et al.. Like the partitas, most of the English suites are of approximately 20 minutes duration and are not really suitable for packaging on a 3-to-a-disc basis without awkward side-breaks. I haven't timed them all but, I'am sure that one or more may give short shrift in relation to the overall timing and that it would be advantageous to have in the can a work like the 'Italian Variations' which could add 10 minutes or so to a short side, as needed.

2) On May 2 and 3 we will be recording Schonberg's song, opus 12 no. 2, with Cornelis Opthof and the 'Variations Chromatique' by Bizet. The Schonberg will wrap-up our complete lieder project and since much of that material has been on ice for up to seven years, I really think it would be desirable if we could make it available on release as soon as possible. As I mentioned on the phone, I'm not quite sure what format the Bizet will adorn. I do think, however, that we might, with all due deference to Peter Munvies, think about a 2, 3, or even 4 record set which would detail a history of the variation form. We've already got quite a bit of material which could be culled from other releases (especially if the project were offered at a bargain rate) and, in addition to the material which we're picking up courtesy of the EBU, we could at some point in the future, record a few more bits of esoterica such as the Bizet which represents a genuinely novel – for the 19th century, anyway, – approach to variation-form.

3) On May 22 and 23, we should be able to wrap-up the French Suite, French-Overture project. Outstanding at the moment, in relation to the first volume of that project, are four movements of the E major Suite (no.6) and the long introductory movement to the 'French-Overture'. The main order of business at that time, however, will be the 'English Suite No. 2 in A minor'. I've scheduled it for a CBC broadcast due this summer and which must be edited during June – hence, the unpredictable sequence involved (no. 1 in A major was included on one of my CBC recitals some years back).

I suspect that once the May dates are concluded, Andy may be in need of, if not a rest, at least somewhat more relaxed schedule. In any event, since I expect to spend a good portion of the summer away from Toronto, it might be advisable to reduce the frequency of our sessions after the end of May. As you know, much of the material which we've been consigning to the can, both during the present sessions and, indeed, for the past few years in New York, relates to my broadcast-contract with CBC. This contract, which stipulates that I program only works which I've not recorded commercially, compels me to be rather inventive in relation to the makeup of these programs and much of the more esoteric material which we've recorded during the past few years (Byrd, Phillip Emanuel Bach, Scriabin, Bizet, etc.) has come about in this way. Within the next few weeks, I'll be working out the details for next season's CBC programs and, at that time, I can send you a breakdown of the material which seems pertinent to our purposes at CBS.

There are, however, certain on-going projects at CBS which we should think about in relation to sessions for next season or, indeed, if time permits, for this summer:

1) Scriabin Sonatas: As you know, no. 5 is in the can at present and our intention was to pair it with one of the other late sonatas on one side of a disc which would contain as the main – i.e. longest – work either the Sonata no.1 or no. 2. The long-term raison d'etre in relation to that project is that it would be nice to combine on each of, say, three discs all the 'Mystery-Chord'² pieces from the later years, which, marvellous creations though they are, do sound a bit of a muchness harmonically, with one of the first three, resolutely tonal, sonatas. Ultimately, this would necessitate lifting the Sonata no. 3 from the Schonberg-Prokofiev album and, since there are 10 sonatas in all, will leave one of the later works outstanding. It is possible, however, since many are very short indeed (little more than 10 minutes, in some cases) that we might be able to wedge three such on the flip-side of one disc, but perhaps we can face that problem when we come to it.

2) Mozart Sonatas: As you know, volume three is already in the can though not yet edited and the only sonatas that remain outstanding are K.457, 570 and 576 (K.545 having been recorded out of sequence several years ago). We should also, probably, do the fantasias in C minor K.396 (the longer of the two in that key – K.475 – was recorded in 1966) D minor, and C major (this piece was included as a filler in the long deleted Mozart-Haydn album of 1958 but it should be re-done in stereo.

The up-coming album will consist of K.310, 330, 332, and 333. It could also include K.331 which was recorded in 1965 but in which, if I'm not mistaken, there were some rather badly misjudged insert-tempi and, although the first

143

movement of that work was provisionally edited at that time, there were, as I recall, sufficient problems with the 2nd movement in this regard to justify doing it, at least, again. There is, in any case, a precedent for moving out of sequence and by-passing one of the consecutively Kocheled sonatas since in volume two we skirted K.310 in just that way.

I think this about all the project-information I can muster at the moment but, as soon as I have the CBC repertoire available, I will be in touch again.

All best for now,
Sincerely,
Glenn Gould

[1]In the early 1970s, on the initiative of the CBC, Gould was invited to contribute a recital to the main concert series of the European Broadcasting Union (EBU). The EBU consists of the state broadcasting organizations of Europe and Great Britain with the addition of some other members, including Canada, through the CBC. As the policy of the EBU was to present live events, Gould's recorded recital was an exception to the rule, which only an artist of his stature could have brought about.
[2]Known as the "mystic" chord, its basic form consists of C, F♯ and B♭ in the bass clef, and E, A, D in the treble clef.

TO WENDY BUTLER   April 30, 1971

Miss Wendy Butler,
CBC

Dear Wendy,

Some thoughts on the 'Hammerklavier'[1]: it is, as I'm sure you know, the longest, most inconsiderate, and probably least rewarding piece that Beethoven wrote for the piano. I say this with some reluctance because, ever since my student years, I've been determined to find some real rewards in it and to document them in a broadcast or recording, or both. On several occasions, years back, I scheduled it for public audition – usually in spots like Dry Gulch, Mont., or Los Yahoos, N.M. but, inevitably, at the last moment, amended a discreet programme change. The piece simply alluded me as a totality and I was determined to unravel its enigmas before letting it go public.

Anyway, as you know, the bio-centenary advanced the day of reckoning – through a too complicated-to-go-into set of scheduling problems it was originally aimed at, and recorded by, December 1970 – and once again, I determined to have a go at solving its considerable mysteries. Well, I don't think I really managed to solve very many of them, but I did attempt some interesting methods of systems-analysis enroute. I decided, for instance, that since the piece is hopelessly unpianistic – not just because it's horrendously difficult (and what's worse, to the untutored ear doesn't sound all that hard) but because it's written with little or no concern for the sympathies and antipathies which exist between various regions of the keyboard – I would attempt an orchestral approach. I would try to link first note with last through sheer conductorial momentum – not speed but rather through tempi coerced into coalescence – and minimize all of the piano-specialty gestures which, annoyingly and perversely in view of Beethoven's essentially anti-instrumental bias, still get in the way of the music so much of the time.

And there are a lot of them to minimize. There are, for instance, many occasions when arabesques of almost Chopinesque delicacy (the second theme of the first movement is one instance) are placed in unrewarding registers (high ones mainly) and separated from their accompanimental voices by at least one octave too much. Most of these problems occur in the first and third movements – the second is short and taut enough to breeze by unnoticed, and the fugue-finale, for all its mathematical tom-foolery and its grimly vigorous attempts to break the neo-Handelian sound-barrier is both fascinating and fun.

But did my orchestral-overview, no-time-for-piano-conceits attitude really tie these four diverse structures together and make them one big work which does work? Not really. There are some moments that work, I think, and some that don't – which, come to think of it, was more or less Beethoven's score too – but at least I've tried it once and won't have to bother my head about it again until 2027.

All the Best,
Sincerely,
Glenn Gould

¹Sonata No. 29 in B♭ major Op. 106 by Beethoven.

TO MRS. JOHN M. JOHNSTON¹   May 13, 1971.

Mrs. John M. Johnston,
SILVER SPRING,
Maryland
U.S.A.

Dear Mrs. Johnston,

Thank you very much for your letter of April 26, for your kind comments about my Bach records, and for telling me about your own endeavours in that direction. I don't want to sound a false note of cheer-leaderish optimism but I am reasonably certain that, if you persevere for any considerable period with the music of Bach, you'll find that its many-layered secrets will be revealed to you.

I would suggest, however, that, in my view at least, the ideal preparation for the contrapuntal pursuits to be found in Bach's music is offered by the music of the English tudor composers – particularly William Byrd.[2] Byrd is very much on my mind these days, since I've just finished a recording[3] which will consist of half a dozen major selections by that composer in addition to three or four shorter items by his compatriot Orlando Gibbons,[4] but quite apart from my own inordinate enthusiasm for the music, I do believe you will find that the keyboard attitude, so to speak, of the tudor masters is, although directed at a very different kind of keyboard, admittedly, not unlike that of Bach, and that their music, as a whole, makes a very worthwhile complement to a study of JSB.

Again, many thanks for your letter.

Sincerely,
Glenn Gould

[1]A fan.
[2]English composer (1543-1623).
[3]*A Consort of Musicke bye William Byrde and Orlando Gibbons.* William Byrd: First Pavan and Galliard; Hughe Ashton's Ground; Sellinger's Round; Sixth Pavan and Galliard; A Voluntary. Orlando Gibbons: Allemande, or Italian Ground; Fantasy in C; "Lord of Salisbury" Pavan and Galliard (Columbia, 1971).
[4]English composer (1583-1625).

TO CARL LITTLE   June 5, 1971

Mr. Carl Little,
CBC Toronto

Dear Carl,

Just to confirm our conversation of Friday morning: I'll be happy to regard the Bach-suite programme as item one of our 71/72 contract and to consider that the 69/70 contract (which it theoretically related to) called for three contributions only. As I indicated the other day, I expect, within the next few days, to have some definite word as to the availability of an historian who can throw some light on aspects of 18th century nationalism. This will provide the intermission feature and, at that time, I'll arrange with Susan[1] for the additional hours needed to effect the studio-to-studio hookup, the editing of the interview, and the packaging of the programme accordingly.

If the Bach programme serves as item one for the new season and is, indeed, designed for Musicscope[2] it would, I assume, be aired subsequent to the EBU recital.[3] (There should be no danger of any CBS conflict viz a viz the Bach repetoire, by the way, since, so far as I know, they have no plans to issue the

French suites prior to the fall of 72.) I assume, however, that the remaining solo recital under the new contract would appear as a 'Tuesday Night' item. If we can get the good Dr. Weaver[4] working on the 'Hammerklavier' in the near future perhaps we can then schedule the other recital for a winter or spring date.

As I mentioned earlier, I think I would like to try a Scandinavian theme for that one – Grieg sonata, Nielsen suite, and possibly a sample of the current Baltic avant-garde. The only possible CBS conflict in relation to it will relate to whatever designs they have upon the Grieg sonata which was put in the can for them and for us last March.[5] As you know, I'm recording Uncle Edvard's concerto with the Cleveland Orchestra in September and both works are intended for release later in the season (possibly the so-called 'convention' release of July 1972).[6] In any case, I'll keep you informed as to the CBS plans so that we can have our own Bergen festival well in advance.

As for the 'Marienleben',[7] I've written to Lois[8] suggesting that my own preference would involve a series of sessions – at least four or five, in view of the complexity of the work – spread over two weekends, (not necessarily consequtive ones) and that a date in the fall subsequent to my Cleveland sessions would be ideal. I do hope that we can prevail upon Mr. Gardner and Co.[9] to look the other way and permit the use of my equipment for that session, although I would like to augment it, possibly on a rental basis, with a four-track so that the crucial decisions as to appropriate voice-piano balance can be reserved for the mix. This is, I think, a most important consideration in regard the transcription not only because of its length and difficulty but also because the green-room acoustics at Eaton's tend to be reverberant in the extreme so that, as I discovered in my recent session with Cornelis Opthof,[10] it is not easy to make a judicious settlement on the spot as to the appropriate ratio of voice to piano.

As you know, I would very much like to turn that recording into a conventional broadcast and employ for that occasion, the Lister Sinclair[11] translation of the Rilke cycle. During the 1962 Stratford Festival we presented the 'Marienleben' as a 'theatrical occasion' and invited John Horton to serve as narrator – reading Sinclair's very fluent translation, two or three poems at a time according to the periods of the story represented. I certainly would not advise doing this on the transcription as such, not only because it would push it over an hour but also because the intrusion of the poetry per se might lose its novelty and point on subsequent hearings. It did, however, have any extraordinary impact at Stratford and I do think we should opt for perhaps a one and one quarter hour period for the original broadcast presentation.

Hope this brings us up to date for the moment.

All best for now,
Sincerely,
Glenn Gould

P.S. I'm enclosing a copy of last Sunday's New York Times re the WTC volume 6 (our first disc originating from Eaton Auditorium sessions) and in which the critic seems blissfully unaware of any change of sound or locale.[12]

[1]Susan Englebert, CBC staff.
[2]It was aired on CBC's "Musicscope" on September 24, 1971.
[3]A recital recorded by the CBC for the main music series of the European Broadcasting Union (EBU), heard in the United States, Canada, and all European countries.
[4]Robert Weaver, then CBC producer of literary programs and chairman of "CBC Wednesday Night."
[5]Grieg's Sonata in E minor, Op. 7 (CBS, released in 1973).
[6]This work was not recorded.
[7]Das Marienleben by Paul Hindemith (1895-1963). Recorded with soprano Roxolana Roslak (CBS, 1978).
[8]Lois Marshall.
[9]CBC engineering staff.
[10]Canadian baritone (b. 1930).
[11]CBC broadcaster and writer.
[12]Recorded in 1969 and 1971. J.S. Bach, The Well-Tempered Clavier, Book II: Nos. 17-24, BWV 886-893 (CBS, released in 1971).

TO RONALD WILFORD
June 8, 1971

Mr. Ronald Wilford,
c/o Columbia Artists Management,
NEW YORK, N.Y.,
U.S.A.

Dear Ronald,

I feel I should let you know about a 50th anniversary TV-salute to the Toronto Symphony in which I'm participating next February. Ancerl,[1] will, of course, conduct and I'm writing because of your comments some months back that we should approach one or other of the major video-cassette manufacturers about the possible utilization of material which we already have in, or will shortly consign to, the can.

Some months back, John Barnes[2] and I tentatively settled on the Mozart concerto K.503, but Ancerl himself at one point had suggested the Grieg (the important consideration was to find a concerto which occupies less than thirty minutes) since we are recording it (with Cleveland) in the fall and since it is, or should be, a cameraman's delight.[3]

Of course, I don't know what sort of repetoire you had in mind but it seems to me that Uncle Edvard's opus 16 deserves inclusion in whichever token library of 'serious' music is initially made available via cassette and, needless to say, if there was interest in it, and a suitable arrangement could be worked out with Ancerl and the TA, I'd be delighted to revise the repetoire for the February programme. It will, by the way, be recorded with 8-track facilities so that we would not necessarily be locked into the TV sound (which, in this case, is intended to serve as a FM simulcast) and if the cassette people were so inclined they could, indeed, remix after the fact.

John Barnes tells me that our 'Emperor' concerto has definitely been sold to NET for next season as well as to the Zweite Deutsche Rundfunk. Do please let me know whether you were responsible for this latter contact so that I can set aside commissions accordingly. John also indicated in view of your conversation with Mr. Buttrose that he would put his Export Sales people directly in touch with the ABC and send a kine to them if they so desired.

Do give me your thoughts on the Grieg when you get a moment and, for that matter, on any other cassette material which you would like to see us schedule for future telecast.

All best for now,
Sincerely,
Glenn Gould

[1]Karel Ancerl (1908-73), Czechoslovakian-born conductor of the Toronto Symphony.
[2]Head of Music for CBC Television in Toronto.
[3]Gould did not record these two works.

TO ROY VOGT[1]

August 3, 1971

Prof. Roy Vogt,
Dept. of Economics,
University of Manitoba,
WINNIPEG,
Manitoba.

Dear Prof. Vogt,

Thank you for your letter. I can well understand your concert about the uses to which your interview-material might be subjected, but I should like to set your mind to rest in relation to the methods by which I intend to employ it.

As I indicated to you at the time of our meeting, I am interested in detailing the widest possible spectrum of opinion which finds shelter under what we might call the Mennonite umbrella. Your comments, therefore, because they provide evidence of a particularly liberal viewpoint and because of your notably persuasive and articulate presentation of them, are a valuable constituent of that testimony.

It is, of course, true that I hope to devise a form for the programme which in musical terms could be called 'contrapuntal'. I really cannot apologize for that analogy, however, because in my view – and I think this view would be shared by most 20th century, as opposed, perhaps, to 19th century historians – counterpoint is not a dry academic exercise in motivic permutation but rather a method of composition in which, if all goes well, each individual voice lives a life of its own. Naturally, even in the most complex contrapuntal textures certain concessions must be demanded of each musical strand as an accomodation to the harmonic and rythmic pace of the whole. It would, however, be true to say that, in musical terms, the more accurate expression of the totalitarian ideal to which you refer in your letter could be found in homophonic music in which one thematic strand – usually the soprano line – is permitted to become the focus of attention and in which all other voices are relegated to accompanimental roles.

It is also true that my personal predilection for what might, I suppose, be termed a neo-Thoreauvian way of life does determine, in some measure, the choice of subjects for my documentaries. Certainly, programmes such as 'The Idea of North', 'The Latecomers' (my documentary about Newfoundland) and the present project do possess thematic ambitions in common. I do not, however, feel that my personal convictions encourage me to distort the interview-material which is made available to me. Quite frankly – and to put it in the most selfish terms – I would do less than justice to my role as a producer if I were to deliberately sacrifice the 'contrapuntal' integrity of one value-system in order to enhance another.

Needless to say, the programmes which I make are very unlike the 'linear' (using the word in the McLuhanesque sense now) documentaries with which radio has traditionally been concerned. If, for instance, I interview a dozen people in the course of a project such as the present one, I obviously cannot attempt a dozen sound-portraits within the structure afforded by that programme. For that reason, as I indicated to you, I make no attempt to identify individual speakers but every attempt to guarantee the fidelity of each piece of testimony in relation, not only to its contextual service within the documentary, but also to the original transcript from which it was evolved.

All best wishes,
Sincerely,
Glenn Gould

[1]Vogt was interviewed by Gould for his documentary concerned with the Mennonites called "The Quiet in the Land." This documentary sustains an on-going tension between the movement away from fundamental Mennonite beliefs on the part of some people and the equally strong adherence to their faith by other Mennonites. It is the third of the Solitude Trilogy.

TO ALBERT PREFONTAINE[1]

c/o 354 Jarvis Street,
Toronto, Ontario
August 12, 1971

Mr. Albert Prefontaine,
DON MILLS,
Ontario.

Dear Mr. Prefontaine,

Thank you very much indeed for your letter and for your very kind comments about my recordings in general and about the partitas in particular.[2] They are, of course, in some respects, the most varied and contrapuntally involved of the Bach suites – just at the moment, however, I'm recording the six 'French' suites[3] which, though much less elaborate in scale are no less touching in their own quiet way – and I'm happy to learn that my recordings of them helped you to become a Bachian convert.

At the moment, I must admit, the music which absorbs me most, however, is that of a somewhat earlier era. I have just finished an album devoted entirely to works by the English Tudor composers, William Byrd and Orlando Gibbons and though it may seem an odd choice, in relation to conventional keyboard repetoire – I've discovered, to my great delight, that their music sits surprisingly well on the modern piano. This is particularly true in the case of Byrd who is, of course, in some respects, the father of modern keyboard writing – more introverted Gustav Mahler to Byrd's decidedly extroverted Richard Strauss – but both masters really produced such an extraordinary and virtually untapped output that I'm particularly pleased to have been able to represent my enthusiasm for it in some concrete way.

Once again, many thanks for your letter and all best wishes,

Sincerely,
Glenn Gould

[1]A fan.
[2]Gould recorded the Partitas No. 1 in B♭ major, BWV 825, and No. 2 in C minor, BWV 826 in 1960 (Columbia), Partitas No. 3 in A minor, BWV 827 and No. 4 in D major, BWV 828 in 1963 (Columbia).
[3]Gould recorded the French Suites, Vol. 1 in 1973 (Columbia); French Suites, Vol. 2 in 1974 (CBS).

151

TO EDITOR, TORONTO TELEGRAM

354 Jarvis Street
Toronto, Ontario
August 26, 1971

Editor
Toronto Telegram
Toronto, Ontario

Dear Sir:

Due to an opening-sentence gambit in Mr. John Fraser's[1] Heintzman-piano story, I seem to have been identified by several of your correspondents with the view expressed therein. I should like, therefore, to put the matter, and my relations with the Heintsman firm, in perspective.[2]

For the past 20 years, I have been party to a gentleman's agreement with the American firm of Steinway and Sons whereby, in exchange for my promise to eschew professional contact with any other piano, they undertake to provide one or more instruments of my choice at all engagements. Such arrangements, incidentally, however tempting a target for anti-trust sharp-shooters, are the rule rather than the exception among my colleagues in the United States and enjoy an historical precedent which dates back to the early decades of the 19th century. It should be obvious, however, that, because of the crucial mating of piano and pianist which is essential for a satisfactory keyboard experience, such 'contracts' are rarely entered into simply as a marriage of convenience. Indeed, I yield to no one in my admiration for the incomparable craft and care which has produced the Steinway piano.

That said, I must point out, however, that on three occasions during the past two decades Steinways were unable, due to transportation mix-ups, to fulfil their commitments and on each of those occasions, with the approval of the Steinway management, I selected a Heintzman as replacement. My relations with the Heintzman Company, consequently, were always most cordial and, in my opinion, they produced (the tense is deliberate since they no longer manufacture a nine-foot or, in lay parlance, 'concert' grand) an instrument which bore favourable comparison with any of that celebrated quartet of pianistic B's – Baldwin, Bleuthner, Bosendorfer and Bechstein – which, indeed, possessed certain tactile characteristics reminiscent of the Bechstein, and which was, in every respect, superior to all imports from the Orient I've come across thus far.[3]

Yours truly,
Glenn Gould

---

[1]John Fraser was the last music and dance critic of the now defunct *Toronto Telegram*. He was the author of an article on the decline of the Canadian piano.
[2]Heintzman and Co. Ltd. is the oldest manufacturer of pianos in Canada. It was based in Toronto (1866-1978), and moved to Hanover, Ontario, in 1978, under the name Heintzman Ltd.
[3]Gould's view on pianos changed. Towards the end of his life he fell in love with a Yamaha concert

grand in New York which he quickly purchased. It was used for his recording of the Haydn sonatas (CBS) and for his second recording of Bach's *Goldberg Variations*, BWV 988 (CBS), the last recording made before his death.

TO HELEN WHITNEY

3 September 1971

Miss Helen Whitney,
NBC News,
New York. N.Y.
U.S.A.

Dear Helen,

Herewith, as promised, some thoughts about future collaborative possibilities. I'm sure I need not point out that since much of the upcoming material was rehearsed in draft from prior to my western trip, the ideas contained herein may well seem old hat to you by now. In any case, here goes:

As I mentioned on the phone some weeks back, the matter of most concern to me at this stage is an essential agreement as to the kind of television we want to do. Needless to say, I am not aware of the importance of a respectable story-line, so to speak, and I will endeavour to come up with two such in the course of this note. But above all else, it seems to me that the process involved is what really should command our attention and I feel that, if we can attain some agreement in principle in that area, all other matters will fall into place accordingly.

Let me say, first of all, that what I object to most in television is its disposability. It seems to me that the easy way out while working in this medium is to rely on the instant access capability which it possesses and to assume thereby that the exposure thus attained is sufficient to justify the one-shot nature of many, even of the most ambitious projects attempted in the medium. I'm reasonably certain, for instance, that if I had occasion to work full-time in the magazine field, I'd come to resent the term 'periodical' and attempt to contrive something which might deserve to be called a 'permanent'; in television, accordingly, I'm reluctant to accept the one-shot status of 'specials' and I feel that we should endeavour to invent something which can be constantly renewed not only by repeats on T.V. but through video cartridge or whatever.[1] All of this may see self-evident, but I've got to get it off my chest first so that I can proceed to talk about more specialized techniques which simply take this process of 'permanence' for granted.

As you know, most of the television programming I've been involved in has been of or about music; by contrast, relatively few of my major radio specials (always excluding conventional broadcast recitals) have been musically derived and, in due course, I will, quite tentatively, make one musical and one extra-musical proposal. Necessarily, however, my experience with music on television has convinced me that in the vast majority of cases it simply does not come alive via the home screen, and the reasons for that failure, I think, are not too difficult to ascertain. The most obvious reason is that most television producers have attempted to bring the ambience of the concert-hall with all proscenium liabilities thereunto pertaining into the home. Inevitably, the results are influenced by this decision and, more often than not, the shooting that accrues, while it may be done with extra-ordinary care and finesse, appears rigid and predictable. I'm not saying that one cannot make the studio-oriented, concert-hall-imitating, video-tape production come alive but, particularly where an orchestra is involved, there are very few occasions, in my opinion, where that vitality has been built into the production.

Significantly, the best video-tape camera experiences I've had have related to solo piano material and very often to a sequence in which, perhaps, just one cameraman was given a certain lee-way and permitted to choreograph a particular segment of music accordingly. Most studio-shot orchestral performances, however, with or without a solo instrument, are depressingly square and unimaginative precisely because the director is, in most cases, required to subscribe to conditions which simply do not belong to the natural vocabulary of the medium. Most orchestral sessions are lit, blocked, and edited so as to infer the conventional realities of the concert-stage and, quite apart from the limitations of time and budget which may be applied to them, they necessarily reflect all the least desirable attributes of those conditions. I am not, as you know, an enthusiastic supporter of the public concert but I can at least concede that the relationship of audience position to stage presentation is one with sufficient variables as to make its reproduction on the home screen, by comparison, limited and unwieldy.

There are, on the other hand, instances of the successful adaptation of orchestral music to the camera and, as I indicated to you during our conversation in Toronto, by far the most impressive of these, to my mind, is the set of films made with various directors for the Berlin Philharmonic with Von Karajan. In the best of these – I think of the superb Dvorak 'New World' by Clouzot[2]– the relationship, or varieties of relationship, which appeared to exist between Von Karajan and the members of his orchestra, takes no cognizance of the conventional audience point of view. The performances are, of course, recorded in advance (dubbed to their own sound-track) – sync problems being their major, and sometimes very annoying drawback – and the disposition of the orchestra viz a viz its relation to the conductor changes from frame to frame. The effect, on one level, is entirely surreal; on a more profound level, however, these films convey the notion of what goes on in the score, of the instrumental balances and modulatory shifts implicit in that score, more effectively than any other musical-visual demonstration I know. They are, in effect, the only orchestral presentations designed for T.V. which I have ever wanted to see more than once. (I have, in fact, seen the Beethoven 'Pastorale' on three occasions already and find that my admiration for it and fascination with it increases with each subsequent opportunity. And the connection between that capacity for repetition and the integral use of the screen is not, I think, accidental).

In any case, so much for the preamble: I will proceed to a pair of concrete proposals directly. The idea which intrigues me most in relation to musical television at the moment – assuming that the employment of an orchestra is possible and desirable – is a look at the birth, development, decline and death of the piano concerto. This would be a project which, because it would follow the course of the keyboard as protaganist, because it would watch the keyboard player rise from the pit, so to speak, flex his muscles viz a viz the large ensemble and then, for any number of reasons which have more to do with social history than with musical form per se, recede once again into the background and in our own day, for all intents and purposes, disappear, would effectively deal with much more than its nominal subject. It would, in essence, cover approximately 300 years of history and by inference, since the formal problems of the concerto are simply an elaboration of other forms, detail, in large measure, the processes of sonata and symphony as well.

What I like about this idea is that, built into its story-line (I hate the word but I can't think of any other) is an excuse not only for many different kinds of music – and hence, for relatively short selections which, generally speaking, work better on camera, in any case – but, necessarily, many different kinds of camera technique, set design, and audio balance. I think that it would be a colossal waste to set forth a project of that kind within the proscenium implications of one set, one basic audio-visual relationship of piano to orchestra. I'm not suggesting that we should do an E. Power-Biggs-style tour of auditoria in order to find a visual raison d'être for each selection; on the contrary, I think that with the right hall, the right orchestra, and imaginative lighting, virtually all of our requirements could be amply met. But I do think that we should take advantage of the variety of styles under consideration in order to fashion an equally diverse set of criteria for the audio man, the lighting technicians and for the cameraman.

I think, in effect, that it should be done with film cameras, but that in order to avoid the sync problems which have plagued the Von Karajan series it should, wherever possible, be filmed as a performance. Needless to say, the whole point of film cameras would be lost if one attempted to do extremely long sections at one sitting – one might as well retreat to the video-tape format – but I think that, within reason, and in relation to any protracted shots of the keyboard, let's say, our battle-plan should carefully stake out those moments where sync problems are likely to materialize and make very sure that such segments are filmed in sequence as a performance.

The other thing that I think we should avoid is any temptation to link the narrative aspects of the programme to the set or sets in which it is performed. I think that if I were to get up and exhort the nation on the subject of some aspect or other of the concerto's evolution while the accompanimental forces were displayed in the background, a great deal of that deliberate unreality in the interests of a higher reality which I would like to see us cultivate would be lost. I think that the narrative segments should be done somewhere else altogether, at home, in the studio, or best of all in many different locations and possibly in situations in which conversational elements would naturally arise. I do believe that, given a chance, most people adjust very quickly to scene changes of this kind, providing the rhythm of the programme is such that it offers them some reasonable yardstick for these changes. I am certainly not proposing that we subvert logical extenuations à la Godard, but simply that we give to the narrative portions of the programme the same independence and integrity that we would try to bring to the shooting of the orchestra per se.

I suspect that, in relation to this project, we are really talking either about a programme which would run, say, to an hour and a half, or, perhaps, of two one-hour programmes. Perhaps not – perhaps we can find a way of telescoping many events into a relatively brief period. Certainly, I would like to telescope, both in audio terms and visually, a number of musical events within one larger structure (very much in the manner of my radio documentary on Stokowski which you heard) but obviously, this could not be done ad infinitum and, at some point, we're going to have to stop and play major segments of music more or less straight through.

I said, earlier on, that I was going to submit a non-musical proposal and, in that category, the idea which comes to mind at the moment is a look at the Thoreauvian way of life as evidenced in present-day America. You will, of course, recognize this as a south-of-the border adaptation of *my* theme – the c.f.[3] (as we used to say in counterpoint class), for 'The Idea of North' and for 'The Latecomers', et al – the relationship of isolation and solitude to one's productive capacity; in effect, to one's life in the world. As you know, most of my radio documentaries, or whatever they are, have variatively examined those concepts and even those which have nominally related to musical subjects have touched upon it (I think I was telling you about the talk between Carlos, the Moog manipulator and Jean LeMoyne, the theologian) and this project would explore much the same ground and attempt to do so (a) in video rather than purely audio terms and (b) in terms which perhaps have special meaning for an American audience.

As I mentioned the other night, I'm much less sure of my ground in relation to this project. The problem, I suppose, is that, for me, audio ideas tend to occur straight-off and, inevitably, I conceive documentary projects in terms of the audio capabilities they afford. If, therefore, we were to embark on a Thoreau[4] opus it would, obviously, necessitate the sympathetic indulgence of one or more inordinately poetic cameramen.

The interesting thing about it, however – the thing which I would incline to zero in on, were it, in fact, a radio documentary – is the degree to which one can find extra-national parallels for all of those quirkily American attitudes which Thoreau reveals in 'Walden'. Obviously, perhaps too obviously, the 'Walden' themes are no longer a peculiarly American property – any more than Ives'[5] music, for instance, with all its anti-academic nose-thumbing which we incline to associate with 'New World' attitudes, can still be viewed purely as an American phenonomen. It would seem to me that the revolt against certain aspects of materialism – indeed, the revolt against television itself in some quarters as a purveyor of those aspects – is interesting not only as a generational phenomena but interesting as well for the way in which it variatively disports itself in foreign climes. Somewhere there, I think, is a superb visual essay but I am not really sure that I am visual essayist enough to attempt it.[6]

We could, of course, adopt the form employed in 'The Idea of North' as film in which an enormously 'busy', superficially anti-videoistic, sound-track was used as the basso-continuo for film material which more often than not commented on it and, in all its better moments at any rate, refrained from any attempt to beat verbal description and audio sensation in general, at its own game. I think of that technique as a dramatic and, indeed, largely unexplored, if somewhat contradictory, T.V. component. And I would, I must admit, welcome the opportunity to try another project involving the same essentially contradictory outlook in relation to the medium.

Needless to say, if we were to embark on any such venture, the audio techniques involved would determine the pace with which we could go about it. They are, as you know, enormously time-consuming (400 studio hours have been budgeted for the editing and mixing of my current project on the Mennonites) but, precisely because they are audio techniques, not really very expensive until such time as the video counterpoints come to hand. I would, of course, need to travel about a fair bit in the preparation of a sound-track like that and to interview a good many people – all interviews outside North America would have to be handled by someone else since I have no intention of breaking my anti-aviation resolve, but I could easily submit fairly detailed lines of questioning which I would like to have pursued – and, then, working from transcripts I would be in a position to plot the audio shapes which we might invoke within it. By way of distinction to the 'Idea of North', this could conceivably be a project in which the video-correlative was plotted well before the audio mix per se. I really do not know how serious a compromise that might necessitate but, while still differentiated from the conventional pictures first and audio second documentary approach, it would allow for an interesting and challenging kind of mix in which I would very much like to be involved.

So there you have it, one project which seems, even at this distance, relatively clear to me and one which, though much less easy to visualize at this particular time, seems, if far more trouble, somehow, much more fun.[7]

Be my guest with both of them.[8] All the best for now.

Sincerely,

Glenn Gould

[1]Long before the video cassette became a commonly used technology, Gould foresaw that video recordings in one form or another would emerge.

[2]Henri Georges Clouzet (1907-77), French film director and scriptwriter.

[3]Cantus firmus. Fixed song or melody, employed by a composer for contrapuntal treatment or manipulation.

[4]Henry David Thoreau (1817-62), American writer and philosopher.

[5]Charles Ives (1874-1954), American composer.

[6]Gould sometimes stated that he had an underdeveloped visual sense.

[7]This project did not come to fruition.

[8]Gould often complained that the problem with trying to adapt concert music to the television medium was the insufficient time for experimentation. He commented that at the CBC there should be a center for video research where ideas could be tested without related production deadlines.

TO JOHN ROBERTS

354 Jarvis Street,

Toronto, Ontario.

September 18, 1971

Mr. John Roberts,

CBC,

Toronto.

Dear John,

Before the dust settles on the EBU affair, and while I still retain in memory the sequence and significance of the events involved, I would like to summatively and, I hope, temperately offer these comments:

As you know, the charges which arose via the EBU telexes and which were primarily, though not exclusively, the product of the BBC's Engineering Department, were five in number. Lacking access to the telex at the moment, I will reproduce them for the record as succinctly as possible.

1) The tape hiss was obtrusive.

2) There were discrepancies in the voice-track level as opposed to the music level per se.

3) The stereo reproduction was slightly out of phase.

4) Noise to signal ratio at 35 decibels was unsatisfactory.

5) The tape was not converted from the NAB curve to the CCIR curve for use in Europe.[1]

On closer inspection, of course, these five changes become, in fact, four. Number four is simply a more precise version of the tape hiss objection – and these four charges break down, it seems to me, into three distinct categories. Number five, while posing as a technical comment is, in fact, an entirely bureaucratic matter; number two is wholly aesthetic; numbers one and three are comments which more properly fall within the domain of an engineering department.

Let me deal with the 'bureaucratic' comment first. As you know, not only were we not instructed to provide CCIR tape for the EBU – indeed all contractual references simply refer to 'one original stereo' and 'one original mono' – there are, in fact, no facilities for conversion available at CBC or, so far as I can discover, in Toronto. It seems to me that if you have further dealings with the EBU and if they continue to take the position that the conversion should be done at the point of origination, it would certainly be wise to invest in the appropriate facilities.

In the meantime, however, I can only lament that we were manipulated into a position whereby we permitted a tape to be sent off without any playback facilities available to audition its output. This is not intended as a criticism of the fine and, I'm sure under the circumstances, ingenious work of the Maintenance Department but I do not feel that the appropriate solution to the problem was to concoct a jerry-built convertor without playback facilities – the lack of which means, by definition, that there is no possible way of ascertaining whether or not the product which was supposedly converted met the requirements of the CCIR curve. I think that it is entirely possible that what we sent off last week was a monstrosity; granted, it is also possible that through foresight, ingenuity, and plain good luck, the Maintenance Department may indeed have pulled off a miracle, but, as I indicated to you last weekend, I would welcome the opportunity, before it's too late, to send either an appropriate NAB copy dubbed on 206 tape without conversion or, as you suggested, to have the master converted in New York and thereby save one generation. In any case, I think that, for the sake of the CBC's reputation abroad, the EBU should be told that, however it may have turned out, the end result was not only not the product of a conventional CCIR convertor but was, in fact, a product in relation to which we were given no playback criteria.

Now we come to what I have called the 'aesthetic' objection – to wit, that the voice-track level was inconsistent with that of the music. As I mentioned to you some months back, I do not believe that, in this day and age, any listener is sufficiently naive as to suppose that, in the midst of a long and difficult programme such as the one embodied in this recital, the artist simply swivels about on the piano stool at the end of each selection and announced the upcoming number accordingly. Personally, I find that the attempt of many producers to enclose announcers comments within the same apparent ambience as the music under discussion is irritating rather than helpful; I am, however, willing to concede that this is a matter of taste for which there can be no pleasing of all parties. I suspect, however, that – as Stanley Horobin[2] remarked – the primary objection registered under this category was not based on anything that was actually heard but rather almost entirely upon something that was seen. A careful scrutiny of the VU meter during most of my introductory comments reveals that the voice-track was dubbed in at a cruising speed, so to speak, of minus 10 db. This, of course, is a rather unconventional level but it was chosen quite deliberately (a) because I prefer in all cases to frame the music by the voice rather than vice versa and to minimize the competition which sometimes results between the two elements and (b) because, with the possible exception of the Bach Variations, each of the five musical selections opened in the pianissimo to mezzo-piano range.

According to the way in which one read this objection, one could also interpret it to mean that there were inconsistencies in the level of the music per se. This, of course, even as regards the first version, is utter nonsense since, in relation to that version, not more than four or five splices were 'levelled' with the help of the 'pot' and, in the second version, since we chose to by-pass the mixing console, there was no dynamic manipulation at all. Mind you, I would like to think that the EBU and their storm-troopers at the BBC would be sophisticated enough in matters of recording technology to allow for the validity of electronic manipulation – I am thinking now of the sort of multi-track mix that we propose with the Scriabin sonatas – but, even in relation to the most conventional radio techniques, the present project simply did not contain any elements which could be objected to on even the most conservative of grounds.

We come now to the more problematic aspect of the telex – the two objections which I have characterized as more conventionally 'technical' in nature. As you know, Stanley Horobin had a rather lengthy chat with Andy Kazdin[3] about comment three – i.e. that certain elements in the tape were 'slightly out of phase' – and Andy, who with an electronics workshop in his basement (including an oscillopscope) and a doctorate from MIT is as qualified to speak on matters of 'phasing' as anyone I know, has assured me, and attempted to assure Stanley, that, in his opinion, the objection as registered is utter rubbish. I mentioned to you on the phone last week some of the technical particulars upon which he based this judgement – a judgement reinforced by an oscillopscopic check of all the material which he produced for us at Eaton's – and, at the very least, it would appear that a clash of philosophies as to the nature of stereo reproduction is involved. I do not want to take the time to recapitulate all of Andy's comments but, since Stanley's concern centered upon the fact that it was precisely in monaural reduction that the 'out of phase' characteristics manifested themselves, I must point out that, out of curiousity as much as a sense of pique, Andy converted to mono a substantial portion of the Bizet 'Variations' and has empowered me to say that, assuming the listener were not so situated in the room as to receive the full and normal benefits of stereo reproduction, he would stand by the word 'indistinguishable' in relation to it. In any event, Andy has offered to speak at greater length with Stanley and, indeed, with any of your technical people who would care to sit in, and since, from a purely theoretical stand-point, his expertise is, in my opinion, second to none, it's an invitation that I would urge you to consider.

Finally, objection one – the hiss problem more suavely rephrased as objection four. As you know, all of our sessions at Eaton's are recorded on 206 tape – the latest and best of Minnesota Mining's products and both of my Ampex 440's are specially adapted to record with that tape. Not so the CBC's machine, however, and on the original mix we dubbed the 206 material on to government issue 175 stock. As you probably know, 175 is an extremely variable tape at the best of times and, even at such times, is guilty of at least 5 db. more hiss level than its successor 206. I feel that this is the one objection levelled by BBC Engineering which I have to take seriously – although I cheerfully confess that I am totally unbothered by the signal to noise ratio even in the original – and I frankly admit that had we chosen to circumvent the CBC console – i.e. to sacrifice the occasional splice-pull in the original mix – we could have dubbed the original stereo product on any remaining Ampex 440, and, consequently, provided you with a version which would have remained faithful to the infinitely better quality obtained on the 206 tape. As you know, at the session for which the maintenance-shop 'convertor' was employed, the technicians also adapted one of the CBC units to accept 206 tape and, since this is a relatively minor adaptation, I do feel somewhat guilty that I did not insist that this be done in the first instance. Unfortunately, however, the 206ness of it all has now been inextricable combined with the quite probably haphazard conversion method which was employed, and it is entirely conceivable, as Andy explained to me, that the felicities of one may be cancelled out by the grotesqueries of the other.

I think this wraps up all the comments that come to mind in relation to the original telex. I understand, from Carl,[4] however, that there was an additional comment forthcoming from some eminence whose name escapes me at the moment to the effect that many of the above problems arose precisely because we chose to – I hope the quote is substantially accurate – employ the 'close-up North American, harpsichord style' pick-up. In view of the fact that I have written a great deal, and talked myself hoarse about the anachronistic attitudes of Europeans generally, and Britons in particular, in regard to microphone placement, I feel I can only greet this particular rejoinder with the silence it so richly deserves.

All best wishes,
Sincerely,
Glenn Gould

cc: Carl Little
CBC Toronto
Gordon Rosch
CBC Toronto

¹This technical letter relates to Gould's radio broadcast for the European Broadcasting Union (EBU). The policy of the EBU was to broadcast major concerts "live" so that they could be heard simultaneously. As a member of the EBU, the CBC offered to provide a piano recital by Gould, but stated that the program would have to be pre-recorded, and distributed individually on tape to all member organizations because he would not undertake a "live" concert. The CBC was not experienced in such projects for European partners, and a variety of technical problems arose. The entire event was fraught with misunderstandings and conflicting views concerning radio music broadcasts and what constituted quality stereo production. In the end the EBU regarded the recital as one of the finest it had ever broadcast.
²CBC engineer.
³Andrew Kazdin, producer at CBS Records.
⁴Carl Little, Assistant Head of Music at CBC.

TO GEORGE ROY HILL¹

354 Jarvis Street
Toronto, Ontario.
September 27, 1971

Mr. George Roy Hill,
Universal Pictures,
NEW YORK, N.Y.
U.S.A.

Dear Mr. Hill,

Thank you very much for your letter and for sending along a copy of 'Slaughterhouse Five'. Having now gone through it twice, I'd be most intrigued to learn about the cinematic notions you intend to apply to it. Certainly a baroque ambience for the Dresden sequences sounds both appealing and appropriately ironic. In any case, we could discuss it, at your convenience, in Toronto and/or, if you prefer, by phone – my number is (416) 922-9573 – and, needless to say, I'd be particularly pleased to have a look at the rough cut when available.

Again, many thanks for your letter and I look forward to hearing from you.

Sincerely
Glenn Gould

¹American film director of *Slaughterhouse Five*, for which Gould provided the music. The novel of the same name was written by Kurt Vonnegut, and although Gould did not care for it, he was intrigued by the possibility of putting together music for an American-made movie. Gould's filmscore consisted of a compote of bits and pieces of Bach, which he arranged and performed with a musical ensemble.

TO JANE FRIEDMAN

354 Jarvis Street,
Toronto, Ontario.
October 23, 1971

Miss Jane Friedman,
CBS Records,
NEW YORK, N.Y.,
U.S.A.

Dear Jane,

Some months back, I promised to keep you posted should any new and offbeat repetoire arise in the course of planning this season's CBC recitals. One such item has indeed come to the fore and, though I do not know whether it will be of any particular interest to CBS, I did feel that I should tell you about it.

As I think I may have mentioned in that previous note, I have been planning for sometime a recital with a 'Scandinavian' theme which would include the Sonata, opus 7 by Grieg.[1] My original choice for a companion piece ran to such now-conventional items as Nielsen,[2] et al, but I decided, on spec, to get in touch with the young American composer, Alan Stout,[3] who has made a fairly extensive study of Scandinavian music and who, in fact, has spent a good portion of his life in those countries. He suggested that the perfect complement for Grieg and the most appropriate up-dating of the Norwegian scene could be found in the music of one Fartein Valen.[4] Exactly, I'd never heard of him either! In the meantime, however, I had discovered that certain of his works were available in a rather obscure Norwegian edition and managed to secure several of his later compositions for piano (he died in 1952) including a set of variations – and a second piano sonata.

Valen's music, among other things, provides the most 'refined' – if that's the appropriate word – utilization of conventional 12-tone techniques this side of Alban Berg. It is, indeed, quite Berg-like in the degree of freedom and casual control with which he manipulates his materials. It does not, however, have any of the frenetic hyper-romantic qualities of Berg and somehow combines an extraordinarily rich harmonic idiom with a practical yet personal disposition of motivic events that reminds me, curiously enough, of the 12-tone works of Frank Martin – Le Vin Herbe,[5] for instance. In any case, some place on the Berg-Martin diagonal lies Fartein Valen and I really do feel, for the first time in many years, that I've encountered a major figure in 20th century music.

I've decided to include his Second Sonata on the aforementioned CBC recital and, although it will be paired on that occasion with the Grieg for which, of course, CBS has another coupling in mind, we could, certainly, devote the 'flip' side of any disc which might include the Sonata to one or more of the other Valen pieces that I've been pouring over of late. The Sonata, I would guess, is about 20-24 minutes, there is a splendid set of variations from more or less the same period – early 40's – as well as some incidental pieces from the last years of

163

his life. I forgot to mention, by the way, that Valen lived as a virtual recluse in those latter years, having been granted some sort of a government pension and that may, indeed, account for the fact that virtually no-one on this side of the water seems to have heard of him. There is also, in the brief biographical note which accompanies the Sonata, some mention of a First Sonata and several earlier (and perhaps un-published) piano works which apparently detailed the various stages of his Schonberg-bound evolution. If I can get hold of these earlier works there might be an even more attractive coupling to be found among their number. In any case, you can now ponder the mystery of Fartein Valen and, in due course, can give me your thoughts as to whether or not we might devote a disc to him.

All best,
Sincerely,
Glenn Gould

cc: Mr. Thomas Frost,
CBS Records

[1]Recital on July 18, 1972 in "CBC Tuesday Night." Apart from performing, Gould also wrote the script and acted as producer. The program was also broadcast by the Norwegian state radio NRK. Gould had an interesting Scandinavian connection – the composer Edvard Grieg (1843-1907) was a cousin of his maternal great-grandfather. The program consisted of the Sonata in E minor, Op. 7, by Grieg and Sonata No. 2, Op. 38, by Fartein Valen.
[2]Carl Nielsen (1865-1931), Danish composer.
[3]American composer and teacher (b.1932), Stout had spent 1954-55 studying at the University of Copenhagen.
[4]Norwegian composer and teacher (1887-1952), whose work Gould promoted.
[5]Swiss composer (1890-1974). *Le vin herbé* is a secular oratorio for twelve solo voices, seven strings, and piano.

TO CARL LITTLE

354 Jarvis Street,
Toronto, Ontario.
November 13, 1971.

Mr. Carl Little,
CBC – Toronto

Dear Carl,

I just wanted to let you know that I'm going to require a certain amount of background sound for the Mennonite project which cannot, as far as I know, be obtained from any of the customary sound-library sources. What I have in mind is the actual ambience of a Mennonite service from which I wish to extract three special effects only: 1) coughs, sneezes and general preparatory titters prior to the service itself; 2) whichever hymns are sung on that occasion, taped from the congregation's point-of-view as opposed to that of the choir or minister; 3) Idle chitchat picked up as the congregation departs after the service.

This can be accomplished in one of two ways – I can contact one of the Mennonite congregations in Toronto (there are, in fact, only two listed in the directory) and explain the project to them or, alternatively, I can turn the whole thing over to Ben Horch[1] and ask him to tape a service at his own church for me. I don't know whether or not your budget allocations make one course more desirable than the other but felt that I should give you a chance to comment, before I make contact either way. If the service is taped in Toronto, it would, of course, be necessary to spring Lorne[2] from his regular Sunday duties – he is now officially scheduled for CBC service on all weekends – and, additionally, I think it would be appropriate to offer some contribution to the congregation involved by way of expressing appreciation for their participation.

All best,
Sincerely,
Glenn Gould

cc: Gordon Rosch,[3]
CBC

[1]Ben Horch was Director of Music for the Mennonite Brethren Bible College in Winnipeg and Founder and Conductor of the Mennonite Symphony Orchestra in Winnipeg. His wife, Esther Horch, was also interviewed by Gould for "Quiet In the Land."
[2]Lorne Tulk, sound engineer who worked closely with Gould at CBC.
[3]CBC budget officer in the Music Department.

TO JOHN REEVES

354 Jarvis Street,
Toronto, Ontario.
November 13, 1971.

Mr. John Reeves,
Producer,
Radio Drama,
CBC

Dear John,

Since our last discussion re the 'quadraphonic specials',[1] I've been able to sort out some aspects, at least, of my contract with Universal Pictures.[2] It appears that, despite vigorous protests on my part, they are going to be quite adamant in regard to the 'thou shalt serve no other employer during the term of this contract' type of clause. The term in question is one of 10-weeks, beginning December 1 and, although I have a long-standing commitment to tape a TV special in the first week of February which I mean to do via a rider in the contract, regardless, it will be exceedingly difficult to push through any other exceptions in relation to it.

During the period, however, I'm going to proceed with as much of the fine-editing of the Mennonite project as possible – this can all be done on my own time, without prior scheduling and need not conflict, in any way, with their right to demand my services on short notice – and it is conceivable that by early in the New Year I might have enough material available to quadraphonize (?) let's say, one scene from the programme. Quite frankly, there is no possibility, given the particulars of that contract, that I could attempt the very sophisticated mix which would be involved in a four-channel version of the programme as a whole, but I do think that I might be able to manage a sort of ten-minute or thereabouts scena which could, perhaps, serve as overture or entr'acte to one of your other programmes. I'm really sorry that this project cannot be released quadraphonically, in toto. As you know, I had originally conceived it in that form and if you are planning any other four-channel experiments for later in the year I would very much like to be included in. For the present, however, I'm afraid that a very modest contribution is the most that my schedule will permit and I look forward to your reaction accordingly.

Sincerely,
Glenn Gould

¹John Reeves was a CBC producer with a profound belief in the emergence of quadraphonic sound as a new medium for recording and broadcasting. At the time of this letter he was planning special quadraphonic broadcasts to demonstrate the validity of this new medium. Gould was convinced that quadraphonic sound would usher in a new era for certain kinds of recordings.
²The film was *Slaughterhouse Five*.

TO DAVID RUBIN

354 Jarvis Street
Toronto, Ontario
December 12, 1971

Mr. David Rubin
Steinway & Sons
New York City, N.Y.

Dear David:

Herewith as promised, the tuner's report re the late and much lamented CD318.¹ I am sure that these details will be substantially borne out by your technical people when they have a chance to assess the damage, but, needless to say, I am most anxious to know whether any parts are salvagable and could be used in conjunction with another instrument.

1. The piano was apparently dropped with great force and the point of impact would appear to be the front right (treble) corner.

2. The plate is fractured in four critical places.

3. The lid is split at the bass end and there is also considerable damage to it toward the treble end as well.

4. The sounding board is split at the treble end.

5. Key slip pins are bent out of line and the force of the impact was great enough to bend No. 10 type screws as well.

6. The force was also great enough to put the key frame and action completely out of alignment, i.e. forward at the treble end.

As I mentioned to you on the phone, Vern Edquist, my tuner, examined the travelling case on Monday morning and reported that there is a deep gouge on the left hand side near the top, and that the wood block inside was torn loose by the force of the impact.

Subsequent to our call on Monday, I had another chat with Miss Mussen and managed to gather together a few more facts about the time and means of transport involved. The piano, according to her records, was crated on September 17 and originally scheduled for pickup by Maislin Transport on September 20 – she believes, however, that because they did not send the appropriate crew on the 20th, its departure was delayed until the 21st. The more interesting set of statistics, to my mind, concerns its return. Again according to her records, it arrived at the border via Intercity Transport (Manifesto No. BUF114949) on October 14 and at what Eaton's refer to as the 'dump' which, I believe, translated, is the customs shed on the outskirts of the city, on October 15. It was cleared by customs on the 18th, delivered to the upper ramp at Eatons, College Street, on the 20th, and installed in the Auditorium on the 26th.

Quite frankly, there are features about this latter report which intrigue me. The most obvious query would relate to the fact that it took them six days (admittedly counting a weekend) to move the piano from the ground floor to the 7th floor Auditorium. I also find it just a bit odd that it would require two days after customs clearance to go from the suburbs to the downtown store. I would ask that you handle these latter bits of information, or more accurately my paranoid suspicions in regard to them, with your customary discretion, but I'm sure you will agree that both questions could stand some elucidation.

I also find it odd that no accident report has appeared in relation to any portion of the trip. Granted, Maislin, Intercity Transport, or Robertson Movers who are, I believe, in charge of local handling for Eaton's, may well have failed to appreciate the degree of internal damage which such a fall would cause, but I should think that the external damage alone – the case etc. – would be more than sufficient to have warranted a report of some kind from the appropriate party.

In any event, I shall leave you to ponder these things and as soon as I have your report in regard to the salvagability of the action, etc., we can pursue the question of a replacement instrument accordingly.

All best for now.

Sincerely,
Glenn Gould

¹This letter reflects the trauma Gould experienced over the damage to his recording instrument, Steinway CD 318. When the piano was repaired, Gould felt it never totally regained its very special sound quality and responsiveness.

TO HUMPHREY BURTON

354 Jarvis Street,
Toronto, Ontario.
December 21, 1971.

Mr. Humphrey Burton,
c/o London Weekend Television.

Dear Humphrey,

Many thanks for your note and for your invitation to take part in Volume 5 of the complete Burton-Gould conversations. Needless to say, I would be enormously pleased to work out something of the sort of the future, but I am afraid that February is absolutely impossible for me and, indeed, most of the spring months will, by all appearances, be little better. Just at the moment, I'm working on the sound-track of 'Slaughterhouse Five' – Universal Pictures adaptation of the Kurt Vonnegut novel – and am bound by a contract which places me at their exclusive disposal until the end of February.¹ I have already had to beg leave in order to fullfil an old promise to John Barnes but, in view of the fact that the final mix will take place during February, I don't feel that I can reasonably expect additional time off.

You ask about recent projects which you've not yet seen: as far as I know, you are fairly well up to date, but there is one project, as yet only vaguely formulated, which you might want to consider, perhaps as a collaboration with John or

Curtis Davis, or both. I'm having a bit of a Haydn fit at the moment and am thinking seriously about a recording of all of the piano sonatas.[2] As you know, I'm not really our average rococo buff but, somehow or other, Haydn is very much the exception to whatever bias I have against that period and I would like to do a major programme – performance largely, I think, though certainly with a reasonable proportion of talk, as well – devoted to his music. I would particularly like to finish off, or perhaps begin and end with something symphonic, directed from the harpsichord. I'm not really sure how well the later symphonies would work in that fashion, but I'm quite confident that the earlier ones would go beautifully and that, given the right mise-en-scene, one could make a compelling and intimate camera statement with them. The middle of the programme, certainly, would involve sonatas at the keyboard – piano, I suppose, though perhaps one could better illustrate the transition from baroque left-overs through 'style galant' to fait accompli classicism by a flugel-switch.[3] In any case, if the idea interests you, let's think about it more concretely.

In the meantime, if you are in North America during February do please give me a shout so that we can plot a conversational course for the future.

All best,
Sincerely,
Glenn Gould

[1]Gould was interviewed on the CBC Radio program "The Scene" on August 26, 1972 regarding his sound track for the film.
[2]Between October 1980 and May 1981 Gould recorded the following Haydn Sonatas: No. 56 in D major, H. XVI/42; No. 58 in C major, H. XVI/48; No. 59 in E♭ major, H. XVI/49; No. 60 in C major, H. XVI/50; No. 61 in D major, H. XVI/51; and No. 62 in E♭ major, H. XVI/52 (CBS).
[3]Switch of keyboards from harpsichord to piano.

TO RONALD WILFORD

354 Jarvis Street,
Toronto, Ontario,.
December 21, 1971.

Mr. Ronald Wilford,
Columbia Artist's Management,
NEW YORK, N.Y.,
U.S.A.

Dear Ronald,

As you requested, I have given some thought in recent weeks to suitable repetoire for DGG[1] and I'm sending along several suggestions which would, I think, make eminent sense in relation to their catalogue. Needless to say, each of these suggestions relate to the assumption that they are represented fairly accurately by the North American edition of Schwann which may not, in the end, be an accurate assumption at all. Each of the undertakings, if selected independently, and in conjunction with a continuing association chez CBS, could form an appropriate embellishment to the rather considerable amount of repetoire already recorded and/or in the 'can' at Columbia. If we were to think in terms of exclusivity with DGG, however, it would obviously be essential to maintain some semblance of the scope and variety of material which our present contract encourages and, consequently, we would then have to examine these projects from the standpoint of overall catalogue balance.

The project which most interests me, at the moment, is a survey of the complete Haydn sonatas. There are, as you probably know, more than fifty in all and, according to Schwann, DGG is represented by only one – no. 44 in a recording by Richter. Obviously, such a project would necessitate many years for completion. With luck, and depending upon whatever policy we adopt in respect to double-bar repeats – I have eschewed most such in my Mozart sonata series – it might be possible to wedge all the sonatas on to ten discs.[2] Again, my experience in respect to the Mozart project has indicated that an average of four sonatas per record is a reasonable allocation and involves no flip side problems whatever – i.e. none of the sonatas needs to be divided intra-movement. It would be quite appropriate, I think, to calculate in the same fashion on behalf of the Haydn project but, since some of the earlier works, in particular, are quite brief, I would not be surprised to find that we might, on occasion, manage five, or even six sonatas, per disc. Obviously, then, an estimate of ten to twelve discs would be realistic and I think that we could manage, if necessary, two Haydn discs a year.

My inclination would be to proceed chronologically and, though I don't want to interfere in the area of marketing policy, to release them initially, at least, in packages of two or three discs each. Each package would then cover approxi- mately one decade of the 3$^1/_2$, or thereabouts, which Haydn devoted to his efforts at the keyboard. I think the chronological approach has a good deal to recommend it; the sense of development from the baroque leftovers of the 1760's, through 'style galant', to the fait accompli classicism of the works written in the last decade of the century, points up very clearly the linguistic transition of 18th century music.

In the event of an exclusive contract with DGG,[3] however, I would be more than a little restless unless subsidiary, if less demanding, projects could be developed as counterpoint to the Haydn effort. In the baroque area, there are several projects which could keep us busy: I have thus far tackled only one of the seven Bach toccatas and that item – no. 7 in E.minor – was recorded for CBS in 1962, released the following year, and hence is well past the five year deadline imposed by our contract.

Since I am already well along with a complete 'French Suite' project for CBS –

nos. 5 and 6 and the 'Overture in the French Style' are in the 'can' already – I feel a moral commitment to complete the project for them. In many ways, the ideal Bach project for DGG would be the six English Suites. Of these, unfortunately, I have quite recently taped, though not yet released, no. 2 in A minor but, perhaps, if we were to trade off the completion of the French Suite project, CBS might permit us to re-record the A minor within the next five years. In any event, the toccatas would involve two discs, the English Suite a further pair, and we could also, perhaps, devote an additional set of discs to the complete Handel suites. There are sixteen of these, more or less, and four discs would seem like a reasonable guess, at this juncture.

All of the above projects, of course, are 18th-century-happy, and it would be important, I think, to uncover some significant 20th century repetoire, as well. As you know, we are presently working our way, and rather experiementally, through the sonatas of Scriabin – the experiement involves the use of multi-rank mike perspectives. If that experiment meets with success, it could, I think, become the prototype for stereophonic – dare one say quadraphonic[4] – wonders to come. We could, in fact, prepare some of the later Scriabin sonatas – thus far, I have taped only nos. 3 and 5 and committed myself additionally to nos. 1 and 4 – for DGG, with or without the employment of multiple perspectives. It would, however, be most important to unveil some entirely off-the-beaten-track repetoire as well.

My current enthusiasm – and mentioned here more as an example than as a concrete suggestion since, if all goes well, I shall record it for CBS fairly soon – is the music of Fartein Valen. He was a Norwegian recluse and, during the last 15 years or so of his life, while pensioned off by his government and in retreat at a farmhouse on the banks of a fjord – I'm not making this up – wrote some of the most extraordinary music of the 20th century. The discovery of Valen is my find of the season – though his music is played from time to time in Europe – -and I plan to include the 2nd piano sonata in a CBC recital during March. There is, at present, no representation for this extraordinary musician in the Schwann catalogue and, while a recording of the sonatas is long overdue, I include his name, as mentioned above, more as a prototype in respect to the kind of project I would like to develop than as a firm commitment re our suggestions to DGG.

In sum, then, I feel that, in terms of solo repertoire and if an exclusive contract is involved, we should think of an involvement with three distinct areas: a) baroque b) Haydn project – supplemented by any or all of the Beethoven sonatas I've not yet recorded (i.e. approximately sixteen of the thirtytwo) and c) late-romantic and 20th-century material.

As I need not tell you, an exclusive contract with a European firm is by no means ideal from my point of view. Much to be preferred, it seems to me, is an arrangement whereby, while continuing our present relationship with CBS, we add, primarily with the overseas market in mind, a substantial body of work for

DGG. Needless to say, of the projects listed above, the one which I would most favour in the event of that situation would be the Haydn sonatas. We now come to the rather troublesome matter of production authority which could, I suspect, make or break a relationship with DGG. As you know, I have enjoyed remarkable autonomy at CBS, both in respect to the selection of repertoire and, quite frankly, that autonomy is an acquisition which I would not willingly relinquish. I think, consequently, that it would be essential to point out to DGG in your discussions with them that, for the past year, all of my recording has been done in Toronto, that I have acquired a substantial amount of professional equipment, and that I would want to continue to make use of the Toronto facilities in relation to any sessions – always excluding orchestral repertoire – which we undertake for them.

As you know, DGG cultivates a rather distinctive, certainly ultra-refined, instrumental pick-up and, while I have an enormous admiration for the quality of work they produce, the recording philosophy embodied in it reflects, it seems to me, a rather more concern-memory-oriented persuasion than I feel the process of recording warrants. I would be most pleased to discuss improvements in my present equipment or, indeed, the acquisition of new equipment with them and I would certainly undertake to ensure that the available equipment would meet their requirements, but I could not, in all conscience, abandon the relatively close-up, highly analytical sound which has been the hallmark of our recording at CBS and which reflects, not only my own predilection in regard to piano pick-up but, more significantly, a continuing persuasion as to the validity of the recording experience as a manifestation divorced from concert practice.

In effect, then, I would prefer to act as producer for my own sessions and this could be done either while utilizing DGG's technical personnel or, perhaps more expediently, one of the two or three technicians who work with me fairly consistently at the CBC and who have participated in the preparation of our various CBS sessions at Eaton Auditorium during the past year. Frankly, I think this latter arrangement would be ideal for DGG since, even if they maintain their Boston studio, we could, in this way, prepare each of the discs for them in master-tape form, and thus supervise all editing at this end. It would simplify their task considerably, would allow me a good deal of peace of mind, and enable me to maintain the close contact with production per se that I have long enjoyed at CBS.

In any event, I leave you to ponder these things and in the meantime, all best wishes.

Sincerely,
Glenn Gould

¹Deutsche Grammophon.
²The project did not come to fruition.
³From time to time Gould reflected on his recording career and wondered if he should move to

another label. Before signing his final contract with CBS he toyed with the idea of not having an exclusive contract with any one company. He thought he might be able to undertake recording projects for whichever company was prepared to be the highest bidder. 'Gould was convinced quadraphonic sound would become the norm.

TO EARL PRICE [1]

354 Jarvis Street
Toronto, Ontario
January 8, 1972

Mr. Earl Price
CBS Records
New York, N.Y., U.S.A.

Dear Earl:

Just a note to bring you up to date on the current status of the CBS Deutschland promo.[2] The voice-track was taped approximately six weeks ago, a four-track was moved into my apartment for two days, and mix was done a month back, and the results shipped off to Dr. Knolke[3] at that time. Two weeks ago, I had a call from her and she professed herself somewhat dismayed with my handling of the German language – not, by and large, from the standpoint of pronunciation as I'd feared, however. Her quarrel, rather, was with the pace at which I'd elected to read the material – 'you should have been driving a Volkswagen, not a Jaguar' was one of the more celebrated sallies. I am sure the comment is entirely justified and, as I pointed out, largely attributible to the fact that, since I had not the faintest notion what I was doing, I fell back on the old ploy 'when in doubt, accelerate'. In any event she feels, I gather, that the result is like playing a 33-1/3 at 78 and that she would like me to read it again 'largo con expressione'.

This, of course, presents enormous problems since the mix – a seamless compot of Bach fugal strands – was, of course, cut to the cloth of my reading pace. She volunteered, however, to send a tape of a real live German reading in an appropriate tempo and suggested that I might wish to imitate same and remix accordingly. I explained to her, that, at the moment I'm involved with the sound-track of 'Slaughter House Five' – and that I have more or less committed myself to a contract which places me at their exclusive disposal until the middle of February. In effect, therefore, there would be no opportunity for me to do the mix again until that time and at that late date, of course, it would not be possible for her to release it in conjunction with the WTC.[4] This was pretty well the state in which we left things by phone – I neglected to mention that thus far, the engineering expenses on the promo clock in at about $500 – and I'm not sure any of us are prepared for another go at that price – but it has occurred to me that perhaps the most practical 'out' in relation to this project would be to re-do only the voice-track – observing the inflective niceties of the tape which intends to dispatch – and let them attempt whatever mix they can manage at that end.

Needless to say, this is a far from satisfactory solution from my point of view; the original mix was, I think, a particularly handsome complement to the text. I feel, however, that I should not jeopardize her release, and that I should, at least, offer to do it in this fashion especially if she can assign some responsible person to attempt a mix not too dissimilar from the montage provided in the original tape. I have, in fact, cabled her to this effect and, in the event you hear about it from her, this will keep you in the picture accordingly.

All best for now.

Sincerely,
Glenn Gould

PS: Any bright ideas as to what we should do with the engineering charges thus far?

[1]Sales and Marketing Manager with the CBS International office in New York.
[2]Gould recorded *Glenn Gould über Bach* (CBS: [Germany] GG1) circa 1972. A bonus disc was released by CBS of excerpts from previous recordings of works by Johann Sebastian Bach.
[3]Dr. Knolke was with CBS in Germany.
[4]J.S. Bach, *The Well-Tempered Clavier*.

TO HARRY GARFIELD

354 Jarvis Street,
Toronto, Ontario.
April 24, 1972.

Mr. Harry Garfield,
Universal Studios,
Universal City,
U.S.A.

Dear Harry,

First of all, let me say how very much I enjoyed our conversation the other day. I'm only sorry that we could not have been in touch directly about this matter at an earlier date. I'm sure that many of the problems could have been solved most handily had that been possible.

Having now slept on your proposal for four nights, I am fairly convinced that my conviction about remaining true to Johann Sebastian Bach's original designs was not misplaced. As I indicated on the phone, I would have no scruples whatsoever about making alterations in a classical score in order to facilitate its transfer to the screen and to accomodate the visual rythum of a picture. Indeed, this is precisely what I did in relation to the last few seconds of the D Major Concerto which is used in the Dresden station sequence. I feel, however, that I should not engage in any such alterations where a recording is concerned. I don't think this stems from any overly puritanical respect for the letter of Bach's law; I simply feel that since any musician can compare the result with the original and any layman, given even a modicum of familiarity with the original, could detect the marks of my handiwork, and particularly since no visual raison d'etre is at hand in the recorded medium, that the enterprise is one in regard to which all musicological sense dictates my absence. (I did, by the way, mention your proposal to our mutual friend, Steve Posen, and it did, as predicted, make his week.)

Assuming no re-write is involved, and assuming that you remain faithful to the Bach original, I feel that the two items which would best justify their representa-tion on a 'single' would be the second movement from the Concerto no. 5 in F Minor (all of which at one time or another is heard in the picture) and the finale from the Concerto no. 3 in D Major. As I indicated on the phone, the latter movement because of pictorial necessities, was not heard in its entirety and you would require the additional material (approximately 45 seconds in all) from Columbia in order to make use of it on the flip-side of the proposed 'single'. For that matter, you would require the original stereo tapes of both items, as opposed to the mono tapes which were requested for the film.

I sincerely believe that this is the only proposal which makes any kind of musical sense, though I am well aware that there may be commercial justifica-tion in one or more of the semi-classical-style adaptations which you proposed. Do let me know if I can be of any assistance and, in the meantime, all best wishes.

Sincerely,
Glenn Gould

TO ROBERT A. SKELTON[1]

354 Jarvis Street,
Toronto, Ontario.
May 23, 1972.

Mr. Robert A. Skelton,
Bloomington, Ind.
U.S.A.

Dear Mr. Skelton,

Thank you very much for your letter of May 3 and for telling me about your most interesting project in the field of Canadian chamber music. Certainly, the three works you have chosen for your thesis do represent a 'wide spectrum of forms and styles', as you suggest.

In regard to my own quartet, a fairly detailed analytical note was included with the recording made some years ago by the 'Symphonia' quartet and released at that time by Columbia.[2] Looking back at it at a distance of almost two decades (it was, after all, begun in 1953) I can recognize in it certain essential attitudes which I have, I think, brought to bear in more recent years on another medium altogether. I am going to send you under separate cover the original sound-track albums of 'The Idea of North' and 'The Latecomers', two documentary dramas which I prepared for CBC in the late 60's and, additionally, a fairly detailed analysis of them which appeared in a recent edition of the Journal of the Canadian Music Council,[3] and which took the form of a conversation with a student at Ryerson Institute of Technology who was, at the time, preparing a thesis based on my radio documentary techniques.

Superficially, 'The Idea of North' and 'The Latecomers' – as well as a current project dealing with a Mennonite community with which I have been occupied for some months and which is tentatively scheduled for release next winter[4] – might seem to have relatively little to do with the outlook and attitudes of the quartet, especially since the latter work is more or less a conventional concert-hall outing for four string players and the two documentaries in question, involving a cast of five and thirteen respectively, not only are not designed as a public spectacle but, in fact, exploit electronic resources to the utmost.

There are, however, certain connecting links which should, I think, be noted: perhaps, most obviously, a concentration on aspects of counterpoint (you will find a more detailed discussion of the multi-linear aspects of the documentaries in the CMC Journal) and perhaps, less obviously, a tendency in each case to celebrate, if not precisely a fin de siecle situation, then at least a philosophy which deliberately sought an isolated vantagepoint, in relation to its time and milieu. Certainly the quartet which, superficially at least, revisited the harmonic world of, let's say, Strauss and Mahler, was an odd sort of creation to turn up in the mid-1950's. (Let me say parenthetically, that because of the intense – really quite Schonbergoan – motivic concentration it employed, the work did not simply revisit the Strauss-Mahler harmonic formulae but rather re-examined them in the light of the cellular concerns of the second Viennese school). It was nonetheless, and despite all rationalization to the contrary, an unusual work for its time and place, and it would be no exaggeration, I think, to stress that aspect of it through which, in effect, I sought to challenge the zeitgeist.

The tyranny of stylistic collectivity in the arts and, more generally, in life styles, per se, has been, I think, the primary theme in most of the works I have attempted and, indeed, in a good many of the articles which I have written from time to time about the musical situation. And, as I have indicated above, I think that, however far fetched the connection may appear at first glance, there is a true fraternal link, both in subject matter and technique, between the vocal polyphany of 'The Idea of North' and 'The Latecomers', and the chromatically concentrated counterpoint of the quartet. Let me caution you that 'The Idea of North' is in glorious mono only, while 'The Latecomers', on the other hand, which involves a great deal of multi-liner vocal activity is best served by stereo speakers set well apart.

I am not sure whether this helps or, indeed, supplies the sort of information you were after but I do want to wish you great success with your thesis and, in the meantime, all best wishes.

Sincerely,
Glenn Gould

P.S. Do please give my best regards to Prof. Gingold.[5]

[1]A fan.
[2]Recorded in 1960, String Quartet Op. 1 (Columbia).
[3]"Radio As Music" from the *Canadian Music Book*. Montreal: Canadian Music Council Journal, Spring-Summer 1971.
[4]"The Quiet In the Land" was broadcast on CBC-FM's "Ideas" on March 25, 1977.
[5]Joseph Gingold (b. 1909), Russian-born American violinist and pedagogue.

TO PAUL ELLERY[1]

354 Jarvis Street,
Toronto, Ontario.
June 17, 1972.

Mr. Paul Ellery,
Epson,
Auckland,
New Zealand.

Dear Mr. Ellery,

Thank you very much for your most interesting letter. I will do my best to answer your questions in regard to Bach, Schonberg, and the recording process – I guess the last two are really, in fact, one question. First, let me deal with the French suites because the answer is much easier to come by: Bach most certainly did write those six delightful miniatures but, so far as is known, had no hand in styling them 'suites in the French Style' or whatever. It is certainly true that as a responsible burgher of the period, Bach would have known a good deal about contemporary French culture and it is also true that on certain occasions – the 'Italian' Concerto being a notable example – he did define his musical outlook according to nationalistic assumptions of one kind or another. Most evidence in regard to the 'French' suites, however, suggests that they derived there not inconvenient title – they do, after all, through the absence of that more vigorous counterpoint associated with the partitas and perhaps also of the breadth and vigour found in the 'English' suites seem to strike a pose of Francophilia – at the whim of a publisher rather than through any design of the composer.

I cannot really provide any pat answer in regard to your question about the preparation of a recording. I have, to be sure, gone on record many times as stating my preference for those sessions to which one can bring an almost dangerous degree of improvisatory open-mindedness – that is to say, sessions in relation to which one has no absolute, a priori, interpretive commitment and in which the process of recording will make itself felt in regard to the concept which evolves. I don't want to overstate the case because, obviously, I could not in good conscience suggest that one approach any session in a state of unpreparedness. I do feel, however, that the recording is in no sense a documentary replica of the concert-hall experience and that, however planned or unplanned a particular interpretation may be, one must take full advantage of the peculiar opportunities the process itself affords. I do not, for example, agree with proponents of the 'Take one-or-bust' philosophy – artists who seem to feel that there is some inherent dishonesty in a multi-take or multi-insert approach to the creation of a musical structure. In my opinion, it is precisely through the unabashed exploitation of those assets which make recording something more than a photographic process by which to capture concert-performance virtues and liabilities that the process it-self can come into its own and make an original contribution to musical tradition.

This does not, of course, quite answer your more specific question in regard to Stefan George and 'The Book of the Hanging Gardens' et al. I absolutely agree with you that one should endeavour to bring to any recording project a backlog of period information which, by the time of the recording, will have become an almost subliminal rather than overt influence. You might be interested to know that I have just recently completed a recording of all the remaining Schonberg lieder[2] – i.e. those that were not included with our performances of opus 1, 2 and 15 issued some years back.[3] Once again, as in 'The Book of the Hanging Garden' the soloist for almost all of the material on the disc was Helen Vanni and some of it, particularly the superb collection of eight songs, opus 6, represents, in my opinion, the very highest level of Schonberg's pre-atonal accomplishment.

I am delighted you enjoyed the seven talks with NZBC[4] relayed some years ago. They, in fact, derived from a series of 21 programs prepared for CBC in 1969[5] and, although I was aware that a third of the series had been heard in New Zealand, I never did find out which seven were involved.

Again, many thanks for your letter.

All best wishes,
Sincerely,
Glenn Gould

¹A fan.
²Songs Op. 3, 6, 12, 14, 48, recorded in between 1964 and 1971 with Donald Gramm, bass-baritone; Cornelis Opthof, baritone; and Helen Vanni, mezzo-soprano, was released in 1972 on Columbia.
³Recorded in 1964 and 1965, with Donald Gramm, bass-baritone; Ellen Faull, soprano; Helen Vanni, mezzo-soprano. Released in 1966 (Columbia).
⁴New Zealand Broadcasting Corporation.
⁵"The Art of Glenn Gould."

TO DRS. S. BROWN AND J.G. HILL

354 Jarvis Street
Toronto, Ontario
August 31, 1972

Drs. S. Brown and J.G. Hill
C/O Brown's Animal Hospital
Don Mills, Ontario

Dear Drs. Brown and Hill:

I want to thank you very much indeed for your special kindness with regard to the stray dog which Mrs. Widman¹ brought to you last week. As you probably know, I turned to Mrs. Widman in the hope that she would be able to place the animal in a suitable home and, as I gather is her wont, she came through in remarkably short order.

It's most encouraging to know that there are people like Mrs. Widman who, quite literally, devote their lives to improving the lot of the animal kingdom and, since I understand from her that you took a special interest in the dog and were more than generous with your time in relation to its care, I do want you to know how very grateful I am.

All best wishes.

Sincerely,
Glenn Gould

¹Gould was referred to Mrs. Lillian Widman, a local animal lover, by her brother-in-law Harry Mannis, a staff announcer at the CBC, after Gould found the stray dog wandering on Jarvis Street near the CBC. Gould had taken the dog to his parents but it posed several problems, first trying to sleep on his mother's bed and, later, attacking a neighbor's child. Because of the latter incident the dog ended up in the Scarborough pound for a two-week quarantine, and Gould wanted to have it released to a good home. (Eventually Harry Mannis took the dog.)

TO JAMES E. JONES[1]

Jarvis Street
Toronto, Ontario
September 12, 1972

Dr. James E. Jones
St. Peters, Missouri

Dear Dr. Jones:

Thank you very much for your letter of July 27, and for your kind comments about my Bach recordings, and my apologies for the delayed reply. I'm sending along under separate cover a photo as you requested.

I do appreciate your interest in my current attitude in regard to public performances. I'm afraid, however, obstinate as it may seem, that it has changed not a whit for well over a decade and, quite frankly, in view of my very time-consuming interests in radio television and film as well, of course, as recording per se, I simply cannot conceive of any situation which could induce me to trod the boards again.

I realize, of course, that for many people – particularly for those of the older generation (I had occasion last year to interview Arthur Rubinstein[2] and he simply could not understand my attitude toward the concert as a medium) – contact with an audience is an indispensible component of their performing craft. In my own case, I confess it was never so; at best the presence of the audience was a matter of indifference; at worst, impossible to reconcile with the essentially private act of music-making. In my opinion, music is much more cogently and creatively served by the recording studio or via any medium which permits one the luxury of second-guessing, so to speak, the interpretive decision. Obviously, film does this, as does radio and television and, for that reason, I've directed my activities toward those media exclusively.

Again, many thanks for your letter and best wishes.

Sincerely,
Glenn Gould

[1] A fan.
[2] Polish-born American pianist (1887-1982). The interview appeared in *Look*, Vol. 35, no. 5, March 9, 1971.

TO BRUNO MONSAINGEON[1]

354 Jarvis Street
Toronto, Ontario
November 12, 1972

Mr. Bruno Monsaingeon
Paris, France

Dear M. Monsaingeon:

Many thanks for your letter of September 26 and for the outline enclosed. I feel that it summarizes most accurately the enormously enjoyable discussions which we conducted in August and, at this point at least, I really have no major alterations to propose.

I would like to suggest, of course – but I am sure you have already borne this in mind – that we continue to leave certain options open in regard to the specific repetoire involved. Quite apart from the already agreed-upon options available – the substitution of one Bach overture for another, etc. – I do feel, for example, that we should not be too firmly tied down to the inclusion of any one major excerpt – i.e. the Chopin B Minor, the Beethoven Op. 106, the Schoenberg Op. 25, etc. – but, rather, should continue to develop our thoughts about the primary points of view to which we seek to give expression and leave the repetoire examples as presently noted as indicative of our overall intention toward the shape of the program rather than as a specific commitment to it.[2] (I have, for example just in the past week, agreed to prepare for release next September a record of my own transcriptions of Wagner excerpts – 'Prelude to Meistersinger', 'Siegfried Idyll', 'Prelude and Liebestod'[3] – and it is possible that we might get some additional use of that material in the context of one or other of the programs). I am sure, indeed, as the year goes on, that other 'off-beat' items may turn up as well and such possibilities alone augur a relatively flexible repetoire outline for the tri-partite series.

I've given some thought to the not inconsiderable problems involved in the translation of the commentary, and/or discussion sequence, into Franch. As you will recall, during your visit to Toronto, we seemed to feel that the obvious strategy would be to record all such conversations in English, have them translated as quickly as possible, and to put them up on the tele-promptor for my benefit, accordingly. The problem with this approach is that it assumes that I can become proficient with the niceties of the language virtually overnight and, although, as I indicated to you, I can read it quite adequately, I think, I should much prefer to have a substantial period of time with which to become familiar with the material and, consequently, be able to deliver it, despite the inevitable reliance on the telepromptor, in an almost improvisatory fashion.[4]

My proposal, then, in regard to the language problem, is this: that at some point prior to your visit, we map out major conversational areas and that, based on the questions which you would like to discuss with me, I draft, in English, a dialogue for the two of us, accordingly. I realize that, generally speaking, scripted dialogue of that kind will have a stilted, laboured quality and will not reflect the spontaneity which we would like to inject into these programs. I have, however, had so much experience in drafting dialogue of a similar nature for radio documentaries in this country – dialogue which virtually defies the listener to bet against its having been created at the moment – that I am absolutely confident this system would work and that, with a French translation returned to me, for example, several weeks in advance, my own security with the language would benefit enormously.

Just last month, for example, I scripted a 45 minute mini-documentary – nominally, on the subject of competitive athletics (to which I stand in determined opposition needless to say) but, in fact, using that subject as a metaphor by which to explore the competitive aspects of our society as a whole.[5] If you're curious about the degree of spontaneity which one can inject into a program by the approach I have outlined, I'd be happy to send you a tape of the program (and a copy of the script too, if you would like one) and you can judge for yourself the effectiveness of the approach. In any event, I do feel that it would make a tremendous difference in relation to our project, and I'd be most interested to have your reactions.

Let me say again, however, that I was absolutely delighted that the general outline you submitted so accurately captured the 'feel', so to speak, of the entire project as we hatched it in Toronto and I am looking forward to it with real enthusiasm. I must apologize, by the way, for not having as yet rounded up the various materials which I promised you. I will make a real effort to do that in the coming week and will get them off to you as soon as possible.

Again, many thanks for your letter and all best wishes.

Sincerely,
Glenn Gould

[1]Producer of television programs in Paris, Monsaingeon enjoys an international reputation for his music programs concerned with such artists as Gould and Menuhin.
[2]Gould is writing about a television series that Monsaingeon was planning with him for the ORTF, the acronym used for the French national broadcasting system at that time. It was called *Chemin de la musique*, and included Gould's commentary as well as performances. Of the works mentioned, only the Suite for Piano, Op. 25, by Schoenberg, was included.
[3]Recorded in 1973: "Siegfried Idyll," "Dawn," and "Siegfried's Rhine Journey" from *Gotterdammerung* (Columbia); *Die Meistersinger* Prelude (Columbia). These transcriptions by Gould were not included in the television series.
[4]Eventually the attempt to get Gould to speak French was abandoned and a French translation of his text was used.
[5]"The Scene" was broadcast by CBC Radio on October 7, 1972.

TO KIMIKO NAKAYAMA[1]

354 Jarvis Street
Toronto, Ontario
November 12, 1972

Miss Kimiko Nakayama
Dusseldorf
Germany.

Dear Miss Nakayama:

Thank you very much for your letter of September 26,[2] which was forwarded to me, and particularly for your very kind and interesting comments.

Needless to say, I am delighted to learn that my Bach recordings are of particular interest to you but, as you quite rightly imply in your letter, it is exceedingly difficult to analyze the interpretive facets upon which one attempts to focus when dealing with any particular repetoire and even more difficult, of course, to attempt a correlation between one's philosophic outlook and the manner in which that outlook assumes musical representation. Quite frankly, I feel that the questions you raise are of such complexity that one would have to deal with them at much greater length than any one letter would permit.

I think, however, that it is possible to isolate certain factors which may have some bearing on my attitude toward the interpretation of Bach's music. One such, certainly, is the lack of instrumental discrimination, so to speak, which Bach exhibits. As you know, a great many of his works are almost interchangeably felicitous when on the harpsichord, organ and, though some would disagree, on the contemporary piano, and I do believe that this instrumental indifference plays an important part in helping us to achieve sufficient freedom so as to articulate our perhaps quite specialized views of his music without embarrassment. In other words, and in contra-distinction to music of the late 19th century, for example, where a very detailed notational style and a very specific instrumental predilection was built in to the creative concept, the music of Bach, in particular, because of its curious combination of structural precision and improvisatory options, encourages one to invest it with aspects of one's own personality. Needless to say, those aspects must be, to some degree at least, harmonious with the basic philosophic and/or religious outlook which permeated much of Bach's music, as well as with the specific contrapuntal design with which all of it was invested.

In regard to this latter facet, I think that it would be fair to say that contrapuntal manifestations in all forms have always held a particular fascination for me and, in recent years, indeed, I have produced a series of radio documentaries – the majority of which have nothing at all, in terms of subject matter, to do that music – in which the multi-voice aspects of baroque and pre-baroque polyphony are applied to the human voice rather than to musical instruments. For example, one such program, 'The Idea of North' – which was about the experience of life in Arctic isolation – opened with a segment in which three characters – not actors it should be added, but rather people who had allowed me to interview them about their life in the north – were permitted to speak – via multi-track tape techniques, of course – more or less simultaneously and to form, in that segment, what would in musical terms, and specifically 'baroque' musical terms, be referred to as a trio-sonata. I cited that as but one example – not by any means the most complex from my documentaries – to suggest that perhaps the sense of linear independence, of simultaneous motivic impressions, has played a particularly important role in my life and in my relationship to music and that, just as in a fugue where the solidity of the structure contracts, as I suggested already, with the improvisatory nature of the interrelationship between the voices – i.e. with the way in which, without damaging or compromising the structure one can illuminate, draw from context, so to speak, individual strands and thereby emphasize that peculiar dichotomy mentioned above – that the possibility for linear invention in the recreation of a work is unquestionably one of the aspects of late baroque literature which particularly fascinates me.

I am not really sure whether this answers your question adequately – as I suggested, to do full justice to it would require a much greater digression – but, in any event, I do hope it helps and do wish to thank you for your letter once again. All best wishes.

Sincerely,
Glenn Gould

[1] A fan.
[2] In her letter Nakayama writes, "I hear something 'dämonisches' (demoniac), something 'übermenschliches' (superhuman) in your music, which I have, so far, never found in any other person's."

TO J. STEPHEN POSEN[1]

GARFIELD, GARFIELD, GARFIELD & GRUBB
Barristers and Solicitors
10001 Galaxy Place
Alamagoro, New Mexico
November 30, 1972

Mr. J. Stephen Posen
C/O Minden & Gross
Toronto, Ontario, Canada

Dear Mr. Posen:

We take pleasure in enclosing a cheque from our client, Mr. Glenn Gould, in the amount of one thousand, three hundred and ninety-two dollars ($1,392.) in regard to your services re his recent exposure to and via Universal Pictures. By consulting those files to which our client repeatedly, selflessly, though regretfully, with but scant success, has commended your attention on several occasions, you will discover that the enclosed amount represents a lesser sum than that submitted according to your invoice – the discrepancy being, in fact, the amount of two dollars and thirty-five cents ($2.35).

This amount is withheld by our client as an act of conscience. Mr. Gould is prepared to testify that he has repeatedly urged against your intellectual – and in view of the merits of the work under discussion, we apply the term loosely – involvement with the novella, Slaughterhouse Five, hereinafter referred to as 'the property'. Ceaselessly, tirelessly, and at great personal cost, our client has devoted many hours of his immensely valuable time in an attempt to dissuade you from any perusal of the aforementioned 'property'. His attempt to preserve the moral integrity and, if we may so express it, essential innocence of your relationship with the 'property' above mentioned having met with no success, our client must now exercise his remaining prerogative – the withholding of any reimbursement relative to your purchase of such property.

Should you wish a precedent in law for the action herein defined, we would direct your attention to the judgment of June 18, 1972, as handed in the case of Lin vs. Lum during the assizes of the County Court, Bangkok – Judge Lae Chin-Ho presiding. As you are undoubtedly familiar with this landmark decision, we need only remind you that the plaintiff Lin had claimed, from the guardian of the defendant Lum, payment plus compound interest for a transaction involving the sale of a quantity of hashish made available to a ward of the said Lum and possession of which had been expressly forbidden to the aforementioned ward by his guardian. In sum, the lengthy judgment avowed that, although the substance in question was not per se illicit within the jurisdiction represented by the court, it was nonetheless incumbent upon the court to base its findings upon that code of ethics which determined the personal and spiritual jurisdiction of the defendant.

We feel confident, dear sir, that the parallel, while not in every respect synchronous with the case at hand, will not be entirely lost upon you. We are further convinced that, through the exercise of proper discretion you will not elect to puruse this matter further and that, in perpetuity and throughout the Universe, you will renounce all rights, claims, liens and attachments upon our client in this matter.

Yours very truly,
J. Henry Garfield III[2]

---

[1]Gould's lawyer.

[2]This humorous letter refers to the film *Slaughterhouse Five*. Garfield is, of course, a Gould pseudonym, based upon the personality of Harry Garfield of Universal Studios, with whom the contract for the filmscore was negotiated and who became affectionately known between Gould and Posen as "Harry Baby," in the true Hollywood tradition, because Garfield persisted in calling Gould "Glenn Baby."

TO PETER SYMCOX[1]

354 Jarvis Street
Toronto, Ontario
December 10, 1972

Mr. Peter Symcox
C/O Canadian Broadcasting Corporation
Montreal, Quebec

Dear Peter:

Many thanks for your kind note and for the most intriquing enclosure.[2] Needless to say, it was a joy to meet you at last and I am very much looking forward to our Schoenberg project next fall. I do hope that, well in advance of the taping, we can plot the visual and narrative aspects of the program in some detail; for the moment, however, I thought it might be helpful to get down on paper some of the musical ideas we discussed.

As I indicated during our conversation in Toronto, I do feel that a most revealing approach to Schoenberg's formative – i.e. pre-atonal – years would be via the lieder route. As you know, on our local project which deals with musical events in the first decade of the century, I'm using Scriabin preludes – some 9 or 10 of them, interspersed with commentary – to suggest something of the momentum involved in that composer's experiments with extended tonal fields. I think that we could define much the same sense of progression vis-a-vis Schoenberg through a judicious selection of lieder chosen, for example, from opera 2, 3, 6, 14 and concluding, perhaps, either with a representative sampling of the George lieder, opus 15 (which, along with the opus 11 piano pieces represents his first plunge into atonality) or, since the latter work is a cycle and on that account, less than ideal for purposes of illustration, the two posthumously discovered lieder (without opus number) the most adventuresome of which has a superb text by Rilke. In any event, I think that half-a-dozen of such songs would reveal very clearly the extent of the post-Wagner influence on Schoenberg's early career and – in the case of the George lieder or the posthumous songs – convey as well his first tentative rejection of the post-romantic milieu.[3]

Since your Toronto visit, by the way, I have secured the Webern transcription of the Chamber Symphony, Opus 9 and it is, I think, a remarkably successful adaptation as well as a work which I should very much like to tackle either with a string quartet or, in its alternate version, with a flautist and clarinetist substituting for violin and viola respectively.

I do feel, however, that, apart from its undeniable value as a novelty, it would take approximately ten minutes longer than the collection of songs suggested above to establish Schoenberg's niche in the post-Wagnerian world and would not reveal the varieties his reaction to that background at all – The Webern transcription, in short, would make it much more difficult for us to set the stage for Schoenberg's ultimate rejection of tonality and, in addition, would tend to bind us to a pictorial situation from which, for at least half the program, there would be no real escape. The songs, by comparison, if you so desire, could be interspersed with commentary, accorded visual supers, and would, in every respect, offer a more flexible and instructive introduction to the program.

As I indicated in Toronto, and always assuming that we move chronologically, the middle segment of the program could then be devoted to solo piano works. In my opinion, the most colourful and most successful work Schoenberg penned for the instrument is the Suite, opus 25 – also, incidentally his first full-fledged 12-tone composition – and it could well serve as centrepiece for the program. Since it is, unashamedly, a collection of baroque dance movements, it also manages to underline the degree of miniaturization for which Schoenberg's first twelve-tone efforts were notable.[4] Should we wish to stress this point even more emphatically – i.e. the fact that, with the initial rejection of tonality came a period of profound doubt and depression which, in turn, resulted in works of extreme compression, even atomization, of thematic material – we could also include some or all of the six miniatures, opus 19. In fact, this might not be a bad idea, in any case, since, although like Pierrot Lunaire and, as a determined anti-Stravinskian, I would have to add, 'LeSacre," opus 19 is certainly one of the linch-pins of history – works more important for the results they engendered (op. 19, I think, a direct descendent of the Boulezian experiments with timbre, etc.) than for any intrinsic merit they possess.

It occurs to me that, perhaps in some very informal way, it might be appropriate, during the middle third of the program or thereabouts, to indicate via a series of very brief examples, the alternative contemporary aesthetics which Schoenberg, for one reason or another, rejected. We could, for instance, do a quick tour around Hindemith, Stravinsky, etc. and, just to keep some sort of perspective, could even introduce in contradistinction to the incessantly evolving Schoenbergoan esthetics, the essentially non-evolving but, in my view, every bit as valid, aesthetic of Richard Strauss.

It's fascinating to conjecture that, in the very year when Schoenberg, in exile, was writing his most vehement protests about war in general, and Hitler's in particular, Strauss was concocting, for the Munich operas the gentlest and most disengaged of all his theatrical works, Capriccio. In short, while all such examples are just that – examples – and many other equally successful antitheses could be found, it is, I think, important to convey some sense of chronological perspective, if only to avoid the really unworkable notion that Schoenberg's was the one true way and that all those who did not, while his contemporaries, see the light, were heretics accordingly. I think that the great advantage of doing a Schoenberg program now as opposed to, perhaps, twenty years ago is that, whereas, at that time, one was, to some extent, in the position of the theorists of Shaw's[5] day – the Shaw of the 90's that is – for whom Brahms and Wagner represented an either/or proposition, so much has happened in the twenty years

187

since Schoenberg's death – not least the 'happening' itself – that we are now, I think, able to make clearer and more balanced assessments as to the real value of his work without allowing partisan positions to cloud our judgment.

The reference above brings me to my suggestion for the program's conclusion – the Ode to Napoleon.[6] Having offered all the arguments I could think of during your Toronto visit as to why it almost never comes off and, in particular, having suggested something of the casting problem involved with the role of the sprechstimme, I still think it's a – or perhaps the – logical conclusion to the program and I would like another go – my 5th, actually – at solving the problems involved. I do feel that if we were able to secure the services of the Orford Quartet[7] – assuming, of course, that they would be amenable to the idea – we could prepare the instrumental contribution literally months in advance so that, as a totality, it could take on the plasticity of a conventional chamber music get-together and, with that secured, add the narrative contribution accordingly.

Form the point of view of his previous involvement with the work, I would have to opt for John Horton who recorded it with me in 1965,[8] though, as I indicated, the recording was rather more deliberate and literal in terms of the deployment of the voice than I should have liked. On the other hand, we are by no means committed to an Anglo-Saxon as narrator though, since the text is by Byron we are, of course, committed to someone with at least, plausible English. Is there, perhaps, someone in French-Canadian theatre with both musical and dramatic experience in more or less equal proportion? In any case, it's an avenue we could perhaps explore at a later date, keeping Horton in mind as possibly the most likely candidate.

Do forgive me for rambling as though this project was a fait accompli – there are many ways to make a program by Schoenberg. This is only one of them, and I am most eager to get your reactions to it – I did feel, however, that it would be helpful to get something down on paper so that we can proceed apace with our plans.

All best for now. I look forward to hearing from you.

Sincerely,
Glenn Gould

P.S. I am sending, as I promised, under separate cover, the recently issued Handel Harpsichord disc.[9]

[1]CBC television producer, Montreal.
[2]No enclosure found.
[3]Gould included four of the *Eight Songs*, Opus 6, No. 1, sung by Helen Vanni in a television program aired on February 20, 1974 in the "CBC Musicamera" series. It was called "Music in Our Time," No. 1.
[4]The Suite Opus 25 for piano by Schoenberg was a work championed by Gould. In 1974 he included it in a telecast for the French state broadcasting organization, the ORTF, produced by

Bruno Monsaingeon as part of a series called *Chemins de la Musique*, and again in the "CBC Musicamera" series on November 26, 1975, in a program called "Music in Our Time," No. 3.

[5]George Bernard Shaw (1856-1950).

[6]Another Schoenberg work championed by Gould.

[7]The Orford String Quartet, a Canadian ensemble founded in 1965, disbanded in 1991.

[8]Gould recorded the *Ode to Napoleon Buonaparte*, Opus 41, by Schoenberg in 1965 with the Juilliard String Quartet and the Canadian actor John Horton as speaker.

[9]Suites for Harpsichord Nos. 1-4 (Columbia) recorded and released in 1972 (CBS).

TO H.A. OVERHOLTZER[1]

354 Jarvis Street
Toronto, Ontario
December 17, 1972

Mr. H.A. Overholtzer
Dundas, Ontario

Dear Mr. Overholtzer:

Thank you very much for your letter, for sending along a copy of your transcription of the Bach Chaconne, and my apologies for the delayed reply.

Let me say, first of all, that I find it, on balance, an extremely skilful adaptation and I do hope that it will eventually find its way to publication. As you perhaps know, I have certain reservations about the whole question of the transcription as a genre. I suspect that these reservations stem from my youthful organ-playing days when, from all sides among my conservatory colleagues, I found myself inundated by piano transcriptions of organ works which I had every reason to believe should remain the property of that instrument.

In recent years, however, (perhaps I've mellowed a bit) I find myself, though still wary, somewhat more amenable to the process as a process. A few years ago, I recorded the Liszt transcription of the Beethoven Fifth Symphony[2] and, although I have great admiration for Liszt's boundless ingenuity, I did learn from that experience a sort of lesson in reverse. I suspect that my exposure to Liszt's transcription technique was not unlike your own to that of Busoni – i.e. that Liszt, even as Busoni, was at once too exploitative and too literal. There are, for instance, many occasions in his transcription of the Beethoven Fifth, and indeed of the other Beethoven transcriptions which I have seen but not recorded, when, in order to faithfully reproduce, for example, material consigned to the double bass or tympany, Liszt compels the pianist to present this material in the least ingratiating registers of the keyboard, and often via rather hackneyed means (tremolandos, et al).

With this in mind, the only suggestion that I feel qualified to offer in regard to your own transcription is that, on a few occasions, you could perhaps delete one

189

or two notes so as to clarify the textures accordingly. A few of these situations related to questions of leading-tone resolution, a few others to octave-doubling and, needless to say, in many such cases, a simple arpeggio would remove the burden of the parallelism. In any case, I hope you won't feel that I'm being hopelessly puritanical with suggestions of this kind since, in all other respects, your transcription impresses me as a work of great quality.

Allow me, however, just in relation to the first page or two, to illustrate the type of situation to which I alluded above: in the first brace, bar 4, I feel that the third beat should either be arpeggiated in a bottom to top fashion, or be deprived of the alto C sharp. Similarly, in the first bar of brace 2, I feel that in the A-E-A combination in the left hand, the parallel move of both A's to D's in bar 9 could be circumvented either by an arpeggio (which would probably have to be imitated by the first beat of the bar in the left hand, as well) or, could profit by a withholding of the upper A in the left hand until the third beat and the subsequent deletion of the tenor D in bar 9. In bar 16, I suspect that the G to E parallelism might cause a problem (although I'm less certain about this one because of the nicely imitative motion of the G to F in the tenor at the bar line) and, if so, A could possibly substitute as a dotted quarter in the tenor at the second beat.

As you will notice, all of these very minor objections fall essentially within the same category of observation, and all of them could be alleviated by a lute-like approach to arpeggiation throughout the work. Indeed, even if questions of octave doubling etc. were not involved, I would recommend this – if not as a written down formula then certainly as an ad libitum suggestion to the per-former – since this approach to keyboard sonority inevitably helps to spread the sound and to simulate the rather tinsel-like clarity which, rightly or wrongly, we associate with the baroque.

One last point will perhaps help to clarify this approach to the work. It seems to me that in bars 33 through 35 the parallelisms between left and right hand will cause trouble in direct proportion to the characteristics of the instrument on which it is played. On a well regulated, carefully voiced piano, it should be possible to articulate the progression as written. I suspect, however, that on the great majority of modern pianos, which are neither well regulated nor care-fully voiced, you will find that less duplicative information (or, once again, the arpeggiated alternate) will help to create a more genuine baroque ambience.

As I mentioned above, I realize that many or all of the points raised stem from what may very well be a needlessly puritanical and, indeed, idiosyncratic approach to the keyboard. Since, however, you did ask for my suggestions and since I do feel that your approach to the Chaconne is a very vital and dynamic one, I did feel that these minor points might merit some consideration.

With all best wishes.

Sincerely,
Glenn Gould

[1]A fan.
[2]Recorded in 1968, Beethoven Symphony No. 5 in C minor, Op. 67 (piano transcription by Franz Liszt) (Columbia).

UNKNOWN[1]

[c. 1972]
YAMAHA DRAFT

Dear Miss *** _____

Thank you very much for your letter and for your kind comments about my recordings etc. and my apologies for the delayed reply.

I'm afraid that my contact with the Yamaha piano has been very minimal, indeed. As you perhaps no, I have played the Steinway exclusively for many years and, consequently have very little opportunity to evaluate other instruments. I have, on one or two occasions, see Yamaha pianos in studios at the C.B.C., but my impression was that these instruments were not intended for concert use and it would be most unfair to judge the quality of the Yamaha product as a whole by that yardstick. Quite recent, indeed, a very celebrated jazz pianist, Bill Evans,[2] was giving a concert in Toronto and mentioned to me that on several recent occasions he had played and was enormously impressed by the Yamaha instruments.

You also asked about my preferences in regard to pianos generally, and while I have no reluctance whatever in replying to the question, I am sure you realize that any such response is a very subjective matter and that the piano which might, for whatever reason, recommended itself to me, would be of no interest to every bit a [blank] and vice versa. In my own case virtually all of the recordings which I have made subsequent to 1960 have been done on the Steinway piano originally built in the late 1930's, and redesigned to my specifications in 1960 – perhaps to be more accurate, I should say, redesigned over a period of years beginning in 1970. For many years prior to that time, I had felt that the instruments which were most congenial to me personally were those built during the 1920 and 1930's and for that reason whenever possible I tried to select for my concerts and recordings instruments of that period. It was, however, not always possible to do so and eventually having experimented with many different action systems, I came to the conclusion, that whatever the piano the one tendency of pianos build in America – and, to some extent in Europe as well – in the last 25 years – which I absolutely abhor, is the tendency to increase the draft of the key – i.e. the distance which the key is permitted to follow when struck – and much – possibly out of some search for a larger or more brilliant tonal quality had displaced many of the peculiar

191

virtues of pianos built in the preceding decades. In my own case I prefer an instrument which is regulated with a touch-block of a slightly shallower than average measurement partly because, assuming all the correltive factors such as after-touch etc. are accounted for, it does, generally speaking, increase ones control over the instrument and provides a more precise and usually more even tonal quality. Needless to say the compensatory adjustments relative to this draft decision are of supreme importance but, all else being equal, it is possible, I think, to generate via the piano an almost harpsi-cord like clarity of sounds which, particularly for music of the 17th and 18th centuries is appropriate now.

I think I should point out that the fact that I no longer give any live concerts whatsoever and am exclusivel6 involved with recordings, radio recitals, television concerts and films, necessarily plays an important part in assisting me to arrive at the preference which I stated above. Or, perhaps, to reverse the example, one might say that the proliferation of large concert halls built in recent years has encouraged the opposite tendency – i.e. the design of an instrument which, though it may possess enormous potentials of senority [sic] and project those qualities with great vitality, doesn't, in my opinion, begin to match for precision a delicacy the much more subtle instruments which are designed 30 or 40 years ago.

In any event, the instrument which I presently use though built at that period has been, of course, totally reconditioned, and it does, I feel, combine the best of both worlds. I do hope that this helps to answer your question and again my thanks for your letter.

Sincerely.

[1]This letter was obviously dictated by phone to Gould's typist, a practice that became a part of his work methods. Although the correspondent is unknown, and the letter is clearly a draft, Gould's comments on the draft of piano keys, and other matters, are of sufficient interest to warrant inclusion.
[2]Bill Evans (b. 1958), American tenor and soprano saxophonist as well as jazz pianist.

TO VIRGINIA KATIMS [1]

354 Jarvis Street
Toronto, Ontario
January 20, 1973

Mrs. Milton Katims
Seattle, Washington

Dear Virginia:

Many thanks for your note of December 10 which reached me via a rather roundabout route – hence the delayed reply. Needless to say, I've kept in touch with Milton's wonderfully inventive activities with the Seattle Symphony via the press and, in view of his extraordinary endeavours on behalf of music in that area you really should not feel 'isolated' in any way. I still remember our performances together[2] with the greatest of pleasure and regret that we never did manage to bring off our Brahms quintet performance.

Now then: allow me to come to the point about your cook book. I simply cannot imagine what 'recipes' you have from me for inclusion in it, and have absolutely no recollection of the 'personal anecdote' to which you refer. I do have a vague recollection of a conversation with you on the general area of culinary pursuits, but I couldn't possibly have contributed any original recipes – it is, I suppose, possible that I cribbed some from friends or family – for the simple reason that, in the best Anglo-Saxon tradition, I'm almost totally indifferent to the process of eating and, quite frankly, can just barely manage to open cans. Furthermore, my basic attitude toward food is that it's a time-consuming nuisance – I have, by the way, become virtually a vegetarian in the past decade – and I would be only too delighted if one could effectively sustain oneself with all necessary nutritional elements by the simple intake of X capsules per day. I realize that this sounds forbiddingly ascetic, but it's a fair reflection of my attitude toward the subject, and I beg to request exclusion from your volume accordingly.

Needless to say, however, I wish you all the best with it and I do hope that my inability to participate will not involve you with layout problems, etc.

My very best to Milton, and, of course, to you.

Sincerely,
Glenn Gould

[1]Virginia Katims, wife of the conductor of the Seattle Symphony Orchestra, Milton Katims (b. 1909), American conductor and violist.
[2]Gould and Katims performed together in Montreal on October 30, 31, 1956, Bach's D minor Concerto and Richard Strauss's *Burleske*. They repeated the same program in Vancouver on February 24 and 25, 1958, and in Tacoma, Washington on February 26, 1958.

TO ELVIN SHANTZ[1]

354 Jarvis Street
Toronto, Ontario
January 20, 1973

Mr. Elvin Shantz
Kitchener, Ontario

Dear Mr. Shantz:

As you may have heard from Prof. Epp, I would very much appreciate the opportunity to tape an interview with you for a C.B.C. documentary project on which I have been engaged for some time.[2] It concerns the Mennonites, most of the interview material was acquired in Winnipeg last year but, due to complications induced by the C.B.C. engineers' strike, it has not as yet been edited as a finished project.

In November, I taped two services at the Mennonite church in Waterloo which will be used as a kind of background material for the program and, on that occasion, had hoped to obtain an interview with you as well. I mentioned this desire to Prof. Epp who suggested that Sunday afternoon following the service might be appropriate but, when I was unable to reach you by telephone on the Sunday in question, had no alternative but to release the crew at 3:00 P.M.

Needless to say, I take full responsibility for this oversight. It was extremely foolish of me not to have called you in advance and to have made specific provision for a particular taping period. In any event, I did want to tell you about the project and I would be most grateful if you would agree to grant us an interview for inclusion in it.

I should point out that this program will not, unlike many others which have been done about various Mennonite communities, be unduly concerned with the purely historical aspects of the evolution of those communities. Inevitably, the history of the communities – the sense of transience, of the threat of materialism, of one's relation to the state, etc. makes itself felt, but what I hope to achieve, primarily, is a 'mood-piece' – a radio-essay dealing with the degree to which, as one of my interviewees put it, the Mennonites are able to remain "in the world but not of the world". It is, in short, a reflective and, I believe, rather poetic program and, if it succeeds, will, I hope, capture the atmosphere of the Mennonite communities and the life style of the peoples involved more faithfully than any recitation of historical facts possibly can.

I do hope that you can see your way clear to give us an interview. If so, and if you can give me a choice of dates when you might be available, I can make the necessary bookings for a technician's services accordingly. I do look forward to hearing from you, and in the meantime all best wishes.

Sincerely,
Glenn Gould

[1] A member of Ontario's Mennonite community.
[2] "The Quiet In the Land."

TO JOHN P.L. ROBERTS

354 Jarvis Street
Toronto, Ontario
January 28, 1973

Mr. John P.L. Roberts
C.B.C.

Dear Mr. Roberts:

Permit me to introduce myself: I am a young harpsichordist and, as proof of my modest ability, enclosed a critique of my disc debut. You may well ask, dear sir, how I, an unknown, was selected for the signal honour of a C.B.C. recording. The reason, though I shall endeavour to spare you the more tiresome fiscal details, relates, alas, not to my artistry – if I may so term it – but to my citizenship. Although a long-time resident of Canada, I am officially 'registered' – to borrow maritime jargon – as an Andorran, and the unusual circumstances surrounding my harpsichord debut were brought about through the intercession of my great-aunt, Elspeth-Yvonne who, for many decades, as you perhaps know, has been an intimate of His Serene Highness, the Grand Duke Willibald-Christoph.[1]

Due to a balance-of-trade deficit incurred when the U.S. Central Intelligence Agency refused re-imbursement for some 120 Andorran passports – the production of which constitutes the major industry of my country – on the unlikely pretense that the essential, if invalid, data contained therein was obscured by goat-milk stains, Andorra achieved an all-but-insurmountable national debt of $223.20. (Perhaps I should point out that Andorran passports, at bulk rate, are valued at $1.86 (U.S.)). Although the C.I.A. refused compensation for what it unfairly described as 'damaged goods', the U.S. government was understandably anxious to avoid an international incident which, in all probability, would have resulted in an armed clash and involved the full might of the Andorran military and, therefore, at the inventive suggestion of aunt Elspeth-Yvonne, the undersigned was engaged to commit to disc, on behalf of the U.S. firm, the aforementioned repertoire described in the enclosed brochure. (In a calculation typical of American Economic Imperialism, it was reckoned that, even if the record failed to capture attention, and consequently royalties, in any foreign market, it would as a mandatory purchase for all Andorrans, recoup the sum above-mentioned before first pressing).

In any event, dear sir, I have no wish to fatigue you with the details which surrounded the production of the disc in question. The burden of this memorandum, rather, is simply to bring to your attention the fact that, as a long-time resident of Canada, my abilities on the harpsichord have gone entirely untapped by the moguls of the Canadian Broadcasting Corporation. Aunt Elspeth-Yvonne has addressed herself to this subject in several recent, and remarkably heated, letters to the undersigned and, in order to redress this sad state of affairs, is threatening a state visit to Canada during which, I fear, her penchant for publicity, as well as her capacity to maintain hungerstrikes in the doorways of government buildings for protracted periods, could not but cause you, dear sir, and your esteemed associates, considerable embarrassment and inconvenience.

It occurred to me, therefore, that in order to forestall her proposed visit, you could, by way of concession, present the undersigned in a series of harpsichord recitals before campus audiences across the country. It is my understanding that the C.B.C. music department sponsors a series of so-called 'Celebrity Recitals' at such campuses, although I have been told that the normal allocation is one such event per artist. However, I feel confident that, with an international incident at stake, with aunt Elspeth-Yvonne's dictum that 'once a celebrity, always a celebrity' in mind, and particularly, in view of my own profound belief that, however expertly manufactured, the recording is but a pale and artificial memento of the concert experience,[2] you will see fit to revise your policy for this occasion and to provide me with a suitable and extensive itinerary accordingly.

Finally, may I add that, although my prime loyalties are, of course, to the culture of Andorra, and although it would be tempting indeed to prepare a program consisting exclusively of music by Andorran composers, I am given to understanding that, in this country, you observe a rather quaint custom known as 'Canadian content'. I should like you to know, therefore, that, in view of this regional peculiarity, I am prepared to forego my own repetoire predilections and, where necessary, to amplify my instrument accordingly. Indeed, out of respect for local sensibilities I have, in fact, prepared a program which opens with my own harpsichord transcription of Oskar Morawetz'[3] First Symphony, continues with a similar transcription of Healey Willan's[4] Second Symphony and, as a grand finale, and utilizing the full range of electronic capabilities at my command, concludes with a superimposition of the two compositions which, if I may modestly say so, includes many unique harmonic effects.

To meet the needs of this repertoire, I have arranged to project the harpsichord sonorities with an SAE 5000 watt quadraphonically-energized RMS linear-phase amplifier (as approved by the E.B.U.) and to channel the sound in four-point super-acrylic woofers and .0075 extended tweeters with cast-aluminum acoustic-lenses for 90° high-frequency dispersion in circular symmetry. These latter speakers, of my own design, (patents pending) will be known as 'Voice of the Stadium' and have already received the Stanley Horobin[5] 'Seal of Good Studio-Keeping'.

I trust, dear sir, that this program proposal will merit your enthusiastic approval and look forward to an early reply from your office. Rest assured that, upon its receipt, I shall forward a copy of your reply along with a placative memorandum of my own to aunt Elspeth-Yvonne.

Yours most sincerely,
G. Herbert Gould

c.c.: Mr. Carl Little

[1]Gould had an irrepressible sense of humor. This parody is reminiscent of the film *The Mouse that Roared* in which Peter Sellers played the female role of an imperious but lovable monarch of a small country that inadvertently came into possession of the "Q Bomb."
[2]The opposite of Gould's true view.
[3]Czech-born (1917) Canadian composer.
[4]Healey Willan (1880-1968), English-born Canadian composer, organist, conductor, and educator.
[5]CBC radio engineer.

TO WILLIAM CLARK[1]

Mr. William Clark
San Diego, California

354 Jarvis Street
Toronto, Ontario
February 14, 1973

Dear Mr. Clark:

Thank you very much for your letter of January 1 which was forwarded to me by Columbia Records just last week, and thank you also for your kind comments in regard to my recordings. I would be delighted to take a look at your music and if I can, to make some relevant comments in regard to it.

I feel I must tell you, however, that I have always had serious doubts about the validity of the sort of judgmental practice which you propose. Basically, I am convinced that one must, of necessity, be one's own best critic and that one should, in fact, be rather wary of any opinion from other sources. I realize, of course, that this goes entirely against the grain of academia – but then so do rather a lot of the odd beliefs that I hold – but I do feel quite convinced that one's creativity is enhanced primarily by the more-or-less single-minded pursuit and development of one's own resources without reference to the trends, tastes, fashions, etc. of the world outside. In any event, if you will accept as a guiding premise this somewhat iconoclastic view and, consequently, the slightly reluctant spirit in which I enter into the enterprise at hand, I will be happy to take a look at your work and to offer whatever useful comments I can.

All best wishes.

Sincerely,
Glenn Gould

P.S. Unfortunately, my 'Quartet' was deleted from the catalogue several years back and, I rather doubt that you could locate it in any conventional over-the-counter sense. It may, however, turn up, as similar bits of esoterica occasionally do, on one of those 'remaindered' lists of somewhat elderly recordings that Columbia publishes from time to time.

[1] A fan.

TO MADAME PABLO CASALS

Mme. Pablo Casals
C/O Dr. Fuhrman
Kew Gardens, N.Y.

354 Jarvis Street
Toronto, Ontario
June 14, 1973

Dear Mme. Casals:

I a writing to you at the suggestion of Mr. Frank Solomon and, needless to say, in regard to my documentary project about Maestro Casals for C.B.C. Radio. As I mentioned when we met at Marlboro last summer, I'm an incorrigibly slow worker, but I'm happy to be able to tell you that the bulk of the editorial work on the program is now complete and, if all goes well, I should be able to finish the project within the next few months. (No air-date has been set, as yet, but I expect it will be premiered during the late fall or early winter months of the coming season).[1] My final 'mix' for the project has been tentatively scheduled for a 2-week period in early August but, while all other ingredients are at hand – stimulating interviews with Mr. Kahn,[2] Mr. Galimir,[3] and with a group of young participants in the Marlboro Festival, not to mention the interview with Maestro Casals,[4] I am in urgent need of one additional component for the program, and hence the present note.

As you know, I want to include many of Maestro Casals' recordings within the program and, of course, drawing upon his enormous discography, this augurs an embarrassment of riches. In one area, however, I am at something of a loss: we have devised a scene within the program in which each of the participants comments specifically about Maestro Casals' rehearsal technique and, in particular, about his rehearsals at the Marlboro Festival. The scene as presently constituted occupies about 12 minutes of the hour-long program and, hence, despite the illuminating comments which give rise to it, it is essential to include some excerpts of actual rehearsal sequences at Marlboro or elsewhere. Mr. Solomon has told me that a substantial archive exists vis a vis the Marlboro sessions but that (a) it will be necessary to obtain the permission of the Musicians' Union in order to utilize musical excerpts and (b) Maestro Casals' permission in order to utilize his comments as represented on the tapes. Negotiations with the Union may be a bit awkward, but Mr. Solomon has very kindly offered to approach them on my behalf. First, however, I must have Maestro's permission to make use of the tapes – (needless to say, only 'dubs' will be required; I realize that the originals must remain in the Marlboro archives). I suggested to Mr. Solomon that, if you so desire, I could prepare a draft of all of Maestro Casals' rehearsal comments which I would like to include in the program and submit it to you for Maestro's approval.

In any event, I will endeavour to reach you by phone during your New York visit in regard to this matter since, quite frankly, I feel that its inclusion is essential not only to the structure of the program but, more important, to an accurate portrayal of Maestro Casals' musical personality, and I very much hope that we can have your permission to make use of it, however selectively.

Do please give my warmest greetings to Maestro Casals and, of course, all best to you.

Sincerely,
Glenn Gould

---

[1]"Pablo Casals: A Radio Portrait," a radio documentary created and produced by Gould, was broadcast on "CBC Tuesday Night" on January 15, 1974.

²*Pablo Casals, Joys and Sorrows*. Reflections by Pablo Casals as told to Albert E. Kahn (New York: Simon and Schuster, 1970).
³Felix Galimir (b. 1910), Austrian-born violinist and teacher.
⁴Excerpts from rehearsal sequences at Marlboro with Casals were included in Gould's documentary.

TO MARGARET IRELAND NAGEL[1]

354 Jarvis Street
Toronto, Ontario
June 14, 1973

Mrs. Margaret Ireland Nagel
New York City, N.Y. U.S.A.

Dear Margaret:

Many thanks for your note, and my apologies for the delayed reply. You are, believe me, terribly missed chez C.B.C. and I do hope that if any of your documentary endeavours bring you up this way in the near future – and I gather that you have several irons in the fire that just might – that you will give me a call.

I would also like to expose you to a TV program which we have just finished and are in the process of editing – an audio-visual essay on the music of the first decade of the 20th century which we have called 'The Age of Ecstacy'.[2] The repertoire is Scriabin, Debussy (my first, and quite possibly last, exposure to M. Claude's oeuvre), Schonberg and Berg. Through the magic of chroma-key and some ingenious deployment of a clavi-lux light-machine during certain of the Scriabin Preludes, Mario Prizek[3] has, I think, come up with some stunning visual comments on the music of the period. In any case, I'd love to show it to you and, if you think the Bizet[4] made for a good guessing game, just wait till I try out a tape we have just finished editing on you! I shall say no more; if sufficiently intrigued, you might even come to Toronto.

All best for now.

Sincerely,
Glenn Gould

¹Canadian pianist, formerly producer at CBC Toronto.
²"The Age of Ecstasy, 1900-1910," broadcast on "CBC Musicamera" on February 20, 1974.
³Canadian TV and film director, producer, writer, and video-director, Prizek joined CBC in 1951. He directed and produced "Glenn Gould/The Well-Tempered Listener" for CBC-TV in 1966 and "Glenn Gould Plays Beethoven" in 1970.
⁴Gould recorded Georges Bizet's *Nocturne* and *Variations chromatiques de concert*, 1971-73 (Columbia).

TO JOHN CAGE[1]

354 Jarvis Street
Toronto, Ontario
October 10, 1973

Mr. John Cage
C/O Artservices
New York, N.Y.

Dear Mr. Cage:

I have been asked by the Canadian Broadcasting Corporation to prepare a centennial documentary on the life and times of Arnold Schonberg.[2] Some years ago, I worked on another Schonberg documentary which took care quite efficiently of the figures and facts relevant to his life and, on this occasion, I would like to move rather farther afield and explore the cultural climate in which he lived and worked in as much detail and from as many vantage-points as possible.

I know that your own feelings about Schonberg are perhaps rather ambivalent but, without wishing to cast you in the role of devil's advocate, I do feel that your views about him, as man and musician, would be of inestimable value to the program. I hope, therefore, that I can persuade you to grant me an interview for it in which we could utilize C.B.C. studios in New York. I should point out, however, that, in the past, I have had surprisingly good results with studio-to-studio type interview – i.e. interviewer in one city, interviewee in another – and that, consequently, if your schedule makes a New York visit inconvenient we could certainly set up something of the sort with the help of an obliging affiliate in some other city.[3]

Since we hope to launch this documentary on an unsuspecting public during the late spring of 1974, I would like to have the bulk of the interviews under wraps not later than January, if possible, and I would therefore appreciate it very much indeed if you could advise me as to your schedule at your earliest convenience.

I do hope that you will be able to take part and look forward to the opportunity of chatting with you.

All best wishes.

Sincerely,
Glenn Gould

---

[1]American composer (b. 1912).
[2]"Arnold Schoenberg: The First One Hundred Years, A Documentary / Fantasy" for CBC Radio was broadcast on November 13, 1974.
[3]Gould's interview with Cage was conducted by telephone.

TO THOMAS FROST[1]

354 Jarvis Street
Toronto, Ontario
October 10, 1973

Mr. Thomas Frost
C.B.S. Records
New York, N.Y.

Dear Tom:

Herewith the information I promised in regard to music clearance for the Schonberg documentary.

As you know, it will include, as have most of my major programs on musical subjects, an almost seamless tapestry of sound – not only the sound of Schonberg's own music but also that of various of his compatriots – and, in discussion with the copyright clearance office at C.B.C., I discovered that, although we have no problem in clearing any of this music for broadcast exposure in Canada, the problems of clearance are greatly magnified when we consider the possibility of foreign distribution in general and European on distribution, in particular. As I believe I mentioned on the phone, it may be necessary, in certain instances, to receive the express permission of the artist(s) involved in various recordings in order to make use of the program in certain foreign markets. The problem is an urgent one because the European Broadcasting Union have expressed great interest in it and this, of course, would involve its distribution to all of the major markets in Western Europe and, because of their affiliate status, in the Iron-Curtain countries as well. Moreover, the Berlin Festival have asked for the rights to it during their proposed homage to Schonberg in the fall of 1974, and I expect that there will be other uses of that kind in addition to more conventional broadcast situations.

For this reason, C.B.C. have suggested that I try to at least simplify the problem of copyright clearance in advance wherever possible. Needless to say, at this stage, I am in no position to choose the works involved or the interpretations of them but, when we discussed this program in terms of its European usage recently, it was suggested that we could at least avoid one major obstacle by endeavouring to compose the entire musical backdrop from the catalogue of one company and by having the permission of that company so to do in advance. (I realize, of course, that in markets in which the permission of the artist is also a factor, the individual concerned would still have to be approached in regard to their specific participation.)

The proposition, then, is simply this: since, in all probability, we could manage to concoct the entire musical track from records currently or formerly available on Columbia, we would very much like to have the advance blessing of C.B.S. for the project – it being understood, needless to say, that such permission does not, in any way, infringe upon the rights of the artist concerned in regard to those jurisdictions where artist-permission is specifically required.

I do hope that you can persuade Business Affairs to give me 'blanket endorse-ment' in regard to your product for this documentary since, quite frankly, the only alternative would be to concoct a supplemental version for foreign usage, which, given the sort of documentaries that I try to make, would, putting it mildly, be a nightmare.[2]
All the best for now.

Sincerely,
Glenn Gould

[1]Producer with CBS Records.
[2]This letter is concerned with trying to overcome the obstacles of copyright for recordings suitable for use in Gould's second radio documentary on Schoenberg, "Arnold Schoenberg, the First One Hundred Years."

TO PETER MUNVIES[1]

354 Jarvis Street
Toronto, Ontario
October 27, 1973

Mr. Peter Munvies
C/O R.C.A. Records
New York, N.Y.

Dear Peter:

Long overdue thanks for the superb 'care package' which you forwarded some weeks back. You're fortunate indeed to have access to two such superb string quartets, and I do wish we could lobby with the powers that be for a collabora-tion with the Guarneri at some point in the future.

I have also asked for a 'care package' to be forwarded to you. As I think I mentioned, I'm rather pleased with the results of the Wagner transcription disc and, since I suspect you are a died-in-the-wool Wagnerian, as I am, hope you like it as much as I do. (I must warn you, however, that the italics re my interpretation of the 'Siegfried Idyll' are very much on 'Idyll' and not on 'Siegfried' – i.e. it is probably the most stately rendition since Knappertsbusch;[2] I've always felt that the piece has an indigenous languor which the 'ruhig bewegt', or whatever, in the score does not adequately delineate.) I think you will find, however, that my tempi for Meistersinger and Rhine Journey are almost alarmingly conventional.

In any event, do let me hear from you soon and all best wishes.

Sincerely,
Glenn Gould

[1]Recording executive.
[2]Hans Knappertsbusch (1888-1965), German conductor.

TO CANADIAN RADIO-TELEVISION &
TELECOMMUNICATIONS COMMISSION

110 St. Clair Avenue West
Toronto, Ontario
C.R.T.C.   February 3, 1974
C/O M. Guy Lefebvre
Ottawa, Ontario

Dear Sirs:

I write in regard to your forthcoming deliberations re the license-renewals of
C.B.C. It occurs to me that the prodigious activities of the Corporation vis-a-vis
Canadian society are, in the main, so very familiar (though, I am bound to add,
so frequently misunderstood) that no words of mine are necessary in order to
persuade you of the inestimable value of the Canadian Broadcasting Corporation to the cultural life of our country.

I do feel, however, that, while various aspects of the arts in Canada are the
beneficiaries of the concern and goodwill of many organizations, both public
and private, the C.B.C.'s quite singular role is to provide an overview of the
interrelationship between society and the arts and, above all, to be concerned
not only with the present status of that relationship – which concern has already
established the Corporation as the nation's most enterprising and resourceful
entrepreneur of talent in the arts – but to be involved as well with the documentation of its history and with the contemplation of its future.

In this regard, I fear, on occasion, that in demographic terms, the enormous
impact of television (which, let me add, I would not for a moment denigrate)
tends, nevertheless, to overshadow, for substantial segments of the public, for
media-analysts, and, perhaps as a by-product of these not uninfluential factors,
for many program directors themselves, the remarkable, indeed unparallelled,
achievements of C.B.C. radio. I would hope that, whatever the outcome of your
deliberations, the C.B.C. will be encouraged to vigorously maintain its creative
path in radio – which remains, in my view, at least, the most direct, most
intimate, and most compelling vessel for the transmission of arts programming,
in general, and the presentation of music, in particular.

Yours sincerely,
Glenn Gould

TO PAUL MYERS

March 11, 1974

Mr. Paul Myers
c/o CBS Records
London, England

Dear Paul:

First of all, long over-due congratulations to you and to Mary on the arrival of
Opus 2. I trust that Nicholas has already bypassed the customary out-of-joint-
nose-stage and has now become John Paul's most devoted PR man.

I'm terribly sorry that we failed to make contact at convention-time last summer, and I do hope that if your itinerary brings you anywhere close to Toronto, you will keep me advised. It would be marvelous to see you again and to hear about your plans, short-term, long-term and, indeed, middle-term, as well.

Earl Price forwarded a pink slip, which I gather functions as a communication from Mr. Walker[1] to his agents in the field, in regard to the February release of our WTC, Volume I.[2] Reading between the asterisks, I gather that 'R and R'[3] were ever so slightly enthusiastic (I trust, sir, you'll notice the subleties of understatement which I adopt when addressing myself to a U.K. audience) and, needless to say, I'm delighted that the English market is now only nine years in arrears in regard to our product.[4] But seriously, I am, naturally, very pleased about its reception. Neither of the magazines has arrived here as yet, but I shall keep a watch for them and would be delighted to learn of whatever future plans Mr. Walker may have in store for his audience, once such minor matters as minority government and economic holocaust have been put to rights.

I do want to tell you about a series of four films[5] which we have recently completed for O R T F. The over-all theme of the quartet was music and technology, though Item 1, being a complete performance of the Bach E Minor 'Partita' was by way of an overture and the remaining programs, utilising a music-to-talk ratio of approximately 2 to 1, allowed us to improvise rather casually, upon what were originally, at least, some rather carefully structured topic outlines.

In any event, I have rarely been so enthusiastic about a work in progress. Being film, rather than video-tape, I cannot, of course, speak for the quality of the 'rushes' which are only now being assembled in Paris. But if I can judge by a Nagra's-eye-view[6] of the proceedings and by the conviction that every member of the crew seemed possessed of a quite remarkable expertise, I suspect the end-product will quite possibly be the best piece of film with which I have ever been involved and, I will, of course, keep you advised as to O R T F's plans for it. It could, indeed, be shown in any English market since they plan to use sub-titles in France.

I would also welcome the opportunity to screen for you a program called 'The Age of Ecstacy'[7] – the first of six CBC (Video-tape) 'specials' with which we survey the 20th century, decade by decade. Given the limitations of video-tape, it was, I think, the most affective mating of music and camera we've managed to date and, in the case of the later poems of Scriabin, which were backgrounded with chroma-keyed light-sculptures – especially prepared by an artist in New York who vigorously avoids all psychedelic implications – some of the most effective television I've ever seen.

I do hope that you will find yourself headed in this general direction in the not-too-distant future so that I can try out some of these extravaganzas on you. In the meantime, do keep in touch and all best wishes.

Sincerely,
Glenn Gould

[1]Robert Walker was Head of Classical Marketing in the London office of CBS Great Britain.
[2]Recorded in 1962. J.S. Bach, *The Well-Tempered Clavier*, Book I: Nos. 1-8, BWV 846-853 (Columbia, released in North America in 1963).
[3]The now defunct publication *Records and Recording*. It had published a review of *The Well-Tempered Clavier* containing mild praise.
[4]In the 1960s and 1970s Gould's recordings were not well received by the British musical press. When Myers arrived at CBS Records in London in 1968 he found that not even half of Gould's recordings had been released in Great Britain. With help from Bob Walker, Myers set about changing this situation. Advertising was undertaken and Myers wrote an article on Gould for the *Gramophone*. In spite of these efforts, the British were slow to accept Gould as an international recording artist.
[5]Produced by Bruno Monsaingeon.
[6]The Nagra was a highly regarded portable tape recorder often used by radio and television journalists.
[7]"The Age of Ecstasy, 1900-1910," broadcast on "CBC Musicamera" on February 20, 1974.

TO ROBERT WALKER

354 Jarvis Street
Toronto, Ontario
April 11, 1974

Mr. Robert Walker,
C.B.S. Records,
London, England.

Dear Mr. Walker,

Thank you so much for sending along the most handsomely produced double-set of the '48', Book 1.[1] Earl Price had already forwarded to me the dealers' advisory which you had sent out some weeks back and, as I mentioned in my recent letter to Paul Myers,[2] was, needless to say, delighted to learn of its reception in the U.K. and, of course, to learn from your letter that Volume II will follow in due course.

Having taken note of the enclosed clipping from Hi-Fi News, and, in particular, of the rather oddly phrased paragraph in that article, I think it should be pointed out that we cannot, in fact, take credit for the rather extravagant post-production processes which they attribute to us. As you know, the only way in which their description of such post-production techniques could be made accurate would be to certify that, subsequent to its U.K. release, the original master had been subjected to an elaborate process of equalization, etc. I have not, as yet, had the opportunity to listen to the disc enclosed, but I am quite sure that, as Paul who was, after all, the producer of Volume I, would testify, no such shenanigans took place.

In a way, I find myself in a rather ambivalent position since, ideally the post-production ingenuity with which they credit us is, in my view, the prerogative of the record producer and artist. Further, their reviewer has undoubtedly taken note of various of my own comments to the effect that the piano used in all my Bach recordings has been 'harpsichordized' and is not aware that the same piano has been used for Prokofiev, Scriabin, Bizet, Hindemith, et al without alteration but that, indeed, the 'harpsichordizing' was simply my way of characterizing a rather unique keyboard sound attained through various manipulations of the action.

So, as I say, I feel rather ambivalent about the matter. On the one hand, the recording philosophy which they attribute to us is, however, anti-realistic, a technique highly responsive to the demands of the recording medium but on the other hand, none of the elaborate processes which they assume would have enabled us to achieve the sounds in question were, in fact, employed.

I leave the matter to your very good judgment; perhaps the most judicious option would be to ignore the matter altogether.

Again, may I thank you for your letter, for the album enclosed, and all best wishes.

Sincerely,
Glenn Gould

[1] J.S. Bach, *The Well-Tempered Clavier.*
[2] See Gould's letter of March 11, 1974.

TO HENRY-LOUIS DE LA GRANGE[1] June 13, 1974

M. Henry-Louis de la Grange
Paris, FRANCE

Dear M. de la Grange:

Thank you so much for your last letter and most particularly for your kind comments about the Beethoven and Wagner discs.[2] Needless to say, I'm enormously pleased that you enjoyed them.

I did want to tell you that, earlier today, we assembled the 'fake' version of our conversation which will be the feature of the 5th program in my 10-week Schonberg series.[3] As you may remember, this is the segment in which, because of the deficient line quality on the day of the interview, we took the New York sound and interpolated my questions plus appropriate 'um' and 'ah' – type responses. Moreover, we managed to do this while locating you at approximately 10:30 o'clock on the stereo screen and positioning my voice at approximately 1:30. The result, miraculously, is a totally spontaneous conversational segment; even though I was absolutely confident we could bring it off, utilizing that technique, I simply had no idea just how well it would work. We are doing a final mix on the show next week and I will then make a dub for you consisting of all the conversational portions of it (as you know, the major musical item was

Barbarolli's recording of 'Pelleas', so that our conversation which precedes it is, in turn, preceded by a five or six-minute interlude in which the 'back-up' announcer, my co-host for the series, Ken Haslam, and I are all 'supered' over a sound-track consisting of approximately four minutes from Ein Heldenleben and two minutes from the Mahler C minor symphony. It is, needless to say, a deliberately 'nutty' segment, but it is, I think, an amusing sequence, especially since a good deal of the interview segment consists of your none-too-enthusiastic views regarding the character of Richard Strauss. In any event, I'm delighted with the way the segment has turned out, and I do hope you'll enjoy it.

As I think I may have mentioned at the time of our various phone conversations, I have yet another use in mind for a certain portion of your interview and that, of course, relates to the much more 'impressionistic' documentary which I have not as yet begun to script, but which is due on air in November and which will, in effect, be a compilation of excerpts from all the interviews previously prepared for the weekly series – plus a few others such as one with Ernst Krenek to be taped later this month, which will not be ready in time for the series per se. In the documentary I propose to 'super' various comments over a non-stop backdrop which will consist, not only of Schonberg's music but of the other 'musics', so to speak, that surrounded him throughout his life. I tried a somewhat similar maneouvre with a documentary on Stokowski several years ago, and can only hope that this one will not become distracted from its subject by the studio techniques at hand. Needless to say, I'll also get you a dub of the documentary when we're finally ready to spring it on an unwary nation.

I do hope that all is going well with Volume II and that your Summer Festival plans (which sound fascinating, by the way) come off on schedule.

All best wishes for now.

Yours truly,
Glenn Gould

[1]French musicologist and Mahler specialist. He is the author of *Gustav Mahler*, vols. 1-3 (Paris: Fayard, 1979-84).
[2]Beethoven Sonatas No. 16 in G major, Op. 31, No. 1; No. 17 in D minor, Op. 31, No. 2 and No. 18 in E^b major, Op. 31, No. 3, recorded for CBS, issued in October 1973. "Piano Transcriptions of Orchestral Showpieces" by Richard Wagner were transcribed by Gould. They included *Die Meister-singer*: Prelude; *Gotterdammerung*: Dawn and Siegfried's Rhine Journey; Siegfried Idyll, recorded in 1973 for CBS. In a letter dated May 1, 1974 de la Grange writes, "I am deeply impressed by the Wagner transcriptions and the Beethoven Opus 31s, amongst your most impressive achievements to date."
[3]Broadcast on the "Music of Today" series on CBC Radio, October 9, 1974.

TO ROBERT CHESTERMAN[1]

June 28, 1974

Mr. Robert Chesterman
c/o Canadian Broadcasting Corporation
London, England

Dear Mr. Chesterman:

Thank you very much for your letter of June 18, and for telling me about your most fascinating project.[2] Needless to say, I would be delighted to see the Stokowski material become part of the project and, always assuming the Maestro's blessing, you're most welcome to make use of it.

I think that, especially since I've long admired your very incisive and particularized interviews with other conductors, I should perhaps offer a bit of background in regard to the deliberately defocused compot which resulted from my interview with Maestro Stokowski. Originally, I had been promised two, three-hour sessions with him and was then asked to share said sessions with the cameramen of NET who were anxious to record as much voice-over material and to shoot as many cut-aways as possible for a documentary on his life and times which they had underway at that time. To make a long story short, Stokowski never quite got used to the idea that my audio needs were utterly different from those of the television program and, since the NET crew insisted on blowing the fuses in his apartment on an average – and I'm not exaggerating – of once every half-hour, and since Stokowski clearly became fatigued toward the end of both sessions, I wound up, in fact, with a grand total of 50 minutes of more-or-less usable material, of which, as you know, approximately 25 minutes found its way into the program itself. When I began to realize that I would not have the opportunity to question him extensively about matters musical, I deliberately set out for a mood-piece and gauged my questions accordingly. I attach this preamble by way of suggesting that, if the material is used in your book, perhaps an editor's note, or something of the sort from you, could convey the rather off-beat ambiance which resulted in the documentary. Certainly, in terms of the somewhat impressionistic result I was after for purposes of radio, I was more than happy with Stokowski's responses. I do feel, however, once again with reference to the particularly incisive questioning to which you've subjected many of the other conductors, that the rather subdued atmosphere of the Stokowski commentary does deserve a footnote.

One last point – a point which I rather hesitate to put into a letter – but here goes: Stokowski has never heard the documentary and I would ask you to go to whatever lengths are necessary to ensure that he does not. This was/is no perverse whim on my part – rather the result of an exchange of letters between Stokowski and CBC Publications who were anxious to issue it as a disc and secured all necessary releases from the record companies involved, but who felt that Stokowski should know in full detail the musical selections chosen to represent his work. His response, without having heard the end result, was that he did not approve of the montage as a documentary technique (these were, perhaps, not his exact words, but it's a reasonable paraphrase).

I found the whole episode (a) amusing, in view of the Maestro's fondness for concocting symphonic syntheses etc, and (b) ever so slightly infuriating. In any event, I have subsequently been advised by several quite eminently-qualified Stokowski watchers in New York that he has, for reasons perhaps best known to himself, a fondness for the "you-make-your-move-then-I'll-make-my-move" type of negotiation and the best advice I could obtain in regard to a discographic future for the documentary was to avoid, at all cost, his direct encounter with it. I was not able or willing to undertake a re-mix and I thought it advisable not to have anything in writing whereby he had offered, as his opinion, the fact that this should be done.

I would suggest, indeed, that in approaching him, and in requesting permission for the use of his voice-track material, you might emphasize that this derived from the interview which CBC undertook in collaboration with NET. I'm sure you will appreciate the diplomatic niceties involved and I look forward to a report on your encounters with him. He's really a very dear gentleman, but he is, after all, a nonagenarian, and one must make allowances.

Do keep in touch. All best wishes.

Sincerely,
Glenn Gould

[1]A radio producer with CBC Vancouver, Chesterman was spending a year in London.
[2]The project was to compile a book of conversations with "distinguished podium figures." Chesterman wanted to include Stokowski's comments from the broadcast Gould had prepared. The book was published as *Conversations with Conductors* (London: Robson Books, 1976).

TO JOHN CAGE

354 Jarvis Street
Toronto, Ontario
July 2, 1974

Mr. John Cage
c/o Performing Artservice Inc.
New York, N.Y.

Dear Mr. Cage:

Just a note to say how very delighted I am with the results of our interview of last Thursday. Your contribution had a most remarkable spontaneity and I'm very grateful, indeed, that you would take time and trouble to participate in our documentary.[1]

In the fullness of time, a grateful Corporation will undoubtedly bestow upon you its usual, miniscule, honorarium, but before that depressing communication arrives, I did want to tell you that a quick check of the just-arrived tapes has more than confirmed my enthusiasm re our conversation.

Again, many thanks and all best wishes.

Sincerely,
Glenn Gould

[1]"Arnold Schoenberg, The First One Hundred Years."

TO GERALD POCOCK[1]

July 6, 1974

Rev. Gerald Pocock
St. Mary's Hospital
Montreal, P.Q.

Dear Father Pocock:

Thank you very much for your letter – indeed for both your letters – and, in particular, for your very kind comments about my recordings[2] and about the "Age of Ecstasy".[3] I am sorry that you were not able to see it in colour since, particularly in the case of the Scribin offerings, the lighting effects were designed to augment the musical architecture (I'm not sure that 'architecture' is quite the right word for a composer who ended up employing one chord ad infinitum, but you know what I mean). You might be interested in a program which we have just completed, and which will be aired, I believe, next January, called "The Flight From Order".[4] It deals with the second decade of the century and features excerpts from Schonberg's "Pierrot Lunaire", Stravinsky's "L'Histoire du Soldat", Strauss' "Ophelia Songs", etc. Curiously enough, your suggestion re Oscar Peterson[5] arrived very shortly after a program proposal of that sort was relayed to me via a CBC executive. It was not, in fact, the first such proposal. Indeed, I seem to recall that, as far back as the late 1950's, Patrick Watson[6] who, at that time, was on staff at CBC, was investigating similar possibilities and, if I'm not mistaken, the proposal came to naught at that time because of Mr. Peterson's schedule. Then, as now, I yield to no one in my admiration for his extra-ordinary ability at the piano. I have always felt that his pianistic gift is most exceptional indeed extra-ordinary and, within the limits of my appreciation for jazz, have listened with great enjoyment to his work for many, many years.

Those limits, however, have not appreciably increased in recent years, and I now feel that the essential ingredient for music on camera is a mutual enthusiasm shared by all parties on hand and that, consequently, this particular mix would not produce the most efficacious result. I would, of course, differentiate between a participatory program of the sort you have in mind and a straight interview-type format; I have frequently had occasion to interview musicians, the nature of whose work eludes me to some degree – John Cage, for example, contributed an interview to a Schonberg series which I have in preparation at the moment and I find that, in the role of interviewer, I'm quite unable to maintain an appropriate objectivity.

In any event, I do hope that, as a jazz enthusiast, you will not be put off by the comments above. I do, needless to say, share your sorrow in regard to Ellington.[7] He was, without question, one of the most inventive harmonists of the century and it seems to me that, at any analytical level, his work will be of interest to all musicians for many years to come.

Again many thanks for your comments and suggestions.

Sincerely,
Glenn Gould

[1] A fan letter from the Roman Catholic chaplain at St. Mary's Hospital in Montreal, Quebec.
[2] In his letter dated May 15, 1974 Pocock wrote, "Your work is a challenge that requires more than mere passive listening. I feel that you help me to grow in further appreciation of the music of each composer."
[3] From "CBC Musicamera," aired on February 20, 1974. Pocock also wrote, "I enjoyed that program more than anything the CBC (or any other network) has brought me."
[4] Also from the above series, broadcast on February 5, 1975.
[5] Canadian jazz pianist (b.1925). In his letter Pocock had mentioned his dream of seeing a National Film Board documentary featuring Glenn Gould and Oscar Peterson.
[6] CBC-TV producer at that time.
[7] Pocock wrote again on May 24, 1974 to say that Duke Ellington (1899-1974), the American jazz composer, conductor, and pianist who was a personal friend of his, had died that day.

TO BORIS BROTT[1]

August, 1974

Mr. Boris Brott
c/o Hamilton Philharmonic Institute

Dear Boris:

Many thanks for your letter and for providing more details about your most exciting plans for next session. As I indicated earlier, I will be happy to participate (given certain conditions which I set forth below) and I do hope that I can in some way make a contribution to the success of the Institute's programme.

In your letter, you referred to a series of sessions devoted to the 'Ode to Napoleon' and/or 'Pierrot Lunaire'.[2] I had not meant to suggest that we should include both works; indeed, given their respective difficulties, we will probably be lucky to do a respectable job with either. I *had* meant to suggest that my own inclination was towards the 'Ode' since you mentioned that you are quite certain of a reputable student-quartet in residence. Needless to say, an added attraction, re the 'Ode', was the employment of one B. Brott as narrator-sprechstimme – a role which would, ofcourse, be denied him in 'Pierrot'.

My feeling is that we could probably work up a decent representation of the 'Ode' given 3 or, preferably, 4 sessions with the quartet (I am assuming, ofcourse, that the sessions would be of approximately 2 1/2 hours duration). I think the most useful schedule would be one which would involve my appearance in Hamilton on a more or less weekly basis – if you would prefer to see a more incisive degree of momentum involved in its preparation we could, ofcourse, plan 2 visits per week over a 2 week span – but, to a large extent, whatever value my visits would have must relate to the amount of work that could be done in the interim and, consequently, my instinct favours a weekly get-together with the quartet and our illustrious narrator.

As you know, I have never before undertaken any role of this kind and I really feel that my presence can only of value if (a) the quartet is thoroughly rehearsed by their respective instrumental tutors prior to my first visit and (b) I can be assured that they will have made acquaintance with the score in toto and not just with their own parts. It really would be most depressing to have to encounter them, on the first occasion in what would be, in effect, a sight-reading session. I realize, ofcourse, that there will be many and varied demands on their time but I do feel that both the provisions mentioned above are absolutely essential (the score, by the way, is published by Schirmers.)

Subject to the following provisions, then, I agree to prepare a performance of the 'Ode to Napoleon' at the Hamilton Philharmonic Institute:

1. The dates involved will be confirmed by mutual consent – I have addressed myself to the question of schedule below – and the sessions will be held in late afternoons or evenings only.

2. It is understood that the Hamilton Philharmonic Institute will have no objection if I should wish to arrange for a film and/or videotape session in conjunction with one or more of the rehearsals involved. I think, frankly, that it is unlikely that I will avail myself of this provision – that it would be more sensible to see how things go on this occasion and, perhaps, if we plan some

future endeavour, to attempt a film session at that time – but I do want to keep the door open for this possibility.

3. No members of the press and no photographers will be permitted at any of the sessions without my permission; the onlookers so to speak, will consist exclusively of the active professional members of the Institute – their number not to exceed 2 dozen on any occasion – and I reserve the right to work exclusively (i.e. without benefit of any audience whatever) with the members of the quartet and the narrator at any or all of the sessions involved.

4. As mentioned above, it is understood that the members of the quartet will be given as much advance instruction in the work, from an instrumental viewpoint and by their respective tutors as possible, and that they will all have made available to them a copy of the score well in advance.

5. It is understood that a piano of my choice will provided for each of the rehearsals and I would be happy to hear from you, in due course, as to the instruments available on the premises.

Finally, the matter of dates: As I mentioned on the phone, my recording schedule during the winter months involves sessions for Columbia during the first weeks of January, February, and March respectively. I would suggest, therefore, that, assuming we opt for the once-a-week format, the sessions should be arranged so as to avoid collision with the following dates: January 4th, 5th and 6th; February 1st, 2nd and 3rd; March 1st, 2nd, and 3rd. My own preference would be for January or February (I cannot, in any event, be available in April or May) and, although I am quite prepared to accept a tentative schedule arranged to suit your convenience, I must reserve the right to substitute one or more of the dates at a later time. (I am sure you will understand that the dates listed above represent only CBS commitments and that various projects for CBC, ORFT, etc. which have not as yet been finalised, may inevitably force a change in plans.)

I do hope that you'll forgive the legalese above. Fond as I am of constructing parenthetic exceptions and exclusions, etc. I realise that you have a monumental job of organisation ahead of you in regard to the Institute's programme as a whole, and I certainly do not want to make your life more complicated in that regard. I do feel, however, that we should have all the 'yes, buts' in writing so that the project can proceed as expeditiously as possible.

I look forward to hearing from you at your convenience and, in the meantime, all best wishes.

Sincerely,
Glenn Gould

[1]Boris Brott (b. 1944), Montreal-born conductor of the Hamilton Philharmonic Orchestra at that time.
[2]In his letter of July 30, 1974 Brott asked Gould "to coach the associates on any works of your choice," while mentioning Schoenberg's *Ode to Napoleon Buonaparte* and *Pierrot Lunaire*, with himself as narrator.

TO LEONARD ROSE[1]   September 22, 1974

Mr. Leonard Rose
Hastings-On-Hudson
New York.

Dear Leonard:

Many thanks for your note. I can assure you that our disc in its various manifestations – as unedited tape, edited tape, acetate and, at last, the final product – has been at the top of my personal hit parade for many months now. The whole project was a great joy and an experience which I hope we can repeat in the future. I had already come by Isaac's[2] enthusiasm, via Walter Homburger and, needless to say, I'm delighted to learn of his PR efforts on behalf of our 'baby'.

The question of the Beethoven cycle is a complex one – certainly not in terms of any ambivalence towards the project on my part but, rather, in terms of the simple realities of my recording schedule. As you know, I have long felt that it was nothing short of tragic that you were not better represented in Mr. Schwann's directory; I believe I even urged you, during one of our first sessions last December, to think seriously about devoting as much time as you possibly could to recording your interpretation of all the major cello repertoire. I have long felt that you are grossly underrepresented on disc and that every effort should be made to remedy that situation. (I also know, ofcourse, that you endured what must have been a most frustrating experience in regard to the Beethoven project, circa 1970, and I certainly feel that all appropriate steps should be taken to get your interpretations of the Beethoven canon, in particular, on disc.)

Now for the problem: As you know, I have recorded very little chamber music – obviously not through lack of interest but, simply because our various cyclical plans have had to take priority. On certain special occasions, however, such as the Gamba project, these have been happily interrupted by collaborations of one kind or another. Primarily, these took the form of the complete Schonberg chamber repertoire (all of the lieder, etc.) and, in fact, our Bach disc is the first 'mainstream' chamber repertoire which I have committed to disc. In the more or less immediate future, however, I have agreed to do the Bach violin sonatas with Laredo,[3] the Hindemith Brass sonatas,[4] and the same composers 'Das Marienleben'.[5] This, then, totals four discs of chamber repertoire (most people take two for the 'Marienleben,' but I am determined to wedge it onto one) to which I am committed during the next two years and since, during that period, I must also complete the Mozart Sonatas, continue with the Beethoven Sonatas, and finish the Bach English Suites etc., I simply do not feel that I could handle any other major chamber project in the near future. The Beethoven cello project,[6] indeed, would obviously consist of not less than three discs (possibly four) and I doubt very much whether I could promise more than one such per year. To sum up then: I would love to do the project with you if we could do it over a period of 3 years, beginning during the season 76-77, which would mean a wrap-up date in the vicinity of 1980, and I'm not at all sure that that sort of schedule is fair to you.

My suggestion, frankly, would be for you to have a chat about the entire matter with Andy;[7] I'll be happy to confirm to him my interest in the project, given the schedule restrictions outlined above, and try to determine whether CBS would be willing to go along with so leisurely a production pace in regard to it. I certainly hope so, because I do feel it is a project that should come to pass, and I'd love to be involved in it.

All best for now,

Sincerely,
Glenn Gould

[1]American cellist (1918-84), Rose recorded with Gould in 1973 and 1974. J.S. Bach Sonatas for Viola da Gamba and Harpsichord, No. 1 in G major, BWV 1027; No. 2 in D major, BWV 1028; No. 3 in G minor, BWV 1029 (CBS).
[2]Isaac Stern (b. 1920), Ukrainian-born American violinist.
[3]Jaime Laredo (b. 1941), Bolivian-born American violinist and conductor. Bach: The Six Sonatas for Violin and Harpsichord: No. 1 in B minor, BWV 1014; No. 2 in A major, BWV 1015; No. 3 in E major, BWV 1016; No. 4 in C minor, BWV 1017; No. 5 in F minor, BWV 1018; No. 6 in G major, BWV 1019 (CBS).
[4]Paul Hindemith. Sonatas, for Alto-Horn in E♭ and Piano; for Bass Tuba and Piano; for Horn and Piano; for Trombone and Piano; for Trumpet in B♭ and Piano with members of the Philadelphia Brass Ensemble (CBS).
[5]Das Marienleben (original version) with Roxolana Roslak, soprano (CBS).
[6]In his letter dated September 13, 1974 Rose wrote, "Do you suppose you might care to record all the Beethoven piano and cello works with me?" He went on to say, "As well as the five sonatas and three sets of variations, all masterpieces, I think we should include the early horn sonata, which Beethoven himself indicated, could be performed on the cello."
[7]Andrew Kazdin.

TO SYLVIA HOCHBERG

December 6, 1974

Mrs. Morris Hochberg
Detroit
Michigan
U.S.A.

Dear Sylvia:

Many thanks for your note re 'La Valse'.[1] I'm delighted that you enjoyed the clip and I do hope that you will be able to see the programme in its entirety in February.[2] I'm afraid, however, that my general francophobia proceeds apace: actually, the current decade-by-decade television series is, if nothing else, a good training-ground since it has compelled me, for the first time in my life, to play Debussy and Ravel. But also, I must tell you, for the last time; actually Columbia have badgered me about a recording of 'La Valse' and I'm afraid that I've dug in my heels at least as firmly as when they have a similar notion some years back about one or other of the Chopin sonatas.

In any case, I had a great deal of fun with 'La Valse' because I found Ravel's own contribution[3] downright unusable for at least half its length; as you perhaps know, he simply wrote out the harmonic foundation of the piece on two conventional staves and added, as a kind of optional extra in very small print and on a third stave, most of the colouristic elements which give the piece its flavour; much of the time, indeed, there is simply no way in which one can incorporate the third-stave elements and simultaneously be obedient to the material on the primary staves. Consequently, I cleared away as much of the lower-stave underbrush as possible and incorporated as much of the third-stave material as I could – admittedly make a few discreet alterations in Monsieur Maurice's voice-leading as I went along. As I say, it was great fun, and I do hope you'll see the programme in February – the Ophelia songs of Strauss and the excerpts from Pierrot made it all worthwhile.

All best for now,

Sincerely,
Glenn Gould

[1]Hochberg wanted Gould to record his transcription of Ravel's *La Valse*, Op. 45.
[2]"The Flight from Order, 1910-1920" was aired on "CBC Musicamera" on February 5, 1975.
[3]Gould is referring to Ravel's own transcription of his orchestral piece *La Valse*.

TO ROBERT PRESTIE

December 26, 1974

Mr. Robert Prestie
Palm Springs
California

Dear Bob:

Many thanks for your note and for the invitation to sit in on Krenek's 75th. Needless to say, I would adore to be present, but what with my flightophobia and a particularly busy schedule during January, I'm afraid that won't be possible.

Has Mr. Krenek mentioned to you the invitation for a CBC concert in his honour next summer?[1] After our interview, I mentioned to the powers that be the fact that his 75th was hard upon us, and everyone in the Music Department felt that the occasion should not go unnoticed. The project has now been assigned to Larry Lake – of the department's newest but most efficient producers – and I gather that he has been in touch with Krenek by phone this past week. The general idea would be to have a representative concert of his music through the decades which Krenek himself would select and which, within the limits of his schedule, he would help to prepare. I gather from Lake that Krenek is currently thinking things over in terms of his various involvements for next summer, but I certainly do hope that it comes to pass.

I must tell you, by the way, that, although the inverview with Krenek was a great success (how could it be otherwise with so articulate a spokesman!) and made a tremendously incisive contribution to my Schonberg documentary,[2] which was sprung upon an unwary nation last month and is to be repeated in January, the audio-quality from whatever station was involved – the call letters escape me at the moment – left a great deal to be desired and, indeed, we had to virtually e q Krenek's voice beyond all reasonable limits. (As a matter of fact, if you ever come across a chap who claims patents on the definitive equalizer, I'll return the original Krenek tape as test-material non pareil.) Mind you, we've all heard of this relaxed Southern-California life-style of yours, but this was ridiculous!

One of the tape copies had a persistent whistle throughout, and unfortunately not in an area where one could equalize it away without doing damage to Krenek's voice; the other had no highs whatsoever (I suspect the alignment of the machine in question, but that's just a guess) and, as mentioned above, we had to apply massive e q at the high and an equally drastic cut at around 100 cycles. On top of that, I swear that there were, not consistently, but frequently enough to get in the way of some of Krenek's most telling points, background noises which, when I first heard the tape, I attributed to improper erasure, but which I later decided were the result of a party, if not in control-room then perhaps in the next studio. At one point, a lady was clearly heard to say "Michael, you come back here this instant" or words to that effect. There is also I must tell you, one memorable moment in which a plane appears to be coming in for a landing directly over Krenek's head. It's really a shame because, needless to say, all these extra-conversational tit-bits had to be left on the floor and, with them, many of the most fascinating points that Krenek made. In any event, the programme in its surrealistic way is a smash and I would love you to hear it sometime. The other participants, by the way, were John Cage, Erich Leinsdorf, Henry-Louis de la Grange, Denis Stevens and, courtesy of a tape from the Schonberg estate, Arnold himself.

Again, many thanks for your note. Do give Krenek my very best and, ofcourse, all best to you.[3]

Sincerely,
Glenn Gould

[1]Gould presented the idea of arranging a concert in honor of the 75th birthday of Krenek to CBC producer Larry Lake. The event took place in 1975 and was recorded by CBC Radio and produced by Lake. Krenek devised the program and conducted the works for chamber orchestra.
[2]"Arnold Schoenberg, The First One Hundred Years."
[3]In 1975 Gould was preparing a Krenek documentary for the BBC. However, he did not complete it.

TO ERNST KRENEK [c. 1975]

Mr. Ernst Krenek,
Palm Springs, Ca.
U.S.A.

Dear Mr. Krenek:

Needless to say. I very much regret, that we were not able to make contact during your Toronto visit.

I had particularly looked forward to a casual intermission – style "interview" with you, but, as Larry Lake[1] perhaps told you, the sudden death of my mother necessitated a change of schedule during the last half of July.

I have heard from all hands, about the tremendous success of the concert. Larry has promised me a sneak preview of the tapes and I'm most anxious to hear what all of my colleagues regard as the highlight of this years' CBC Festival. I gather there have been some preliminary discussions re a Toronto production of KARL 5,[2] no-one seems quite sure how best to coordinate the prospective sponsoring agents – i.e.: the University of Toronto, the CBC etc., though everyone I've talked to seems to feel that the Canadian Opera Company – which devotes most of it's time to Puccini re-runs but which, nonetheless, would be the only local organization (always excluding the CBC) capable of a totally professional production – is probably, for all the obvious reasons, out of the picture.

My own feeling is that if the project could be brought off, the most likely collaborative effort would involve a link-up between the University of Toronto and CBC television. To the best of my knowledge, no such collaboration has taken place in the past but I do think that a Canadian premiere of KARL 5 would be a landmark event and that we should all pull whatever strings are currently dangling in order to bring it about.

All best wishes
Glenn Gould

[1]CBC Radio producer and composer.
[2]*Karl V*, Op. 73, an opera written by Krenek.

TO PAUL KUHNE[1]   [c. 1975]

Mr. Paul Kuhne
Berlin

Dear Mr. Kuhne:

I cannot tell you how sorry I was to hear of the passing of Mr. Schiller,[2] but I do appreciate your letting me know. I remember him so clearly for his extraordinary kindness during my various visits to Berlin and I would ask that you extent my deepest sympathy to his family.

I regret to say that the wonderful instrument which I bought from you in Berlin is no longer in my possession. I want to add quickly, however, that my admiration for its unique qualities was in no way diminished during the time that I used it in North America. I found, however, that the specific qualities that made it so remarkable an instrument for concert use were less well suited to the recording studio. You will remember that my great enthusiasm for it was due, in large part, for the extraordinary legato quality of its sound which served one so well in a recital. The problem was that when transferred to the recording studio, especially with regard to the baroque repertoire, of which I recorded a great deal, and when used with rather close microphone adjustment such as is the North American tradition, that this same quality rather worked against the contrapuntal clarity that I wanted to achieve.

Recordings are now the main part of my activity and I have in the last couple of years made several experiments with one piano which I found particularly suitable for Bach recording. By making the key-draft somewhat shallower than customary and similar adjustments, we have, I think, achieved a rather exceptional clarity for contrapuntal styles. I am going to send to you one of our recent recordings and I hope that you will agree.

Again, thank you for writing to me, and with all best wishes.

Sincerely,

¹Paul Kuhne was affiliated with Steinway & Sons in Berlin.
²Employee of Steinway & Sons in Berlin. Initially Gould fell in love with the German Steinway mentioned. An example of its sound can be heard in his recording of the intermezzi by Brahms: Op. 76, Nos. 6 and 7; Op. 116, No. 4; Op. 117, Nos. 1-3; Op. 118, Nos. 1, 2 and 6; Op. 119, No. 1.

*TO KATHLEEN McILHATTEN*¹   January 19, 1975

Ms. Kathleen H. McIlhatten
Alexandria
Virginia

Dear Ms. McIlhatten:

Thank you very much for your letter and for your kind comments about my Brahms Intermezzi disc et al.

I do not have any plans at the moment to record any of the Wagner-Liszt transcriptions. (As you perhaps know, I did prepare a set of my own Wagner transcriptions for records in 1973,² and I elected to do that largely because I felt that the great majority of the Liszt transcriptions which I was able to see either dealt with early operatic excerpts or, in the case of the more mature works, with example which, in my opinion, do not really lend themselves to keyboard adaption – the Liebestod, for example.)

I'm sure its really just a matter of taste, but my own conviction is that, contrary to its turn-of-the-century usage, the piano is most successfully employed as a vehicle for contrapuntal, as opposed to homophonic, music and, again in my opinion, the works of Wagner which lend themselves most readily to the keyboard are those which least depend upon orchestral colour and/or in which the structural contours can be delineated abstractly as counterpoint. For that reason, I selected the 'Meistersinger Overture' the 'Siegfried Idyll' and, with some reservations, 'Dawn and Siegfried's Rhine Journey'. The reservations re the latter transcription pertain to the long-sustained 'Dawn' sequence and not to the

'Rhine Journey' per se. (You might be amused to know, by the way, that I have recently taped for TV my own transcription of Ravel's 'La Valse'.)

Again, many thanks for your letter and all best wishes.

Sincerely,

Glenn Gould

¹A fan.
²*Die Meistersinger*: Prelude; *Gotterdammerung*: Dawn and Siegfried's Rhine Journey; Siegfried Idyll (piano transcription by Glenn Gould) (CBC).

TO DAVID ROSSITER

June 26, 1975

Mr. David Rossiter
Manager, Classical Department
CBS Records
ENGLAND

Dear Mr. Rossiter:

Many thanks for your letter of May 19, and my apologies for the delay reply. First of all, my I say what a pleasure it is to greet a fellow 'flightophobic'.¹ (Does this mean that you will be lucky enough to avoid the upcoming Convention in Toronto? – I'm desperately searching for an excuse myself!)

What can I tell you about Hamilton today? Well, lacking your present age, I can't be sure how long you've been away but it's a fair gamble that you've missed the thrill of taking the Burlington by-pass minus the toll-gates which were removed a few years ago. For all cultural data, I refer you to Boris Brott who, as you perhaps know, conducts the BBC Welsh Orchestra as well as the Hamilton band.

Anyway.... I do thank you for your kind words and for the many recent releases for the UK market. Needless to say, I can't resist the invitation to nominate my own 'top 40', but I'll get to that later on, if I may.

Let me deal with the Hi-Fi News article first: I am aware of their existence, mainly because of some baroque nut who keeps complaining about my inverted cambiata or whatever but, from their representation on local news-stands, would never have guessed that they had supplanted 'Records and Recordings' in the Avis position ("We're No.2 and we try harder" and all that). In any event, "inverted cambiata(e)" notwithstanding, I'd be happy to see them run a piece – the only problem being that, with my present schedule, I couldn't possibly do an original article for them for at least 6 months and you'd like (understandably) to tie it to the Beethoven release in November.[2] Would it not be possible for them to make use of some article already circulated on this side of the water,or, indeed, one which is about to be. In next month's issue – i.e. the August issue, available here by mid-July – of 'High Fidelity' I have a piece of approximately 6,000 words called "The Grass is Always Greener in the Outtakes".[3] It is, in fact, appearing in 'High Fidelity' and in the 'Piano Quarterly' simultaneously but I retain copyright control and there would be no problem whatever about releasing it to Hi Fi News.

Whether it's the right article for the occasion is another question altogether. It is a sort of Kinsey report on the way in which people can, or think they can, identify splices. My own recordings, with on exception, provided the raw material and apart from a few general observations at the outset, it's tipped quite noticeably in the direction of statistical tables et al. The problem vis a vis the UK readership I should think, would be that it assumes rather a lot on behalf of the readership – i.e. assumes that the reader will be, in some measure, aware of my prejudices on behalf of recording techniques etc. This is obviously no problem over here since I have written frequently in related areas of 'High Fidelity' and other magazines but, since this piece simply takes for granted that the reader has encountered these notions before and uses that encounter as a launching-pad, I'm not quite sure whether it would stand on its own feet in foreign climes. In any event, I'm going to forward a xerox of a xerox to you and you can let me know what you think. The copyright, as I have indicated, is no problem and I would imagine that it or any of the other High Fidelity-style pieces would be unlikely to run into more than a very small percentage of the Hi Fi News readership who had already made their acquaintance.

Needless to say, as part of the continuing conversation of "Glenn Gould" with glenn gould" I'd be happy to tackle that elusive subject yet again. Prior to the High Fidelity "interview"[4] I did write a Glenn Gould vs. glenn gould piece about Beethoven[5] – turns out I'm not too fond of his music – which, because of its more concentrated subject, was, I think, particularly effective and which could also be available (it first appeared in the Toronto 'Globe and Mail' and was subsequently picked up by a couple of other outlets but, once again, I hold the copyright). Any original piece will however require the kind of time which I simply don't have available at the moment and I do hope that you can talk Hi Fi News into making use of an existing piece rather than waiting around for something new. I have several pieces due within the next 6 months – notably an article about Ernst Kreneks's 75th Birthday celebrations[6] and another about the theologian Jean LeMoyne[7] but I really don't think that either of those would be quite what Hi Fi News is after. Do please tell me by the way that, even if I were to do an original piece, for them I would insist upon retention of copyright and would expect to make use of it in some magazine over here.

And now to TV, film etc. The Scriabin-Schonberg reference in an earlier letter to Robert Walker, was almost certainly about a programme that metamorphosed into a musical-pictorial view of the first decade of the century and which ended up with inclusions from Berg and Debussy as well.[8] It also was the first of a projected 7-part series (3 currently in the can) which will deal with the 20th Century, decade by decade. All of these programmes are on video-tape, as opposed to film, and if one only were to be selected I would strongly recommend No.2. It was called "The Flight from Order", it was about the years 1910-1920, and it was, I think, the best musical programme on video-tape we've produced thus far. The programme (my commentary is presented between each item) consists of:

1. One of the 'Visions Fugitives' of Prokofiev;
2. Ophelia-Lieder of Strauss;
3. The first third of 'Pierrot Lunaire';
4. the last 4 segments of the L'histoire Suite and
5. My own transcription of 'La Valse'[9]

CBC plans to re-schedule the programmes once the series is completed in three years time but, there would be no contractual problem in an independent sale of one of their number – as a matter of fact, I believe "The Flight from Order" has, in fact, been sold to Germany.

As far as film ventures of recent vintage go, the most interesting project would probably be the four films made for ORTF last year and shown by them in December.[10] I haven't yet seen them, but the crew seemed to be exceptionally engaged with what they were doing and I've had very good reports from Paris. If you want to contact them directly (keeping in mind, ofcourse, that the structure of ORTF has changed in recent months) the producer was Bruno Monsaigneon and the director was Francois Ribadeau. They were, by the way, done with French sub-titles but I'm sure it would be possible for them to work from a pre-subtitled print.

Now to radio interviews. Apart from the conversations with John McClure,[11] which I am sure you know, there really is no interview of a conventional sort available. Every couple of years or so, I attempt to undertake in addition to the production of major documentaries, a short series on something or other for radio – the most recent being a 10-week survey of Schonberg – in which I act as commentator and/or co-conversationalist. In 1969, in fact, we did a 21-week series which was, in effect, a glorified discography but which allowed some leeway for zaniness and in which I was able to turn up as my own critic, variously disguised in such accents as might be appropriate to those gentlemen who co-authored the notes for the American editor of my Beethoven-Liszt 5th Symphony. (If you are not familiar with that particular cover do let me know and I'll arrange for Earl Price to send it to you.) In any case, always assuming the waiting time above-mentioned, I'd be quite willing to undertake a radio interview with myself possibly using a format that I tried out in CBS Bach Promo some years ago. In that one, I played a variety of characters engaged in a sort of 'records' under discussion format and over-dubbed until the approximate ambience of a real studio round-table discussion had been achieved. That tape, incidentally, could be obtained via Earl Price and, come to think of it, might work quite well with an appropriate explanatory set up of some kind. Its running time, as I recall is, approximately 15 minutes.

Finally, the top 40 nominations. I'm reluctant about this because I feel that you obviously are able to anticipate the unique needs of the U.K. market, not only in terms of your catalogue but other companies as well, and that I really should leave all such choices to you. However. . . . I would like to recommend to you Vol.I of the Bach concertos (alias concertos 3, 5 and 7) the Scriabin-Prokofiev disc, the Hindemith sonatas, Beethoven Op.31's ;and, whenever you think the inverted cambiata(e) specialist might be ready for it, the Mozart Sonatas, in part or in toto. In reverse order: I'm extremely biased in favour of the Mozart set (the 5th and last volume, as you probably know, is a convention release) despite, or perhaps even because of, the fact that I'm really not all that fond of Mozart. The albums have, ofcourse, raised alarm among the North American critical fraternity and I'm reasonably confident that, given the infinitely greater conservatism of their British colleagues, you'd have the scandal to end scandals on your hands, and that's why I suggested that perhaps a bit more listener-preparation is in order. In any case, in a year or so, the 5 albums will be brought together in a package[12] and I'm going to write a major essay, quite possibly using a "conversation with" form, and attempt to explain that as RVW[13] said of the 4th Symphony "don't know if I like it but do know that I meant it".

The Hindemith Sonatas are, in effect, the inauguration of a fairly extensive Hindemith campaign. We're presently at work on the brass sonatas (as a matter of fact, I'm recording the Horn sonata next week) and next year we'll do what I believe to be the first-ever recording of the *original version* of 'Das Marienleben'. I mention the Op.31 simply because I love the works and have a reasonable affection for the disc but I do realise that it may well duplicate material already in your catalogue and, quite frankly, am really not sure that the Prokofiev-Scriabin and the Bach concertos have not been released in the UK. We do expect to complete the Bach concerto set within the next year or so – a remake of No.1 which was done only in mono in 1957 and the transposed 4th Brandenburg (alias No.6) have yet to be done, and perhaps it might be more sensible to await the completion of the set. I really think that these are decisions which I should not enter into, but I'm very grateful that you did give me the chance and look forward to getting your reactions to the suggestions above. In the meantime, do let me know whether I can be of any assistance chez ORTF, CBC, or whatever, in regard to your TV plans and all best wishes.

Sincerely,
Glenn Gould

[1] An allusion to Gould's fear of flying.

[2] Beethoven, *Seven Bagatelles*, Op. 33, and *Six Bagatelles*, Op. 126 (CBS).

[3] *High Fidelity*, Vol. 25, No. 8, August 1975.

[4] "Glenn Gould Interviews Glenn Gould about Glenn Gould." *High Fidelity*, Vol. 24, no. 2, February, 1974.

[5] "Glenn Gould Interviews Himself About Beethoven." *The Piano Quarterly*, Vol. 21, no. 79, Fall 1972.

[6] "A Festschrift for 'Ernst Who'???" a book review of *Horizons Circled: Reflections on My Music* by Ernst Krenek in *The Piano Quarterly*, Vol. 24, no. 92, Winter 1975/76.

[7] "An epistle to the Parisians: Music and Technology, Part 1," *The Piano Quarterly*, Vol. 23, no. 88, Winter 1974/75.

[8] "The Age of Ecstasy, 1900-1910."

[9] "The Flight from Order."

[10] *Chemins de la Musique*.

[11] Columbia Records producer and executive, New York.

[12] Mozart, *The Complete Piano Sonatas*, including "Mozart, A Personal View," Glenn Gould in conversation with Bruno Monsaingeon (Columbia, released in 1979).

[13] Ralph Vaughan Williams.

TO PAUL MYERS

6th February 1976

Mr. Paul Myers
c/o CBS Records
London, England

Dear Paul,

First of all, let me be the first to wish you Merry Christmas for 1976 or, if you insist upon being a stickler about these things, the last to do so for 1975. When it came to Christmas-card time, you and CBS were interchangeably linked in my mind with the old Theobalds Road address and I simply could not find any current stationery which took account of the move to Soho Square. At any rate, however late in the day, the top of the Season to you.

I'm delighted to know that you'll be able to participate as interviewer on behalf of the Strauss project. Needless to say, I was sorry that we did not get a chance to discuss a 'cast-list' in more detail before you left New York (though your Mack Sennett description of those last few hours in New York was almost worth it) and I want to use this occasion to throw out a few ideas in regard to possible participants from the U.K. etc.

As you know, my major documentary pieces at CBC alternate between musical and non-musical subjects – i.e. the Schonberg centenary salute was followed by 'The Quiet In The Land' which, in turn, will be followed by the Strauss project, etc. In any event, I am less and less interested in fact-laden musical documentaries, more and more interested in creating a sense of mood and occasion,! using the subject as a springboard, so to speak. In the case of the Schonberg, indeed, I tried to alert the listener to this fact by styling it a 'documentary – fantasy'. Whether or not I do something similar with the titling of the Strauss program, I certainly mean to adopt essentially the same approach to its structure. Almost certainly it will involve a more or less seamless tapestry of sound – not necessarily only that of Strauss himself; in the case of the Schonberg program, and excluding his transcriptions of the "Emperor Waltz" and "Brahms G minor Quartet", it took me twenty-one minutes to 'set-up' the first genuine bit of Schonbergiana – the remainder of those twenty-one minutes have been devoted to an over-view of his predecessors and contemporaries – Strauss, Mahler, etc. I may or may not take the same approach in regard to the Strauss show, but the point is that, either way, it will constitute an omnipresent wall of sound upon which I will pin the comments of our various interview-guests and that, consequently, an excess of facts – the sort of thing that the perceptive listener can derive from a quick glance at Grove's – is quite lost in that sort of environment. What we need, I think, are people who are so supremely well-informed about Strauss and his period that they simply take it as read that biographical data per se is simply not needed but that their presence is useful precisely because they can, through their very secure knowledge of his life and times, comment, however, idiosyncratically, on that subject,

I think we did mention the possibility of inviting Norman Del Mar[1] and, if I recall correctly, you indicated that he is every bit as articulate in person as his books would seem to suggest. I still think it's a splendid idea and I'd very much like you to go ahead and issue the invitation on my behalf or, if you prefer, and can get me his address, I'll write directly to him and outline the project as well as your participation as interviewer. Just let me know which approach you'd prefer.

What would you think of Barbara Tuchman? She wrote – in 'The Proud Tower',[2] if I'm not mistaken – very sensitively about Strauss; in fact, if I recall correctly she used him as Leitmotif for an entire chapter. I haven't read it for some time but I recall thinking that she was bang on in all her references to Strauss though not quite so accurate when she came to talk about the Schonberg of 'Pelleas and Melisande' as an 'atonal' composer. In any event, once again subject to whatever knowledge you may have of her abilities before a microphone, I think it would be a marvelous coup to get her. (Did I mention, by the way, that it looks like I may be able to pry an interview out of the daughter of Hugo Von Hofmannstahl?)[3]

I want to keep the 'cast-list' down to a manageable level. I used only five 'characters' in the Schonberg show – Ernst Krenek, John Cage, Henri-Louis de la Grange, Erich Leinsdorf,[4] Denis Stevens[5] – and it worked out very well indeed. In the case of Strauss, I will probably go to a 90-minute format and could possibly afford six or even seven participants, but certainly not more. I also want to leave room for an idea that is still very much on the drawing-board but which might, I think, be effective – taking a group of young students and asking them what, if anything, Richard Strauss means to them. If for no other reason then their struggles to differentiate between the younger generation's distaste for Strauss and enthusiasm for Mahler (somewhat like the beat generation's adoption for Hermann Hesse and rejection of Thomas Mann) it might be a fascinating ploy.

In any case, if you are able to secure Tuchman and Del Mar at that end, I think I could fill out the rest of the 'cast-list' on this side of the water – except, possibly, for one idea which I'm almost embarrassed to mention – braced? – ready? – Ken Russell![6] I know it sounds completely nutty, and it probably is, but if only for sheer comic relief it might be kind of fun to capture him on tape. What do you think? Do you know about his conversational abilities, etc.?

Why don't I leave these three suggestions with you, give you a call in London after you've had time to make up a 'guest-list' of your own and/or investigate the availability of Tuchman, Del Mar and – dare I say it again – Russell, and we can then discuss how best to proceed. Since I can balance off the cast more effectively at this end once I know the material that is likely to be forthcoming from London, I'd prefer to wait for your interviews to be done before attempting any of my own and consequently, although we have the entire calendar year to play around with in terms of the production, I would like to get the U.K. interviews under wraps not later than May if we can.[7]

All best for now, I'll let you reflect on this a bit and contact you by phone in a couple of weeks.

Sincerely,

Glenn Gould

[1]English-born conductor and author of three-volume study *Richard Strauss* (London: Barrie, 1965).
[2]American author (1912-89) and winner of two Pulitzer Prizes. *The Proud Tower* (New York: Macmillan, 1966).
[3]Poet and librettist to Strauss (1874-1929). Gould was not successful in obtaining the interview.
[4]Erich Leinsdorf (b. 1912), Austrian-born conductor.
[5]English violinist, musicologist, and conductor (b. 1922) interviewed by Gould.
[6]Contemporary British film-maker.
[7]Gould's documentary on Richard Strauss called "The Bourgeois Hero" was broadcast on CBC Radio in two parts on April 2 and 9, 1979.

TO BARBARA TUCHMAN

MUSIC DEPARTMENT

Miss Barbara Tuchman
Cos Cob, Conn.
U. S. A.

354 Jarvis St.
Toronto
Ontario, Canada
14th April 1976

Dear Miss Tuchman:

The CBC has asked me to produce a 90-minute radio documentary on the life and times of Richard Strauss and I was wondering whether I could persuade you to participate in it. The program is not intended to be a technical study of his work but, rather, as with earlier programs on Schonberg, Casals, Stokowski etc. a 'mood-piece' in which we will attempt to capture something of the spirit of the man and of the turbulent times through which he lived. I would like to include the views of:

a) people who knew him personally;

b) younger folk who may be able to throw some light on the rather baffling matter of the disrepute into which so much of his output seems to have fallen, at least in the eyes of the musical community; and

c) people like yourself who have achieved an historical overview of his career – needless to say, I'm thinking of the extraordinary sixth chapter of 'The Proud Tower'.

We expect to have on tape in the near future the views of among others, Sir Georg Solti.[1] Rolf Liebermann[2] and John Culshaw[3] and I would be absolutely delighted if you could see your way clear to grant me an interview.[4]

My usual procedure in relation to this type of documentary production is to interview each of the participants for an hour or so – my questions being left on the cutting-room floor – and eventually put together a collage of opinion – pro, con, or, if need be, in between. We have at our disposal the CBC studios in New York and, for obvious technical reasons, I would prefer to do the interview there, but, if that is not convenient for you, I could certainly arrange to take a technician and a Nagra or whatever to Cos Cob. The program is not scheduled for broadcast until next year but I would like to wrap up all the interviews not later than this summer so that the editing and mixing can begin in the fall.

I do hope that you'll be able to take part and look forward to hearing from you.

Sincerely,
Glenn Gould

[1]Hungarian-born (1912) British conductor.
[2]Swiss composer and opera manager (b. 1910).
[3]English record and television producer.
[4]Tuchman declined, saying "I am so involved in a book on an entirely different subject that I cannot switch my attention at this time."

TO PAUL MYERS   25th May 1976

Mr. Paul Myers
c/o CBS Records
London, England

Dear Paul:
Herewith the long-delayed question-suggestions re the Strauss interview:[1]
1) The working title of the program, as I may have mentioned, is "The Bourgeois

Hero" and, consequently, I would like to explore the somewhat conflicted nature of this man who was for a good part of his life at the center of the Austro-German avant-garde and, for an even greater number of years, entirely beyond the pale in so far as his more radical colleagues were concerned. In short, I want to explore Strauss' relationship to the zeitgeist.

I know that you're well aware of my own feelings in regard to this matter; we've discussed it many times and, as I recall, our views are remarkably similar – i.e. that one should not be required to conform to the standards of one's colleagues and should be allowed to proceed according to the motor-rythms of one's own artistic conscience. In any case, for the purpose of these interviews, our views, except as a subliminal message, are irrelevant; what I do want, however, is a lively exchange of views on this subject which can be related productively to the extraordinary length of Strauss' career, the *apparent* retrogression in terms of technical derring-do, and the quiet metamorphosis of Strauss' stylistic development.

Last year, during my interview with Erich Leinsdorf for the Schonberg program, he talked about the fact that, as far as he was concerned, Strauss' autumnal works (Metamorphosen, Capriccio, etc.) do not represent the miraculous rebirth of the composer's inspiration for which they are so often given credit. He tossed this off as an aside and, since our time was very limited and the program in any case was Schonberg, I did not bother to challenge him further on the subject. Had it been a conversation about Strauss, however, I would certainly have wanted much more than just his overview of the matter – I would have wanted as much supporting evidence as he could muster ("well, they're full of cliche's, the harmonic ground-plans are altogether predictable, etc."). Certainly, many people, like Leinsdorf, do not agree with my own view of Strauss' anti-mainstream swim and, without forcing the issue upon them in any disagreeable way, I would like as much productive dialogue in this area as possible. The dialogue does not, needless to say, have to take the form of an exclusive analysis of Strauss' life and times; all the obvious historical parallels are available – Bach being perhaps the best example – and, within the context of the 20th century, one could certainly contrast the Strauss fixation on tonality with the restlessness of Schonberg, the recklessness of Stravinsky, the cabalistic caution of Webern etc. There are really endless ramifications and, eventually, one comes up against the whole question of what, if anything, society has a right to expect from an artist and other, similar, high-falutin' digressions. Those digressions, however, are precisely what will make the program worthwhile and my highest hope for it is that the particular subject of Strauss will lend itself as a spiritual continuo, so to speak, that the specific comments made about him and his work will, in the course of the 90-minutes at our disposal, take on universal ramifications.

2) Despite everything I've just said, I would like some discussion of the peculiarly Straussian musical traits – the six-four chord which drove Stravinsky wild, the predilection for triadically formulated themes, the relationship between key signature and mood (i.e. E flat major equals adventure in the early works, resignation in the later ones, and so on). Further, I would be deliriously happy if you could arrange for a cross-over in terms of one or more of the sort of ideas proposed above. For example, if Del Mar was to say that 'Metarmorphosen' for example, is, to quote my own recent Streisand article, "twenty-three solo strings in search of a six-four chord", it would be very helpful to have either some continuity of that idea or, alternately, some rebuttal of it from, for the sake of argument, Solti. Please don't feel that it's necessary to strain for any particular effect but cross-overs of that kind give me a marvelous opportunity to plan my non-stop background score accordingly. In any event, one can usually seize upon two or three controversial ideas expressed by one guest and work them, with all innocense, into a question addressed to the next.

I would like to allow each of the guests as much latitude as possible when discussing the relationship – musical, not personal – between Strauss and his major colleagues – Schonberg, Stravinsky, etc. This does, of course, touch upon personal relationships – i.e. Strauss' assistance to Schonberg in the latter's pre-atonal days and subsequent disavowal of Schonberg's work and ideas – but what I have in mind here, primarily, is a sense of the vigorous musical happenings to which Strauss remained blithely indifferent. The important thing, in this regard, is to give me the opportunity to stitch into the musical fabric as many quotations from works of composers other than Strauss as possible and to suggest something of the musical ferment of the period through which he lived accordingly.

3) On the personal level, I think it would be fascinating to explore, among other things, the *apparent* imbalance (or so it seems to me) between an artist who produced some of the most unashamedly voluptuous scores of the century and, accordingly to all reports, endeavoured to conduct them (and just about everything else, for that matter) in a most remarkably restrained manner, who turned, especially in his early years to themes of decadence and yet lived a life of remarkable circumspection. It occurs to me that this aspect of Strauss' character is yet another variation on the theme explored under (1) above and that the ability to stand outside his own creation, while leaving the listener the impression of the most intense emotional involvement, undoubtedly played a part in his (to put it mildly) ambivalent relationship to the politics of zeitgeist.

As far as other personal memorabilia is concerned, I'll happily take whatever I can get (especially from someone like your singer – what is her name? – who may not feel equally at home in all areas of discussion) but by and large, I'd like to see the personal anecdotes inextricably intertwined with a more profound level of observation and analytic perception. For instance, if, in the course of an anecdote about the Strauss – von Hofmannsthal collaboration, somebody opined that Hofmannsthal's frequently patronizing attitude towards Strauss, especially in the latter years of their association, encouraged Strauss to pursue a type of composition (or, at any rate, a type of operatic subject) which implicitly discouraged a continuation of the Salome-Elektra harmonic manner, the subject immediately takes on another and more interesting dimension. One could speculate further that maybe all composers should do away with hectoring librettists, that perhaps all outside influences, especially for a man of Strauss' temperament, constitute a very real danger etc. etc. This latter sequence is simply by way of illustration and not necessarily something that you need explore, although I'd be happy to see you look into it if you feel so inclined.

I would also be most grateful for a few lines from one or two of the participants on the reaction to Strauss' music by today's younger generation – i.e. some comment upon the rather curious situation through which Mahler has been taken up by the younger musicians as though he were the musical equivalent of Hermann Hesse (which, come to think of it, maybe he is), while Strauss, employing exactly the same musical tools (though admittedly putting them to a different sort of purpose) has been, by and large, ignored. I particularly need this kind of comment, however brief it may be because, although my own interview plans are still open pending the receipt of the material from you and from Bruno Monsaingeon in Paris, I do want to assemble a group of piping young voices (albeit very articulate ones) and try to fathom this, to me, quite inexplicable situation.

I hope that the outline above will give you an idea of the sort of program I'm after. Given your expertise as an interviewer, I should probably keep absolutely silent and just let it all happen naturally. In any event, I know that whether you use the handful of ideas above or elect to discard them and strike out on an entirely different path, the interviews will be fascinating to hear and a tremendous contribution to the program.

Finally, a couple of technical points:

– Please be sure that they record at 15 ips non-dolby; that, if two machines are available, two first-generation copies are made at source (I realize that this would not be possible if a portable Uher is involved with Solti) but that, in any case, duplicates are made and sent under separate cover to Canada.

– I would also be very grateful if the materials could be done and/or converted to NAB at that end; however, we can discuss all such errata after you have the interviews in the can.

– Within reason, and always excepting the ambient vagaries of location 'shoot-ing', I would like to keep essentially the same pick-up quality for each of the interviews. This is particularly important for the sake of those scenes where I simulate actual conversational situations from material which has, of course, been the result of separate interviews.

– Depending upon the personality of the guest, I would be very happy to have a couple of throwaway lines such as "I absolutely agree with you" or "Well, I certainly can't agree with that". The purpose is to enable me to enhance the reality of the aforementioned simulated conversations and, consequently, any such line should be rendered in an absolutely natural tone of voice and as though part of a longer sentence or thought. Such comments, of course, may arise naturally in response to such questions as you may pose, but one can't count on that and I have found that a few throwaways of that kind are invaluable at a time of editorial crisis.

– If possible, try to make sure that the mic is directional; since I want the characters to seem to be talking to each other and not to you, or to Bruno, or to me, it is important that while each of us be as noddingly supportive as possible, the interviewers' presence in all cases should go undetected.

I'll alert Jill Cobb at CBC Toronto to our plans so that if any backup is needed from Toronto (requisitions, etc.) they can be prepared without delay.
All best for now. Do let me know what happens when you contact our subjects.

Sincerely,
Glenn Gould

[1]Because he refused to fly, in devising documentaries with an international cast Gould had to use trusted colleagues elsewhere in the world as his interviewers. This letter is a briefing document for Myers to enable him to provide an interview that would fit Gould's concept of the project.

TO INTERNATIONAL MUSIC COUNCIL

Toronto, Ontario
29th May 1976

International Music Council
c/o Mr. John Roberts
C B C, Toronto

Dear Colleagues:[1]
I want to take this opportunity of extending greetings and good wishes to the members of the International Music Council on the occasion of International Music Day, 1976.

Many years ago, one of the great musicians of our time, Maestro Leopold Stokowski, described the then infant sciences of recording and film-making as 'a higher calling'. Implicit in his evaluation, which I share, was the perception of a technological network through which the many musics of the world would at last become the common property of all mankind. I would hope that International Music Day would occasion a contemplation of the time of charity and creativity which bind music and media in a union which far surpasses the sum of its seemingly pragmatic parts for, in the past few decades, we have witnessed the creation of that network which now, quite literally, encompasses the earth.

Sincerely,
Glenn Gould

[1]This letter was requested by John Roberts, then on the executive of the International Music Council, a non-governmental organization of UNESCO, in Paris, that links national music councils and other music organizations around the world. Gould's letter was one of many, collected from renowned musicians, to support the idea of the universal importance of music, for use on October 1, International Music Day.

TO GHYSLAINE GUERTIN-BELANGER   5th May 1977

Mme. Ghyslaine Guertin-Bélanger
Montreal, Quebec

Dear Mme. Guertin-Bélanger:
    Many thanks for your letter of March 25th and my apology for the delayed reply. Your thesis is indeed an interesting one and I am only sorry that I am able to offer very little help. Music critics have never numbered among my favorite people and, even during my concert-giving years, I made no concientious attempt to maintain a review-file. Since, moreover, I have been affiliated with another agent for approximately 10 years and since all files relevant to my touring experience were the property of my original agent, I really feel that you should look to a more propitious source for the materials that you need for your thesis.[1]
    I do, however, wish you well with it and am certainly most gratified that you thought of me and my Bach interpretations in connection with your most interesting endeavour.
    All best wishes,

Sincerely,
Glenn Gould

[1]The title of the dissertation was *Sémiologie et critique musicale à propos de l'interprétation à l'orgue de l'Art de la fugue par Glenn Gould*. A revised version of it will be published by the Presses de l'Université de Montréal. Geoffrey Payzant furnished the author with the material that Gould had not saved.

TO ROBERT L. DOERSCHUK[1]

[c. 1977]
c/o Music Department
354 Jarvis Street
Toronto, Ontario M5W 1E6

Mr. Robert L. Doerschuk
c/o Contemporary Keyboard Magazine
Saratoga
California, U. S. A.

Dear Mr. Doerschuk:

Thank you very much for your letter of November 3rd which has just been forwarded by CBS.

Needless to say, I am delighted to learn that we are in essential agreement on the subject of competitions, and I'm most happy indeed that my Musical America piece[2] was of some interest to you. I must confess that the 'reform' or 'restructuring' of competitive festivals is not a phenomenon to which I have given any thought in the years since that article was written. Five years ago, I did produce a deadly serious satire for radio[3] which took, as its target, various types of competition – it was in fact, keyed to coincide with the 1972 Olympics and the Spassky-Fischer chess encounter in Iceland – but, so far as I can recall, the script only touched once, and very lightly, upon the subject of musical competition, specifically.

My own competitive experience – excluding the usual round of conservatory examinations, etc., was, I'm happy to say, nil. Mind you, I have the impression, at any rate, that in the late 40's and early 50's, there were far fewer such events and that they played a less significant role in career-formation. In any event, in response to your question, I was not 'tempted';[4] indeed, I cannot remember a time when my views as to the essential immorality of the competitive process were substantially different from those that I would want to convey today and attempted to convey in the December '66 article.

All best wishes.

Sincerely,
Glenn Gould

---

[1]Assistant editor of *Contemporary Keyboard Magazine*.
[2]*High Fidelity/Musical America*, Montreal Report: "We, Who are About to Be Disqualified, Salute You!" Vol. 16, no. 12, December 1966.
[3]"The Scene," aired for CBC Radio on October 7, 1972.
[4]Doerschuk asked, "was there ever a period in your career when, as a young pianist, you were tempted to enter the competitive arena?"

TO THOMAS HENIGHAN[1]

June 26, 1978

Dr. Thomas Henighan,
Conference & Fair,
Ottawa.

Dear Dr. Henighan:

Many thanks for your letter, for telling me about your plans re "Canada in the Global Society", and for the invitation to participate.[2] I would be delighted to co-operate in any way possible; the problem, quite frankly, is that, given an August deadline and a number of commitments which will keep me occupied for the balance of the Summer, I could not contribute an 'original' film or video-tape. I will, however, be most happy to grant permission for the re-run of material (in toto or via excerpts) which might be applicable.

Off-hand, three possibilities come to mind:

(1) *The Menuhin 'conversation'*
This sequence was filmed last week and was intended to follow a rather carefully drafted 8-minute script which I prepared and which dealt with the relationship of music and media; it was shot in a sound studio control-room, and its primary emphasis was, of course, on the technology of recorded sound. It did, however, wander into some rather more speculative areas which may well be included in the finished product – i.e. in its appearance in the series 'Music of Man'. I say 'may' because, although my original script accounted for every 'and', 'if', and 'maybe', Yehudi proved constitutionally incapable of following a prepared text. The result was that, although the general outlines of the original script were adhered to, it was used essentially as a scaffolding; we shot at a ratio of 4 or 5 to 1 and, obviously, I cannot determine which points will emerge with greatest emphasis in the final, edited product. I'm confident, however, that it will have a pleasantly convivial tone (Mr. Menuhin converses delightfully, even if he can't read a script!) and, since it is planned as an 8-10 minute segment, the length is suitable for your purposes. The big question mark, however, relates to CBC's editing schedule. I have no idea when this particular segment will be put together, though I'm sure that John Barnes could give you some idea of their plans in this regard.

(2) *Radio as Music*
This was a film of approximately 30 minutes duration, prepared by the CBC for World Music Week 1975, and never aired publicly. It included a conversation with the Director, John Thompson (who *did* follow the script) and dealt with many of the same issues which occupied us in the Menuhin scenario. The focus of this film, however, was on my radio documentary techniques – it simulated, for example, the mixing of a rather busy, vocal-polyphonic sequence form "The Quiet in the Land", a documentary about a Mennonite community – but it used these

235

techniques as a 'basso continuo', so to speak, upon which other, less specific, points could be supered. It's big plus, of course, is that it is a known quantity, and I would think that it would lend itself to excerpting in the event that its present length proves unmanagable.

(3) There is a film of approximately 40 minutes duration – the second in a series of four made for ORTF in 1974[3] – which examines the methods and morals of technology with, I think, extraordinary precision and insight. It simulates various recording techniques (including an 8-track multi-perspective performance of some Scriabin preludes – an excerpt from which will also be included in the Menuhin scene) and is framed by a conversation with its producer, Bruno Monsaingeon. The conversation is in English and the films were sub-titled for their appearance in France. Permission for its use would have to come from INA – the organization which represents ORTF product in export markets and, specifically, from Mme. Jeanne-Marie Rousseau, c/o INA, Distribution Internationale, Voie des Pilotes 94360, Bry-sur-Marne, France.

I must warn you, however, that correspondence with INA can lead to confusion compounded. If you are considering this film, I would recommend a telephone call to Madame Rousseau. It will also be necessary to have permission from M. Monsaingeon, but I'm sure that he'll be eager to co-operate. His address is 8 Bis, Rue Blomet, Paris 15. Needless to say, permission for the use of 'Radio as Music' or the Menuhin segment would have to be obtained from John Barnes at CBC.
All best wishes.

Sincerely,
Glenn Gould

c.c. John Barnes

[1]Henighan was Co-ordinator of "Conference and Fair, Shaping the Future: Canada in the Global Society," August 23-27, 1978.
[2]In his letter of June 2, 1978 Henighan wrote, "we might well be interested in your exchange with Mr. Menuhin in so far as it deals with the theme of the arts and technology."
[3]*Chemins de la Musique/Glenn Gould: L'Alchemiste*, produced by Bruno Monsaingeon, and broadcast on ORTF on December 7, 1974.

TO JOHN FRASER[1]   July 4, 1978

Mr. John Fraser,
c/o Globe & Mail,
Peking, China.

Dear John:
Many thanks for the note, and your enthusiasm for – you didn't say, so I'm assuming it was for the recent Globe review; I've been scribbling away rather

compulsively of late – hence the confusion. As a matter of fact, I'm going to ask the O'Dacre Express to forward a Sunday New York Times Magazine piece about Stokowski which appeared a few weeks back. And before you read it – always assuming, of course, that you haven't already – let me assure you that I disclaim any responsibility for the dumb, bland title (In Praise of Maestro Stokowski). My title (Stokowski, in Six Scenes) was deemed too academic and/or arcane; moreover, it necessitated roman numerals for scene – demarcation and roman numerals, apparently, do not conform to Times' style. Nevertheless, 'Stokowski in Six Scenes' (plus a brief preamble) defined exactly how the piece was made and, when I pull some of these things between covers eventually, it's going right back where it belongs. Anyway, hope you like it.[2]

Now then: I think the prospects for a China documentary are fascinating, even though the prospects for a visit by me to the Orient are nil. As you know, I don't fly – haven't for sixteen years – and no assignment, no matter how enticing, will get me aloft again. Furthermore, with each passing year, I become more committed to a sedentary existence and less willing to contemplate any form of travel. An auto trip to N.Y.C. is a major event in my life these days and even if a slow boat to China did exist, I would not be on it.

On the other hand, an alternative springs to mind: interview-material by J.F., production by G.G. Moreover, there is a precedent. I am currently working on a two-year-overdue documentary about Richard Strauss for which, although I handled those interviews which could be done in North America (albeit by phone – I don't budge for any project) the overseas interviews were done in London, Vienna, and, most important, Munich, by friends who hang out in those parts. The Munich interviews, for example, (Wolfgang Sawallisch, Wolfgang Fortner) were conducted by Jürgen Meyer-Jösten (head of music for Bavarian radio) and were based on a list of questions which I submitted to him. (Needless to say, when Harry Mannis gets around to recording the credits, Jürgen Meyer-Jösten will be acknowledged as 'Production Assistant', or words to that effect; billing, in your case, is, of course, negotiable.)

The big question is: can we find an approach, however oblique, which justifies such a program? I don't think the world is waiting for a Lowell Thomas-style 'China-today' epic, and I doubt that 'a history of acupuncture' could be made into exciting radio fair. What I would like, as in all my documentaries, is a 'mood-piece', essentially. Above all, what intrigues me is the possibility of relating a China-essay to the general theme of my so-called 'Solitude-Trilogy' (The Idea of North', 'The Latecomers', 'The Quiet in the Land'). Each of those programs dealt with aspects of isolation – 'North' with individuals in isolation, 'Latecomers' with a community in isolation, and 'Quiet in the Land' with a religious dimension of the same these. Suppose – and this is strictly off the top of my head – we could do a program about 'The Last Puritans' – with apologies to George Santayana. Matter of fact, I like the title and I particularly like the relationship it could have to my 'Solitude Trilogy' (Quartet!) – i.e. the political dimension of isolation.

What say you? Obviously, I'm open to thematic suggestions and, needless to say, it would have to be determined whether CBC is open to any such project. My current contract with them allows me to work entirely out-of-house – i.e. in my own studio and in my own time – but program subjects must be agreed upon by mutual consent.

Do let me know your reactions; I'm getting more intrigued by the minute. The Strauss project will be my major radio production this year, I would not be in a position to attempt the 'Last Puritans' (like it!) for at least a year, so we would have plenty of time to develop an approach to the project.[3]

All best for now

Sincerely,
Glenn Gould

P.S. Your dispatches are a constant delight; trust the new car has had its 1000 km check-up.

[1]John Fraser was the Peking correspondent of *The Globe and Mail* from October 1977 to October 1979.
[2]The *New York Times Magazine* published this article, based on Gould's documentary on Leopold Stokowski, without knowing that it was also being published in *Piano Quarterly*. When this was discovered, Gould's colleagues at the *New York Times Magazine* were not amused.
[3]Nothing came of the proposed project of a radio documentary on China.

TO ROBERT SUNTER[1]

January 30, 1979

Mr. Robert Sunter
CBC

Dear Bob,

Herewith, a few notes about 'The Bourgeois Hero'. The program is in two 'acts' (approximately 44 and 50 minutes, respectively) and consists of six 'scenes' – the first two in 'act one', and the remaining four in the 'second act'. Each 'scene' is devoted to a different aspect of Strauss's life; scene 2 (at 32 minutes, by far the longest) involves a discussion of his musical development through the first forty years – it ends with the composition of Salome – and a rather hard look at his character, including some speculations about the relationship with Pauline. Scene 3 examines his reactions to such colleagues andéor contemporaries as Mahler, Schoenberg, Stravinsky and Webern, Scene 4 concentrates on the Hoffmanstahl connection, Scene 5 on Strauss's activities during the Hitler period, and the closing scene is devoted to his final years and to some speculations about his prospects re posterity. I've left any mention of 'scene 1' for last because it's less concerned with Strauss, per se, than with providing an introduction for our 'cast'; each of the eight characters takes the opportunity to reminisce about some incident which, however obliquely, connected them to Strauss.

I should point out that, despite the different subject matters under discussion and excluding, of course, the full stop at the end of 'act one', all of the 'scenes' are connected by musical 'dissolves'; there are no pauses or other points of demarcation and, in fact, music runs throughout the program, with but one exception: a few seconds of the opening and closing speeches, in which Jonathan Cott first quotes from Nabokov on the subject of 'remembrance' and, at the conclusion of the program, offers his own, Strauss-inspired, revision of the quotation, are presented a cappella.

The cast is as follows:

Jonathan Cott	– American critic, poet, and anthologist
Stanley Silverman	– American composer
Henry Levinger	– German-American critic – and the only person I know you managed to spend a year in the celebrated pad at Garmischpartenkirschen
Geoffrey Payzant	– Canadian philosopher
Norman del Mar	– English author and conductor
John Culshaw	– English author and record producer
Wolfgang Sawallisch	– German conductor
Wolfgang Fortner	– German composer.

The music consists of excerpts from Salome, Elektra, Die Frau ohne Schatten and Capriccio, from Macbeth, Till Eulenspiegel, Thus Spake Zarathustra, Ein Heldenleben, and Don Juan, and from the Oboe Concerto, the Bourgeois Gentilhomme, Alpine Symphony, Metamorphosen, and Four Last Songs.

Hope this helps. All best wishes,

Sincerely,

P.S. Jill tells me that you are specifically interested in the details of 'act one', so perhaps I should point out that the music in that segment involves the excerpts from the 'Oboe Concerto', the five tone-poems mentioned above, and Salome.

---

¹Head of Music for CBC Radio at the time of this letter.

TO CAROL MONT PARKER[1]

P.O. Box 500, Station A
Toronto, Ontario M5W 1E6
Sept. 30, 1979

Mrs. Carol Mont Parker
Huntington, New York

Dear Mrs. Parker:

Many thanks for your note. I wish I had a simple explanation – or, indeed, any kind of an explanation – to account for this rather unusual phenomenon (if I did, I'd patent it.)[2]

The fact is, however, that it's as much a mystery to me as to anyone else who has heard it, or, indeed, has heard it described. I am, by the way, quite used to skeptical glances and suggestions from friends that I have simply invented his improbable story and am probably smuggling in tuners under cover of darkness; needless to say, no one has ever explained why that would be a useful or sensible thing to do, but the passing reference to it in the Times was the first occasion on which I've gone 'public' with a mention of it. I recall that, approximately a year after its last tuning, – i.e. some time in 1964 – Emil Gilels practised at my apartment before a Toronto concert, made some appropriately pleasant sounds (in German) about what a fine instrument this was, and, when told that it had not been tuned for more than 12 months, (at that time) gave me a look which suggested that something had been lost in the translation.

The piano, moreover, sits more or less in front of a radiator and, with no humidifier in sight, and, though the odd unison does go astray from time to time, it seems to have a self-correcting capacity in that regard. It is, as I said above, a mystery, and I really can't shed any appropriate amount of light on the subject, and, as with most mysteries, it's perhaps best not to try.[3]

All best wishes.

Sincerely,
Glenn Gould

[1] A fan.
[2] In her letter of August 18, 1979 Mrs. Mont Parker asked, "Did I understand correctly that your piano has not required tuning for 20-odd years, and if this curious fact be true, HOW SO?"
[3] This letter refers to Gould's Steinway, which was used as a practice piano in his penthouse on St. Clair Avenue in Toronto.

TO RUSSELL HERBERT GOULD [c. 1979?]

Dear Father

I've had an opportunity to give quite some thought to the matter of your wedding and specifically to the invitation to serve as your best man.[1] I'm sure that, under the circumstances, you (and Mrs. Dobson) would prefer to arrange a private service – one in which any such conventional ceremonial gesture would be inappropriate; in any case, while I appreciate your kindness in extending the invitation, I regret that I must decline. Needless to say, I wish you much happiness, and I would ask you to pass on my good wishes to Mrs. Dobson.

Most sincerely,

[1]We cannot confirm that this letter was mailed. It was discovered in draft form in Gould's journal with no date, nor a signature. His father remarried January 19, 1980.

TO THE EDITOR, ESQUIRE MAGAZINE

354 Jarvis Street
Toronto, Ontario
October 25, 1979

The Editor
Esquire Magazine
New York, N.Y., U.S.A.

Dear Sir,

At the risk of seeming like a spoilsport, I must take issue with Martin Meyer's variations on that hoary fable in which the late George Szell[1] is reputed to have advised me of new uses for a piano stool. The story has, of course, cropped up in other publications, though usually in a somewhat more decorous version, and, to say the very least, it now suffers in your pages from what we in the record business refer to as generation-less – i.e. lack of fidelity due to excessive dubbing.

Dr. Szell never did dispose of any such pronouncement to my face or in my presence – indeed, if he had done, the Cleveland Orchestra would have been obliged to find themselves a new guest soloist in a hurry – though it is certainly possible that this rather heavy-handed witticism, retold and retouched by the maestro, eventually fell into his file of "snappy retorts I wish I'd get off at the time". In any event, since a measure of humour was not among Dr. Szell's more memorable qualities, either personally or professionally, it strikes me as a singularly tasteless inclusion in Mr. Meyer's celebration of his remarkable discographic achievements.[2]

Sincerely,
Glenn Gould

[1]George Szell (1897-1970), Hungarian-born American conductor.
[2]This letter is a repudiation of a story, of which there are several versions, related to an appearance

with the Cleveland Orchestra. During a rehearsal, the conductor – George Szell – was reported to have become impatient while blocks were placed under the legs of the piano. Gould not infrequently arranged for this to be done in order to achieve the ideal distance between himself and the keyboard. In one version, Szell was said to have muttered, "Perhaps if we were to slice one-sixteenth of an inch off your derrière, Mr. Gould, we could begin." Gould remembered another as "I vil personally stick . . . one of zose legs up your rear end," or other words with the same meaning.

TO JOHN DIAMOND[1]   30th March 1980

Dr. John Diamond
Valley Cottage, N.Y.
U. S. A.

Dear Dr. Diamond:

Thank you so much for your letter of May 1979. Unfortunately, it was mislaid and I apologize for this delayed reply.

I most certainly agree with you about the therapeutic effects of music and musical performance; I have always believed that if this relationship does not exist, it *should* exist. At the same time, vis-a-vis my own work, I prefer not to attempt to ascertain from precisely what source any therapeutic value might be forthcoming. Perhaps it's nothing more than superstition on my part – not unlike the reluctance of jazz musicians who frequently refuse to learn score-reading in case some magical communicative ability will disappear in the process. In any case, I was fascinated to learn about your studies, very much enjoyed reading B.K., and can think of no higher compliment than your kind words about the therapeutic value of my own work.

Yours sincerely,
Glenn Gould

[1]Dr. John Diamond was the author of BK: *Behavioral Kinesiology; how to activate your thymus and increase your life energy* (New York: Harper & Row, 1979). He wondered if Gould would be interested in participating in the measurement of the therapeutic value of his music making.

TO DELL[1]   [c. 1980?]

You know

I am deeply in love with a certain beaut. girl. I asked her to marry me but she turned me down but I still love her more than anything in the world and every min. I can spend with her is pure heaven; but I don't want to be a bore and if I could only get her to tell me when I could see her, it would help. She has a standing invit. to let me take her anywhere she'd like to go any time but it seems to me she never has time for me. Please if you see her, ask her to let me know when I can see her and when I can. . . .

¹This is a mysterious letter found in Gould's hand-written journals for 1980. If there were other such letters, they have not survived. The exact date is difficult to determine, as is Dell's identity.

TO SUSAN KOSCIS[1]   [no date]

18/24 Koscis

I've heard a malicious rumour to the effect that I either do not play, or do not play with any enthusiasm, the music of the so-called romantic composer – music of Chopin and Schubert and Schumann for ex. Now, if the list were to stop right there, the rumour would be indeed well-founded . . . In my entire prof. life, I've played exactly one work by each of the composers I've just mentioned.

I find that the piano music written in the first half of the 19th cent. (when all of those composers were active working) – distasteful. I find it mechanistic. I find that it's a real product of the industrial revolution, exploits the newly developing capacities of the keyboard – and I also find it cloyingly sentimental, full of parlor tricks. But, and its a big 'but' . . . when you come to the second half of the 19th century, that's another story altogether. Because it was dominated by the incomparable lyrics of R.W.[2] and I happen to be – and have been all my life – a dyed in the-wool Wagnerian (I tried to give some proof of that devotion a few yrs. back when I rec. my own trans. of such things as Siegfried R.V. and the Meister Preludes.)

But the problem for those of us who worship Wagner and the post-Wagnerian composers like Strauss (who followed in his wake), is that they wrote almost nothing for the piano. The orch. was then inst. the piano was, at best something at which to [blank] idlers and prepare first drafts. Wagner in fact, when he wrote for the pno. at all did so with astonishing ineptitude. Strauss, on the other hand, [blank] meticulously, indigenous – he didn't attempt to treat the pno. as a sub-orch. (As a matter of fact, we have just finished a rec. of R.S. solo piano music – most of which by the way was written at the ripe old age of 15.)[3]

However, the rec. I've been asked to tell you about is not of music by Str. but rather that of music by Brahms and I'm prf. it off as long as I can because like most [blank] I have rather ambivalent feelings about Brahms.

Brahms was not immune to treating the piano mechanistically – some of his famous pieces – the Variations on themes of Handel and Paganini for ex. do exactly that. On the other hand, he could also write with remarkable gentleness and restraint – esp. at the very end of his life. About 20 yrs. ago, I rec. my only prev. Brahms album (it's still in circ. and it consisted of Intermezzi – [4]

[1]Although this letter is an incomplete draft, Gould's revealing comments about the music of the nineteenth century are worth including.
[2]Richard Wagner.
[3]*Glenn Gould Plays Strauss.* Five Pieces, Op. 3, SWV 105; Sonata in B minor, Op. 5, SWV 103 (CBS, released in 1983).
[4]Johannes Brahms. Four Ballads, Op. 10; Two Rhapsodies, Op. 79 (CBS, released in 1983).

TO THE EDITOR[1]

c/o Music Department
354 Jarvis Street
Toronto, Ontario
September 9, 1981

The Editor
Publications Committee
Canadian Music Council
Ottawa, Ontario

Attention: Mr. Guy Huot

Dear Sir:

I much enjoyed your June issue[2] which included Mr. Eric McLean's[3] delightful reminiscence of my early concert years. A remarkable percentage of Mr. McLean's anecdotes were in fact, accurate, a good many of the remainder fell into the close-enough-for-government-work category (my debut with the Toroto Symphony for example, did not take place "under Sir Ernest MacMillan at the age of 15"), but rather under Sir Bernard Heinze at the age of 14) and still others, while rather wide of the mark, factually, make such sparkling copy that they may well find their way into my own anecdotal repertoire.

In the latter category, I must cite the witty dialogue in which I am alleged to have participated following an appearance in "an old folks' home in Winnipeg". Now, to my shame, I confess, that I have never appeared, professionally or otherwise, in Winnipeg or elsewhere, before an audience of senior citizens. I did once give a dinner-hour recital at a United Church Mission for the unemployed but that was in Toronto, not Winnipeg, I was eleven at the time, not twenty-six as in Mr. McLean's story, and since my programme on that occasion was exclusive and perhaps rather perversely devoted to waltzes by Chopin and Liszt – not works which were to form a conspicuous feature of my repertoire in later years – I feel certain that, if this is the event Mr. McLean has in mind, he could hardly have omitted that uniquely distinquishing detail from his account.

I do realize, of course, that there is no correspondent so irritating as the nit-picking recipient of such a good natured and well-intentioned memoir as Mr. McLean provided for your readers and, indeed, I would not presume to indulge myself in these prefatory challenges to his memory but for the fact that, in one of his anecdotes he provides such a virtuosic compote of mis-information that I feel compelled to set the record(s) straight.

The tale in question concerns my 1957 debut with the New York Philharmonic under the direction of Leonard Bernstein.

> The setting is "The Green Room after the performance, (in which) he played the Beethoven No.2. . . . with his own cadenza. Glenn was standing apart from the others with his overcoat draped over his shoulders, and his hands encased in wool gloves – remember, this was May, in New York, and indoors. . . .

> Leonard Bernstein came over to our corner. "Glenn, that was tremendous," he said with genuine enthusiasm. "We'll have to record it – we must make a record together." "Glad you like it," said Gould non-committally. "We'll talk about it." But when Bernstein had returned to his friends the twenty-four year old Gould, leaned confidentially towards me: "He's not ready for it."

Now, the first problem with this story is that my debut with the New York Philharmonic took place not in May 1957, as Mr. McLean alleges but in January of that year. The mid-winter date, of course, in no way excuses my outrageous indifference to sartorial etiquette – indeed, I have been known to hang out backstage in exactly the same garb during August heatwaves – but it does call into question the balance of Mr. McLean's recollection of the event, and in particular, the allegation of my rather snotty aside concerning Mr. Bernstein's 'readiness' to record Beethoven.

The fact is, that in April 1957, one month prior to the events Mr. McLean recalls in such elaborate detail, Mr. Bernstein and I recorded the Beethoven 2nd Concerto in Columbia's 30th Street studio and a glance at my discography which you very kindly included in your issue will reveal that the work was not only recorded but also released in that year.

In any case, by May of 1957 when Mr. McLean sets his account, I had repaired to Berlin in order to check out the collaborative capabilities of another up and coming Beethovenian, Herbert von Karajan.

My favorite part of Mr. McLean's story, however, is his recollection that I played my own cadenza. In fact on that occasion as well as in the subsequent recording with Mr. Bernstein, and during all other performances of the B Flat Major Concerto, I played Beethoven's cadenza – that imaginative, late-Beethoven quasi-fugal reflection upon the themes of his youthful essay. But, as anyone who knows my determination to threaten Beethoven with a measure of stylistic ambiguity and contrapuntal complexity will attest, it's an understandable (though surely flattering) mistake.

Sincerely,
Glenn Gould

[1] Secretary General of the Canadian Music Council.
[2] *Musicanada*, No. 46, June 1981.
[3] Critic, historian, and pianist, McLean became music critic for the *Montreal Daily Star* in 1949 and remained there until it closed in 1979, when he moved to the *Montreal Gazette*.

TO WILLIAM GLENESK

110 St. Clair Ave. West
Toronto, Ontario
M4V 1N4
May 22, 1982

Rev. William Glenesk
c/o St. James United Church
Montreal, Quebec
H3A 2E4

Dear Bill:

Many thanks for the letter of March 25, and my apologies for the delayed reply. Thanks also for the first-class piece on Adler[1] which I hadn't seen before.

There were two rather spooky things about your letter – or, rather, not about the letter per se but about its timing. The first was that 'Reader's Digest' had contacted me about a month earlier with the (unwelcome) news that they planned to run, in the May issue, an abridged version of a piece which appeared last fall in 'People' and which was remarkable, in equal parts, for its compilation of cliches and absence of insights. I asked them whether there was anything I could do to discourage its publication; alas, there was not and I will admit that their abridgement was at least less irritating than the Urtext.

In any case, I knew that they would certainly not consider two profiles (however different) on the same subject and that knowledge made me feel less guilty about not getting back to you at the time.

The second spooky thing about your letter was that, during March and April, I was working on the score for 'The Wars' – a Nielsen-Ferns, N.F.B.,[2] Polyphon (Germany) co-production – based on Timothy Findley's novel,[3] and, during the week in which your letter (with the Adler enclosure) arrived, I was writing two excerpts for, believe it or not, harmonica; they're designed to sound as though they're being played by a doughboy a short distance down the trench. The first excerpt is a short set of variations on the theme of Brahms, the second an arrangement of 'Abide with Me' (both of which themes play a significant leitmotivic role in the score) and together, needless to say, they constitute my first professional exposure to the harmonica. In fact, my ignorance of the instrument was such that I had to ask what the lowest note of the average government-issue harmonica might be – middle C, it turns out, but it's not covered in your average text on orchestration. Anyway, just at that moment your letter arrived; how about that for coincidence.

By the way, I'll look forward to your reaction to 'The Wars'. I think it's a remarkably fine picture – very understated, rather slow-moving, interesting particularly for what it leaves unsaid and unshown. It's a sort of Canadian 'Winter-Light' – the only Bergman film I can relate to – though not quite as well sustained structurally. Hope you enjoy it.

All best for now; keep in touch.

Sincerely,
Glenn Gould

¹Peter Herman Adler, Czech-born (1899) American conductor.
²National Film Board of Canada.
³*The Wars* by Timothy Findley.

TO PETER LUST

Glenn Gould
P.O. Box 682
Don Mills, Ontario
M3C 2T6
June 12, 1982

Mr. Peter Lust
Pointe Claire, Que.

Dear Mr. Lust:

Thank you so much for your letter of March 18th[1] and my apologies for the delayed reply.

I was absolutely fascinated with the Karl Bohm[2] – Felix Schmidt[3] interview; it's one of the most vivid and compelling pieces of musical journalism I've encountered in a long time. It also painted a picture of Bohm (or perhaps I should say allowed Bohm to paint the picture himself) quite different from my rather stereotyped image of the man. Somehow, probably as an outgrowth of my impression of his conducting, I had always imagined him to be a relaxed, genial, even slightly complacent grandfather figure, and I was quite astonished to encounter, via the interview, this crotchety, outspoken, black-sheep-uncle character. It's an outstanding portrait and I do hope you'll pass on my congratulations to Herr Schmidt and, indeed, to Alison Ames, whose translation was exemplary (one could almost swear that Bohm had been speaking in English throughout).

As regards my own reaction to an interview with Herr Schmidt, however, I must point out once again (as I indicated to you on the phone some months back) that my own interview style – obviously, unlike that of Karl Bohm – lends itself best to occasions which involve – perverse as it may seem – minimum spontaneity and maximum deliberation. As I mentioned during our phone chat, I have, on a number of occasions during the past four or five years, written either the answers to questions submitted or, in some cases, indeed, both questions and answers, and tried to do so in a style which, so far as I can judge, most readers have accepted as representing spontaneous conversation with the interlocutor in question. (I'm sure you'll understand that, for obvious reasons, I can't tell you which 'interviewers' specifically allowed me the privileges to which I've alluded.

Needless to say, in the case of Herr Schmidt,[3] whose questions are invariably thought-provoking, I would not presume to act as my own interrogator; nevertheless, because of the success of various other interviews of the kind mentioned above and the relative lack of success of interviews which resulted from more casual conversational contacts, I'm quite determined that, in future all major journalistic efforts will be executed in this fashion.

Again, with many thanks for the remarkable piece and with all best wishes.

Sincerely,
Glenn Gould
(for Glenn Gould Limited)

[1] In his letter of March 18, 1982, Lust asked Gould if he would consent to being interviewed by Felix Schmidt.
[2] Karl Böhm (1894-1981), Austrian conductor.
[3] Felix Schmidt (b. 1934), German author of *Das Chanson: Herkunft, Entwicklung, Interpretation* (Ahrensburg: Damokles Verlag, 1968).

TO MEL HINDE

Glenn Gould
P.O. Box 682
Don Mills, Ontario
M3C 2T6
August 14, 1982

Mr. Mel Hinde
c/o Sony of Canada Ltd.

Dear Mr. Hinde:

Just a note to extend a very belated 'thank you' for your great generosity in loaning us the PCM-1600 (at Sounds Interchange) a couple of months ago. I was most anxious to check out the digital results of a New York session on which my analog dubs were flawed. Fortunately, it was a false alarm – the Sony product was in superb shape – but I'm most grateful for your help in tracking down the problem.

I've asked Ray Roberts to drop off a copy of 'The Six Last Haydn Sonatas'[1] – my first release utilizing the Sony system. (Around the end of next month, a new version of Bach's 'Goldberg Variations' is being released[2] and I'll see that you get a copy of that as well.) I think the clarity and immediacy of the sound, on both discs, is quite remarkable and I hope you share my enthusiasm for the digital result.

All best wishes.

Sincerely,
Glenn Gould

[1]*Haydn: The Six Last Sonatas.* No. 56 in D major, H. XVI/42; No. 58 in C major, H. XVI/48; No. 59 in E♭ major, H. XVI/49; No. 60 in C major, H. XVI/50; No. 61 in D major, H. XVI/51; No. 62 in E♭ major, H. XVI/52, 1982.
[2]*J.S. Bach: Goldberg Variations,* BWV 988, 1982. These were Gould's last two recordings, both performed on a Yamaha piano.

TO THERESA XIMENES[1]

Glenn Gould
P.O. Box 682
Don Mills, Ontario
M3C 2T6
Miss Teresa Ximenes   August 14, 1982
New York, N.Y.

Dear Miss Ximenes:

Thank you very much for your letter of July 29th.[2] I'd be delighted to have you make use of the Bach C Major Prelude and Fugue in your film. As it happens, animal welfare is one of the great passions of my life, and if you'd asked to use my entire recorded output, in support of such a cause, I couldn't possibly have refused.[3]

Good luck with your film and all best wishes.

Sincerely,
Glenn Gould

[1]A fan.
[2]This is the last dated letter in the Gould collection at the National Library of Canada.
[3]In his will, Gould made the Toronto Humane Society one of his major beneficiaries.

CHRONOLOGY

1932   Glenn Herbert Gould, born September 25, in Toronto, to Russell Herbert (Bert) and Florence (*née* Greig) Gould.

The home of his childhood and early manhood is 32 Southwood Drive in the Beaches district of Toronto.

Studies piano with his mother until ten years of age when he attends Toronto Conservatory of Music (now the Royal Conservatory of Music).

1940-47 Studies theory with Leo Smith.

1942-49 Studies organ with Frederick C. Silvester.

1943-52 Studies piano with Alberto Guerrero. Receives ATCM (Associate, Toronto Conservatory of Music) at twelve with highest marks in the country.

1945   Organist debut, Eaton Auditorium Toronto (December 12).

Begins studies at Malvern Collegiate Institute, Toronto.

1946   Debut with orchestra as soloist with Toronto Conservatory of Music Orchestra conducted by Ettore Mazzoleni in first movement Piano Concerto No. 4 by Beethoven (May 8).

1947   Debut with Toronto Symphony Orchestra conducted by Sir Bernard Heinze in Massey Hall. Complete performance Piano Concerto No. 4 by Beethoven (January 14).

First public recital as a piano soloist for International Artists, Eaton Auditorium, Toronto (October 20).

1950   First broadcast for Canadian Broadcasting Corporation (CBC) "Sunday Morning Recital" (December 24).

Finishes his Sonata for Bassoon and Piano.

1951 Tours western Canada. Debut with Vancouver Symphony Orchestra (October 28).

1952 Television debut with the CBC. First pianist to be televised by the CBC (September 8), official opening of CBC Toronto television station CBLT.

    Montreal debut, Ladies' Morning Music Club, Ritz Carlton Hotel (November 6).

1953 First commercial recording (with Albert Pratz, violinist) for Hallmark label, Toronto.

    Performs Piano Concerto Opus 42 by Schoenberg with CBC Symphony Orchestra conducted by Jean-Marie Beaudet (December 23).

    First concert appearance at the Stratford Festival, Ontario.

1955 Recital debut, Washington, in Philips Gallery (January 2).

    Recital debut, New York, in Town Hall (January 11).

    Following day Gould signs an exclusive contract with Columbia Records.

    Finishes his String Quartet, Op. 1.

1956 Debut recording for Columbia Records, Bach's *Goldberg Variations*.

    Tours Canada and the United States in the fall.

    Montreal String Quartet records Gould's String Quartet, Op. 1 as a transcription recording for CBC International Service (now Radio Canada International).

1957 Debut New York Philharmonic Orchestra, conducted by Leonard Bernstein, Carnegie Hall, Beethoven Piano Concerto No. 2 (January 26).

    Conducts pick-up orchestra on Chrysler Festival for CBC television with Maureen Forrester as soloist (February 20).

    First overseas tour. Recitals in Moscow, Leningrad, and Vienna. European orchestral debut with Moscow Philharmonic Orchestra (May 8). Plays with Leningrad Philharmonic Orchestra (May 18) and the Berlin Philharmonic Orchestra under Herbert von Karajan (May 24-26).

    As his performing career develops he "escapes" as often as possible to his parents' cottage at Uptergrove on Lake Simcoe, north of Toronto, where he works in solitude and enjoys the country.

1958 Second overseas tour. Plays with Hart House Orchestra of Toronto under Boyd Neel at Brussels World Fair (August 25). Other concerts in Stockholm, Berlin, Salzburg, and Florence. Gives eleven performances in eighteen days in Israel.

1959 Performs first four of the five Beethoven piano concerti in London with the London Symphony Orchestra conducted by Joseph Krips. His last European concert is in Lucerne at the Lucerne Festival (August 31).

    Receives an injury from a technician at Steinway & Sons in New York. Gould sues Steinway in 1960 and the company agrees to an out-of-court settlement.

1960 Symphonia String Quartet records Gould's String Quartet, Op. 1.

    National Film Board of Canada release two half-hour films, *Glenn Gould: Off the Record* and *Glenn Gould: On the Record*.

American television debut with the New York Philharmonic Orchestra and Leonard Bernstein (January 31).

Concert, Gala Performance for the Orchestra Fund, Montreal Symphony Orchestra, Montreal (April 19). Made three appearances at the Vancouver International Festival (July 27, 29, and August 2).

1961   Active at the Stratford Festival Ontario as a co-director and performs with other co-directors Leonard Rose, cellist and Oscar Shumsky, violinist.

Gould consolidates his reputation as a television commentator as well as a performer with CBC television program "The Subject is Beethoven" in which he collaborates with cellist Leonard Rose.

Adjusts to living in a penthouse at 110 St. Clair Avenue West.

1962   Gould develops his writing career with "Let's Ban Applause!" in *Musical America* (February) and "An Argument for Richard Strauss" in *High Fidelity* (March).

Performs Piano Concerto No. 1 by Brahms with New York Philharmonic. The conductor, Leonard Bernstein dissociates himself from Gould's interpretation (April 6, 8).

Gould's first music documentary for CBC Radio, "Arnold Schoenberg: The Man Who Changed Music" (August 8).

1963   Columbia Records releases Gould's performances of the six Partitas by Bach.

CBC telecast *The Anatomy of Fugue* includes Gould's own composition *So You Want to Write a Fugue*.

Delivers the Corbett Music Lecture *Arnold Schoenberg: A Perspective*, at the University of Cincinnati, Cincinnati, Ohio (April 22) and the MacMillan Lectures at the University of Toronto (July).

1964   Receives Doctor of Laws, *honoris causa*, University of Toronto.

Last public concert given in Los Angeles (April 10).

Retires from concert stage.

1965   CBC Radio broadcast "The Prospects of Recording" (January 10), later adapted as an article for *High Fidelity* (April 1966).

1966   "Conversations with Glenn Gould," four BBC television programs recorded in Toronto with Gould interviewed by the BBC's Humphrey Burton.

Records Beethoven's Piano Concerto No. 5 (The *Emperor*), Opus 73 with Leopold Stokowski.

CBC TV program "Duo" with Gould and Yehudi Menuhin (May 18).

1967   CBC TV program "To Every Man His Own Bach" (March 29).

"Centennial Performance," CBC television program. Soloist with Toronto Symphony, conducted by Vladimir Golshmann (November 15).

Releases recording of music by Canadian composers Istvan Anhalt, Jacques Hétu, and Oskar Morawetz in honour of the Centenary of Canada.

"The Idea of North," the first of the three radio documentaries known as "The Solitude Trilogy," is broadcast (December 28).

1969   Awarded $15,000 Molson Prize by The Canada Council.

        Creates and produces radio documentary "The Latecomers" (November 12), the second
        in "The Solitude Trilogy."

        Article, "Should We Dig Up the Rare Romantics? . . . No, They're Only a Fad," published
        in the *New York Times* (November 23).

1970   Television program, "The Well-Tempered Listener": Gould in discussion with Curtis
        Davis. Gould performs on piano, harpsichord, and organ (February 18).

        Recital for CBC Radio on "CBC Thursday Music" includes uncharacteristic repertoire:
        Sonata No. 3 in B minor, Op. 58 by Chopin and a group of "Songs Without Words" by
        Mendelssohn (July 23).

        Television version of "The Idea of North." CBC TV (August 5).

        CBC TV "Glenn Gould Plays Beethoven"; includes Concerto No. 5 in E♭ major, Op. 73
        ("Emperor") with The Toronto Symphony conducted by Karel Ancerl, in honor of
        Beethoven Bi-Centenary (December 9).

1971   Creates and produces radio documentary, "Stokowski: A Portrait for Radio" (February 2).

        Radio broadcast for the European Broadcasting Union (EBU), broadcast throughout
        Europe and by the CBC in Canada.

        Recorded music by Bach, Bizet, Byrd, Grieg, and Schoenberg for Columbia Records.

1972   Provides music for American film, "Slaughterhouse Five" directed by George Roy Hill.

1973   Purchases Steinway CD 318.

1974   Series of four television programs, "Chemins de la Musique" produced for the ORTF,
        France.

        CBC radio documentary, "Casals: A Portrait for Radio" (January 15).

        CBC TV, Musicamera, "The Age of Ecstasy," the first of a four-part series called "Music in
        Our Time" (February 20).

        CBC radio documentary, "Arnold Schoenberg the First Hundred Years: A Documentary/
        Fantasy" (November 19).

1975   CBC TV Musicamera, "The Flight from Order 1910-1920," "Music in Our Time" series
        (February 5).

        Florence Gould dies (July 26).

        Video, *Radio as Music* produced for the conference *An International Exhibition of Music
        for Broadcasting*, Toronto. It deals with Gould's innovative approaches to creating radio
        programs.

        CBC TV, Musicamera, "New Faces. Old Forms 1920-1930." "Music in Our Time" series
        (November 26).

1977	Records the English Suites of J.S. Bach for CBS Records.
	CBC radio documentary, "The Quiet in the Land." The third of the Solitude Trilogy (March 25).
	CBC TV, Musicamera, "The Artist as Artisan 1930-1940," "Music in Our Time" series (December 14).
1978	Article, "In Praise of Maestro Stokowski," *New York Times Magazine* (May 14). This was a reuse of material first published in *The Piano Quarterly*, in two parts in the same year under the title "Stokowski in Six Scenes."
1979	CBC two-part radio documentary, "Richard Strauss: The Bourgeois Hero" (April 2, 9).
1979	TV, "Glenn Gould's Toronto," City Series, directed by John McGreevy. John McGreevy Productions (CBC telecast September 27).
	"Glenn Gould Plays Bach, No. 1: The Question of Instrument," a CLASART film, is released.
1980	CBS Records, *Glenn Gould Silver Jubilee Album* (two records). Includes the Ophelia Leider, Op. 67.1 (three songs) sung by Elisabeth Schwarzkopf accompanied by Gould, and a Glenn Gould Fantasy.
	"Glenn Gould Plays Bach, No. 2: An Art of Fugue," is released by CLASART.
1981	"Glenn Gould Plays Bach No. 3: Goldberg Variations," a CLASART film is released. Bruno Monsaigneon is director of "Glenn Gould Plays Bach" series.
1982	Second recording of "The Goldberg Variations" by Bach is released by CBS Records.
	In August Gould turns to having himself taped as a conductor and directs a performance of the chamber version of Wagner's "Siegfried Idyll" with local Toronto musicians.
	On September 27 suffers the first of several strokes.
	Gould dies, Toronto General Hospital at 11.30 a.m. on October 4.
	Ecumenical Memorial Service (Anglican, Catholic, Jewish, Salvation Army) for Glenn Gould, with several thousand people present, St. Paul's Anglican Church, Toronto (October 15). Music is provided by leading Canadian musicians as a tribute to Gould.

INDEX

Italicized page numbers denote letters written to the indexed subject.

255